THE MASCULINE MYSTIQUE

THE

MASCULINE MYSTIQUE

THE POLITICS OF MASCULINITY

ANDREW KIMBRELL

BALLANTINE BOOKS ■ NEW YORK

Library of Congress Cataloging-in-Publication Data
Kimbrell, Andrew.
The masculine mystique / by Andrew Kimbrell.
p.   cm.
Includes index.
ISBN 0-345-38658-2
1. Men—United States.   2. Gender identity—United States.   3. Masculinity (Psychology)—United States.   4. Sex role—United States.   I. Title.
HQ1090.3.K55   1995
305.32—dc20   95-13408
                                                                      CIP

Designed by Ann Gold

Manufactured in the United States of America
First Edition: August 1995
10   9   8   7   6   5   4   3   2   1

*This book is dedicated
to my brother Mark, and to Greta,
Alice, and Andy*

CONTENTS

ACKNOWLEDGMENTS

This book is the result of several years of discussions, research, and interviews. To thank all the hundreds of men and women who have written to me, and all those that have contributed to this book, would require a book in itself. They know who they are, and many of their names are found in the pages of the book and in the footnotes. I am especially indebted to the ideas of Robert Bly, Harris Breiman, Warren Farrell, Benjamin K. Hunnicutt, Ron Henry, Ivan Illich, Sam Keen, Aaron R. Kipnis, Robert Mannis, Lewis Mumford, and Jeremy Rifkin; each has contributed much to my thinking as reflected in this work, though they bear no responsibility whatever for what I have done with their ideas.

I am also deeply indebted to my brother, Mark Kimbrell, and to Jay Walljasper for their invaluable ideas and for their early encouragement for my writing on men's issues. Thanks are also in order to Eric Utne and David Shipley for getting my work on men's issues before the public.

I would like to especially thank my editor at Ballantine Books, Sherri Rifkin, for her many excellent editorial suggestions and for her grace, humor, and persistence in shepherding *The Masculine Mystique* through its many stages. I am also grateful to Jeff Kellogg for reviewing and sharpening the manuscript and for his help in researching the book. My agent, Matthew Bialer, also provided welcome support and encouragement throughout the writing and editing of the book.

I would like to thank my wife, Kaiulani Lee, for her perceptive editorial recommendations, and also for her love and patience as I once again combined being a full-time writer with being a full-time public interest attorney. Finally I would like to thank my children, Kaiulani and Nicholas, for being a constant source of joy, courage, and inspiration.

INTRODUCTION

"You go to work and you support your family and you're the breadwinner and you're the man—that's all your responsibility, that's your life."

"One Monday after my regular Sunday visit my lawyer telephoned me to say that the judge had ruled against me, that I would no longer have any visitation. For no reason I wouldn't be able to see my boy again. I was stunned—just devastated. My son, my beautiful boy, had been yanked from me again, all of a sudden he was gone."

"Everybody knows that war and death are scary, but then they just don't think about it anymore. They forget about it and go back to doing what they were doing. But I was there, I saw it—and somehow I can't forget about it. I can't get rid of it that easily."

"I had never given unemployment a thought. Total shock. Came home, didn't even know my own name—and was that way for quite a while—didn't care. I mean, I thought the whole world had stopped. It was the most devastating thing that ever happened to me. I had been through a serious surgery—it didn't affect me one-tenth of what this did."

"For most injuries I took the needle from the team doctor. I didn't want to disappoint my teammates or the school—I sucked it up, no matter how bad it hurt, and went out to play. I mean, I was young and so wild about winning."

"They called to say that our son had taken his own life. He'd shot himself. We knew that he'd been depressed, but he never said anything. He never told us he was in trouble. He never asked for help."

"Living in a shelter. You try and explain it. But people treat you like they've lost all respect for you as a man, you're a failure— like you're unclean, like you're contagious. 'God, keep away, I don't want to get that from him.' That's the exact feeling you get from people."

"My father never put his arms around me. Never touched me. Never hugged me. It probably wasn't his fault, but he was never there, never, when I needed him most."

"There she was, I mean gorgeous, just lying there, and I couldn't get it up. She kept looking at me and I couldn't get it to work. I just kept thinking, 'What's the matter with me? What's wrong with me?' It was my worst nightmare come true."

"There's only two worlds: Either you work every day in a normal nine-to-five job with a couple of weeks' vacation, or you're dead. . . . Working, it's like breathing. It's something you don't think about: you just do it and it keeps you alive. When you stop, you die."

"It took the heart attack to stop me. Before that I never thought about my health, just didn't occur to me. I never went to the doctor. The way I saw it, I had a job and responsibilities. I just couldn't afford to be sick."

"You know I look back on it, all those years, and I ask myself, 'Is this what it's all about? This is it?' "

As a lawyer and activist, teacher and lecturer, friend and brother, I have had the privilege of working with and listening to a broad spectrum of men like those quoted above. Over the years I have learned that there is something terribly wrong in the lives of most men. Whatever age, political persuasion, race, or creed, these men share a common condition. They feel bewildered, out of control, numbed, angered, and under attack. Numerous social forces, including the increasingly difficult task of breadwinning and the financial and personal devastation of divorce, have eroded their lives to the breaking point. Everywhere I turn, I see the tragic, intimate toll that these realities are taking on men—the undermining of men's health, the suicide of so many young men, lives spent in meaningless work or joblessness, broken marriages, the inability to properly father their children, the lack of any real relationship to the natural world.

It is equally evident that men face their current crisis in the midst of a fundamental confusion about their gender identity. In 1963 Betty Friedan wrote that "American women no longer know who they are."[1] Over the last several years men have been experiencing a similar turmoil. They are locked into rigid stereotypes and financial responsibilities but are also being jolted by economic dislocations and rising demands for a change in gender roles. As a result men have been left confused, without a coherent or sustainable concept of their own masculinity.

Whatever their injuries, fears, or confusions, one thing is certain: Whether at work or at home, whether in the doctor's office or on the battlefield, most men will "keep it to themselves." They are locked into a code of denial and silence. When men talk person-to person or in small groups, there is usually a tenacious reluctance to speak about their problems or to show emotion about their condition. Unfortunately when men do break through and open up to discuss their concerns, or complain of constricted and reduced lives, they are often labeled by men and women alike as "whiners."

Compounding the silence, few in academia or the media have seriously described or analyzed the myriad problems confronting today's men. As author Myron Brenton has noted, "The great outpouring of words about the contemporary American woman these past few years has made it seem that the male either had no problems or didn't count enough to have them aired."[2] The personal and social crisis that so many men face therefore remains "the problem that has no name."[3]

This book unveils the hidden crisis for men. It provides a portrait of the American man that is very different from the one routinely presented in the media, and at odds with the image most men themselves attempt to present. It will reveal some grim and little-known statistics that describe the economic, social, and psychological condition of the vast majority of American men. We will see that most survival, health, and economic statistics show a disproportionate negative rate for men. We will review the indisputable evidence of the massive ongoing impoverishment of the quality of most men's personal and public lives.

The book describes how the crisis for men also involves the degradation and undermining of the timeless concept of masculinity itself. We will see how older, generative concepts of masculinity have been destroyed over the last several generations and how in their place a little-known defective mythology about masculinity has been indelibly encoded into our social structures and psyches. Men live and breathe this myth on a daily basis. It is the basis for many of their dysfunctional daydreams and most of their nightmares. It has now led society into a dangerous "misandry," a belief that masculinity itself is responsible for most of the world's woes.

I have put a name to the dysfunctional and reductionistic modern mythology about the nature of men: the masculine mystique. The masculine mystique is one of the principal influences on human behavior in our time. It has become omnipresent in the lives of men and women; we have ceased even to notice it. Though virtually ignored, it is as destructive for men as the feminine mystique is for women. Not only did it help bring men into their current crisis but it has also kept men from protesting their victimization, and even led them to support a system that has meant a near-fatal undermining of their gender. No one can understand the behavior of men in our society without coming to terms with this pervasive mystique.

What is the masculine mystique? How did it come to have such a tragic hold over men? Who are its principal purveyors, and why? The first two sections of this book investigate this powerful yet virtually unexplored mystique. The mystique's origins are traced back to a continuing historical trauma that accompanied the dawn of the modern age. The mystique became, over several generations, a central component of our economic system and our military might. It was promulgated by some of the most powerful institutions—and most prominent scientific and philosophical figures—of recent history.

As this book describes the current crisis for men, and the masculine mystique, it also seeks to provide an understanding of the new "men's movement." It chronicles how in recent years a small but growing percentage of men have begun to openly address the hidden crisis for men and how they are struggling to break the masculine mystique. These men are joining together to recover the lost elements of masculinity, mourn the lost fathers and sons of the last decades, and reestablish their relation to one another and to the earth. Together they are searching for ways to fundamentally challenge the social structures responsible for the problems of so many men.

Media commentators, and many in society at large, do not seem to know how to react to the new energy among men. Demonstrations of fathers in front of courthouses demanding equal custody rights, millions of "angry" men voting out incumbents, or thousands of men venturing into wilderness retreats to drum, dance, and rediscover the mythic dimensions of masculinity, cause chagrin, fear, and amusement. *Newsweek* magazine heralds the advent of "White Male Paranoia," conservative commentators caustically term the men's movement the War of the Wussies, certain feminists see the new behavior of men as the long-awaited and feared "backlash." Others are simply puzzled.

This book closely examines the men's movement. We will travel to the courtrooms, legislative sessions, government agencies, schools, and health care facilities where the new "masculinists" are fighting the current battles over the bodies and minds of boys and men. We will listen to an array of men—veterans, workers, the unemployed, divorced fathers, African Americans, businessmen—who have not remained victims of the masculine mystique but rather have become the courageous and prophetic vanguard of the men's movement. Through a description of their actions and by a careful analysis of current political, economic, and social alternatives, we will see that, though daunting, the problems of men can be addressed and the masculine mystique shattered.

The concluding sections of this work explain how the men's movement can avoid being merely reactionary, faddish, or single-issue oriented, and can now move forward to refashion a sustainable concept of masculinity and create nothing less than a new politics of masculinity. These sections outline numerous specific steps that need to be taken if men are to address the crisis that has engulfed them and their masculinity. The book concludes with a manifesto of personal and political means and goals by which men can form a cohesive political movement. It is hoped that such a movement among men can help spur a transformation of masculinity for the next century—one that moves men away from the masculine mystique toward a generative and sustaining image of the masculine. A political force based in this transformation could have enormous impact in the years ahead. In fact, as the politics of masculinism develop, they, like feminism, could fundamentally alter our society.

PART I

THE HIDDEN CRISIS

1

FACING THE FACTS

Our civilization is a dingy ungentlemanly business;
it drops so much out of a man.   —Robert Louis Stevenson

or several years I have been involved in litigation and lobbying on what are termed men's issues. In addition I have often written about and lectured on the urgent need for a national men's movement. During this time, both in the public media and personally, I have repeatedly met with confusion and consternation over the very concept of "men's issues." Most men and women I encounter respond to the idea that men are experiencing oppression with surprise, humor, and sometimes even outrage. The questions tend to be the same: "Why are you writing (talking) about men's issues?" "Why are men whining?" "Why are men angry?" "What is this discussion of a masculine mystique?" "After all," they ask, "aren't men the privileged half of our society?" "Isn't calling for a men's movement as meaningless and ironic as calling for White Power?"

I confess to a lingering frustration over these routine responses. Virtually every statistic on health or survival, and most on economic well-being, show that despite rumors and myths to the contrary, the vast majority of men are being devastated by our socioeconomic system. Though American society continues to empower a small percentage of men, and a smaller but increasing percentage of women, it is causing significant confusion and anguish for most men.

This work was written to address the growing crisis for men and masculinity and to provide a blueprint for a transformational political movement for men. However, for the many Americans who see no need for such a movement (or book), clearly a preliminary task is in order. They need to face the facts about men. We begin therefore with an overview of the grim condition of the American male—for many, a long-overdue glimpse into a hidden crisis.

■ *Though few are aware of it, men's life expectancy has dropped dramatically as compared with women's over the last several decades.* Due to a variety of causes including accident, suicide, disease, and stress, far too many men are dying ahead of their time. Through 1920 the life expectancy of males and females was roughly the same.[1] Since that time, and increasingly in the 1970s and 1980s, the gap between the genders has widened. Now women are expected to outlive men by approximately seven years. Currently African-American men have the lowest life expectancy of any population group (64.6 years). White males have a lower life expectancy (72.9 years) than do African-American women (73.8 years) or white women (79.6 years). During the last thirty years the ratio of male mortality to female mortality has increased in every age category.[2]

■ *Annual statistics show that America's leading fatal diseases target men far more often than women.* Heart, lung, and liver disease, cancer, and hypertension remain inordinately higher for men than for women. For men between the ages of twenty-five and sixty-five, the death rate from heart disease is about three times that of women in the same age group. Though heart attacks are also the number-one killer of women, almost three-quarters of women who die of heart attacks are seventy-five or older. By this time the average man has been dead for over two years.[3]

Men are also at an increased risk, over women, of developing and dying of cancer. Over the last thirty years the overall cancer death rate for men has increased 21 percent, while the rate for women has remained about the same. Each year over 55,000 more men than women develop cancer, and 30,000 more men than women die of cancer. In every age group men's probability of developing invasive cancers is greater than women's. Overall men have a one in two chance of developing cancer while women have a one in three chance.[4]

Male-specific cancers (e.g., prostate and testicular) have reached epidemic proportions. Each year an estimated 200,000 men are diagnosed with prostate cancer, and about 38,000 will die of it.[5]

Men also suffer disproportionately from a number of potentially life-threatening stress-related diseases, including hypertension and peptic ulcers. Men are of course the primary victims of the growing AIDS pandemic.

■ *Men are the primary victims of crime, violence, and murder.* Rates of violent crimes and theft victimizations remain significantly higher for men than for women. Black men are at the greatest risk of becoming victims of crime, white men have the second-greatest risk, then black women, and finally white women.[6] A 1994 Department of Justice study found that though violence against women is increasing, men were being victimized by violent crime at a 63 percent higher rate than women.[7] Moreover, since 1976 the rate of murders for men has increased by about 10 percent, while remaining virtually unchanged for women. As of 1992, men were about three and a half times more likely to be victims of murder than women.[8]

■ *Men comprise the vast majority of those killed or seriously injured on the job.* Men represent 55 percent of the workforce but 93 percent of all job-related deaths.[9] Further, over two-thirds of all serious workplace injuries and diseases happen to men.[10] Part of the accident toll is due to our nation's hazardous workplaces. Men still represent approximately 98 percent of the workforce in the nation's most dangerous professions. Thousands of men are killed on the job each year. Every day almost as many American men are killed at work as were killed during an average day in the Vietnam War.[11]

■ *America's men are far more likely than its women to suffer from alcohol or drug addiction.* It is estimated that close to 75 percent of all alcoholics are men, and 50 percent more men are regular users of illicit drugs than women. Men also represent close to 90 percent of all those charged with drunkenness, 80 percent of liquor law violators, and over 86 percent of those arrested for driving under the influence of alcohol. Men also are about 84 percent of those charged with drug abuse violations.[12]

■ *Recent studies show that men are chronically underdiagnosed for depression and other mental diseases.* Men are far less likely to be diagnosed for depression than women when the same symptoms are present. A 1991 report indicated that clinicians failed to diagnose depression in two-thirds of male patients who were suffering from well-recognized symptoms of the illness. Additionally, private psychotherapeutic professionals often avoid men, who are perceived as threatening. As a result men are more likely than women to be referred away from private care and to public mental health clinics, which are generally understaffed and underfunded.[13]

■ *Males in the United States are the suicide sex.* While suicide rates for women have been stable over the last twenty years, among men they have increased rapidly. Overall men commit suicide at four times the rate of women. Approximately twenty-five thousand men take their own lives each year.[14]

■ *The health and violence crisis for African-American men is especially acute.* African-American males have the lowest life expectancy of any segment of the American population. They are especially at risk for cancer. The cancer-death rates for African-American men is significantly higher than that for white males.[15] Black males also suffer from mental disorders at a far higher rate than black females or whites. National statistics on in-patient admissions to state and county hospitals show that black males are institutionalized at more than twice the rate of white males or black females, and over four times more than white females.[16]

Black males also have the highest rate of violent crime victimization. They suffer 60 percent more violent crime than white males or black females, and more than 150 percent more than white females. Black males aged sixteen to nineteen are particularly at risk; their violent crime victimization rate is almost double the rate for white males and three times that for white females in the same age group. Additionally, black males aged twelve to twenty-four are almost fourteen times as likely to be homicide victims as are members of the general public.[17]

■ *Boys in the United States are diagnosed and treated for a variety of behavioral and mental disorders far more frequently than girls.* Boys are twice as likely as girls to suffer from autism and eight times more likely to be diagnosed and medicated for hyperkinesis (hyperactivity). Over 700,000 boys are being drugged for this "disorder" every year. Boys stutter more and are diagnosed as dyslexic four to nine times as often as girls. Young boys are admitted to mental hospitals and juvenile institutions about seven times more frequently than girls of similar age and socioeconomic background.[18]

■ *America's young men (ages fifteen to twenty-four) are far more likely than women of the same age group to commit suicide or become addicted to alcohol and drugs.* Young men in this age group die at a rate more than three times that of women of the same age. They take their own lives about five times as often as women in the same age group. They suffer alcohol dependency and serious drug addiction at many times the rate of women of the same age group.[19]

■ *Hundreds of thousands of young men are taking steroids and growth hormones.* Approximately 500,000 young men are regularly taking dangerous and toxic "body enhancing" substances, including anabolic steroids and genetically engineered human growth hormone, in an attempt to fulfill the current stereotype of the male body or to enhance their performance in sports.[20]

■ *Men are suffering an epidemic of sexual dysfunction.* Recent studies show that more and more men are experiencing a variety of sexual problems. So-called impotence has become especially prevalent, now affecting more than 20 million American men. Each year there are approximately half a million outpatient visits and thirty thousand hospitalizations for "impotence," at a cost of around $150 million. Causes include increases in prostate cancer, psychological stress, abuse of alcohol and drugs, and the impacts of environmental toxins.[21]

■ *Despite the view that boys are favored in the classroom, boys are faring far worse than girls in our nation's schools.* Those punished and rejected by our school systems are overwhelmingly boys—incidents of corporal punishment and suspension are far more common with boys. Boys consistently represent a disproportionate number of those with low grades at virtually all primary- and secondary-school levels. Eighth-grade boys are 50 percent more likely to be held back a grade than girls. And according to the U.S. Department of Education, eighth-grade girls are twice as likely as boys to aspire to a professional, business, or managerial career. In high school two-thirds of special education students are boys. Over 60 percent of high school dropouts are boys.[22]

■ *Men are now less likely than women to attend college and less likely to graduate from college.* Currently 46 percent of men attend college versus 54 percent of women. Forty-five percent of men graduate from college, whereas 55 percent of women graduate.[23] Women also represent 59 percent of all master's-degree candidates.[24]

■ *This generation has witnessed a dramatic drop in real wages for the average working man, while that of women has increased.* Men in the unskilled-labor market have seen their wages drop over 25 percent over the last decade.[25] Real wages for men under twenty-five have experienced an even more precipitous decline. Over the last two years, wages paid male high school graduates were 26.5 percent less than in 1979. The recent drop in wages has not been limited to the young or undereducated. College-educated men over forty-five have also seen their yearly pay descend by 18 percent over the last five years. In each of these categories women have experienced an increase in annual real wages.[26]

■ *Recent economic trends have left millions of men permanently unemployed or underemployed.* The United States has transformed itself into a postindustrial society over the last twenty years. As America's economy becomes ever more high technology and service oriented, traditional blue-collar male jobs (i.e., factory, construction, and transportation) have become scarce. During the 1980s the number of men (twenty-two to fifty-eight years of age) who were working full-time, year-round declined by over 10 percent. By 1991 the number of men working full-time year-round (fifty to fifty-two weeks) was declining by 1.2 million each year, while the number of women working full-time was increasing by 800,000. Agricultural work for men has also declined. Over 600,000 farmers have lost their land in the last decade (farmers are 79 percent male).[27]

■ *Male heads of household now have less net worth than women who head households.* Due to increasing male unemployment and the demands of child and alimony support, there has been a dramatic decline in the income of male-heading households. According to the U.S. Census Bureau, women who are heads of households now have a net worth 23 percent greater than that of men who are heads of households.[28]

■ *The economic and social crisis for men is especially dire for African-American men.* African-American men suffer unemployment rates twice as high as those of white men. Moreover they are far more likely to be jailed and far less likely to gain an education than African-American women. One out of four African-American men between the ages of twenty and twenty-nine is either in jail, on probation, or on parole—ten times the proportion for African-American women of the same age range. Also, more African-American men are in jail than in college, and there are 40 percent more African-American women than men studying in our nation's colleges and universities. Even black males who succeed in becoming college graduates suffer economically. Their salaries are far less than white male college graduates' and less than both white and black female college graduates'. By contrast black female college graduates now make slightly more than white female college graduates.[29]

■ *The millions of American male veterans who have returned home from war with broken bodies or minds have been grossly neglected.* One in three American men is a veteran. The toll of war and our national neglect of these men has been high. Fifty thousand Vietnam War veterans are blind, and 33,000 are paralyzed. It is estimated that nearly 100,000 Vietnam veterans have committed suicide since the end of the war, almost twice the number of men killed in battle.[30] Researchers also estimate that 20 percent of all Vietnam veterans and 60 percent of combat veterans were "psychological casualties." Within the first decade after the war a presidential review found that 400,000 Vietnam veterans were either in prison, on parole, on probation, or awaiting trial. Now 25 percent of the men in prison are Vietnam veterans. Furthermore, on any given night an estimated 271,000 of the nation's veterans are homeless.[31] Adding insult to injury, government reports show a shocking lack of adequate hospitalization and mental health facilities for veterans.

■ *The problem of homelessness is primarily a problem of single adult men.* Homelessness is often perceived as a problem primarily of women and children. About 10 percent of our homeless are children, another 10 percent are adults with children (a majority of whom are women). The rest, approximately 80 percent, are single adults. Out of that total about 80 percent are single men. From these statistics a picture of the homeless emerges that is different from that usually portrayed. Of all the homeless adults, single or with families, 70 percent are men. And of all homeless people—adults or children—men represent 58 percent of the total and boys 7 percent.[32]

■ *Millions of fathers have lost meaningful contact with their children as family courts discriminate against men in child custody decisions.* Throughout the United States, divorce is reaching epidemic proportions. One recent estimate is that two-thirds of all first marriages will end in separation or divorce. Slightly more than half of all divorced couples have children eighteen years of age or younger at the time of their separation. Each year there are approximately one million divorces which affect one million children. Fathers and children have been the biggest losers in divorce and custody wars. Mothers initiate divorce actions at over twice the rate of men, while, in many jurisdictions, men receive physical custody of children in only about 10 percent of all contested divorce cases.[33]

Discrimination against fathers by custody court judges and lawyers is a major factor in fathers losing custody of their children. A New York State Task Force survey revealed that nearly three-quarters of attorneys surveyed believed that child custody awards are "often" or "sometimes" based on the assumption that children belong with their mothers rather than on independent facts. Over half of the attorneys believed that judges "always" or "often" employed a maternal preference in custody awards, and 24 percent of attorneys believed that judges "rarely" or "never" gave fair and serious consideration to fathers seeking physical custody of their children. Nineteen ninety-two statistics on child support awards show the result of the discrimination practiced against fathers in New York State courts. The courts issued 65,536 support awards involving 94,788 children; only 3,537 (3.7 percent) were given primary residence with their fathers.[34]

Approximately six million American fathers are now divorced "visiting" fathers. The plight of these men and their children is virtually ignored. Due in part to custody orders, move-away mothers, psychological stress, denied visitation by the mother, remarriage, and relocation, about 40 percent of children see their nonresidential father once a year or not at all.[35]

The toll on the mental health of fathers is high. The suicide rate for divorced men is four times that of divorced women, and higher than that of other men. Divorced men also have higher rates of drug and alcohol abuse and depression than single or married men or single, married, or divorced women.[36]

■ *Men are increasingly torn between the necessities of their job and their desire to have time for their families.* In a 1993 poll, fathers were asked what part of their lives they would "most like to change." Almost three-quarters of those polled said, "I'd spend more time with my children." This represented a nearly 20 percent increase in this response since 1984.[37] Fathers' conflict over spending more time with their children is exacerbated by their continuing role as the primary breadwinner. In 1991, among married couples with preschool children, 77 percent of all fathers were employed full-time, year-round, compared to only 28 percent of all mothers.[38]

■ *Men face serious discrimination in the criminal justice system.* Overall, 94 percent of those incarcerated in U.S. prisons are men. The male incarceration rate is more than 16 times higher than the female incarceration rate, though females are charged with nearly 20 percent of all crimes. Men are less likely than women to receive a plea bargain. They routinely receive longer prison sentences than women for the same offense. Men also comprise virtually 100 percent of those executed in the U.S. each year.[39]

■ *The increasing number of men now heading single-parent households are given virtually no social or government support.* Fathers now head over 1,300,000 single-parent households. This is the fastest-growing trend in parenting in the United States. Many of these new single-parent fathers need support in order to cope with their new financial and personal responsibilities. While numerous government and private programs have been designed for the single mother, programs to aid the single father are almost nonexistent.[40]

■ *As life in the workplace "harness" undermines men's health and their ability to parent, it also makes men obsolete after they retire.* Older men, with the exception of the tiny minority who are part of the power elite, are viewed as little more than useless when they can no longer fulfill their primary role as productive workers. Of course old age in our society too often means obsolescence, vulnerability, and alienation, regardless of gender. However, it is especially cruel for men. Due to the stresses of their lives, fewer men reach old age than women. However, for those that do, it is often traumatic. America's elderly men commit suicide over five times more often than women of the same age. Their health is often far poorer than that of their female counterparts. They are twice as susceptible to cancer and more vulnerable to other chronic illnesses. Furthermore men over sixty-five are twice as likely to be victims of violent crime as women in their age group, and almost four times as likely to be hospitalized for alcohol-related medical problems.[41]

As society begins to face the hidden crisis for men—a reality marked by disease, premature death, suicide, addiction, homelessness, violence, the increasing stresses of work and divorce, and obsolescence in old age—perhaps it will come to better understand the need for men to address this increasing tragic toll on men and boys. Perhaps men and women alike will no longer view the idea of "men's issues" with humor or surprise but rather with empathy and understanding. Perhaps those confused by the concept of a men's movement will see its importance and understand its vital role in addressing this hidden crisis.

2

JUST LIKE A MAN

So God created humans in his own image, in the image of God they
were created, male and female they were created. —Genesis 1:27

The male model involves a relative degree of obsession, egocentricity,
ruthlessness, a relative suspension of social and personal values, to
which the female brain is simply not attuned.

—Anne Moir and David Jessel[1]

Gender remains among the most alluring mysteries and won-
ders of creation. Throughout the natural order the attraction
and interaction of male and female are the basis of the regen-
eration of much of the living world. Even today in the midst of
our highly technologized society, our survival is still inseparably
linked to the continuing fertility of animals and plants. Our lives remain dependent to a great extent on the communion of genders.
Most immediately, it is in human femaleness and maleness that we
all have our personal origins, and our hope of the continuance of
family, community, and the human species itself.

The ancients consistently celebrated the generativity of masculinity and femininity. Rituals and sacraments were enacted to

bring forth the gender powers and to express gratitude for their bounty. Female-fertility carvings and pictures are among the oldest artifacts we have from several ancient civilizations. Representations of the phallus were also common and especially important as objects that, it was believed, could renew the fertility of the earth. Numerous traditional societies had spring planting festivals that involved a dance around a ceremonial phallus to encourage bountiful crops. The maypole dance, still occasionally practiced today, evolved from this early custom.

Feminine and masculine are also seen as universal creative principles, the yin and the yang, extending to all reality. Premodern civilizations have routinely related these gender opposites to the phenomena of the natural world—night and day, heaven and earth, land and sea, rain and soil. Medieval European mystics saw the male and female as part of a cosmic "sacred marriage," with the sun and air being associated with the masculine and the moon and water with the feminine. In the Hindu marriage ceremony the groom says to the bride, "I am sky, you are earth," and she replies, "I am earth, you are sky."

Traditional societies were also well aware of the dark side of gender and sexual attraction. They teach that gender has a horrific shadow reality. Their myths often depict entranced sexual union that leads not to creation but rather to frenzied Dionysian destruction. Motherhood and femininity are transformed from the essence of nurturing to the specter of Gorgon and Harpies and to the smothering, vengeance, and murder personified in a Medea. Even the most primal and creative of male father gods, whether Odin, Shiva, or Yahweh, are often presented as brutal, destructive, and even genocidal.

Though often surprisingly consistent, gender symbolism in the past was not uniform. Geography, economics, and other exigencies often helped to determine how each community would refashion the timeless complementarity of masculine and feminine. Many historians have seen gender definitions as a social mirror as each culture re-creates sexual identities in its own image.

Our modern culture is no exception. In fact we have redefined the genders as no other culture before us has. Over the last several generations we have relentlessly shattered older prototypes of masculine and feminine. In their place we have created new myths and mystiques of the masculine and feminine to better fit our industrial social system. Remarkably this transformation of gender in the modern age has gone largely unexamined.

WHAT IS A MAN?

When each of us attempts to picture what a man is, our projections will likely be a somewhat confused hybrid of personal and social associations. If we had a strong male presence in our childhood, our conception of the masculine may be colored by a family figure—father, uncle, husband, or brother. However, in that so many men for so many generations have been absent from the home, most people may not have a strong male family figure with whom to relate.

In the absence of a familial masculine image, the media have played a crucial role in defining modern masculinity. Author and media expert Jerry Mander reminds us that "we evolve into the images we carry in our minds. We become what we see."[2] It is likely that most men and women have internalized a collage of simulated male images, ranging from the paterfamilias in *Father Knows Best*, to the destructive male machine, "the Terminator."

No matter how varied each of our individual responses, our collective masculine images are firmly stereotyped and have been for decades. These socially accepted versions of masculinity permeate the lives of boys and girls as they get older, and are set by the time we are adults and assume our economic and social roles. Research over the last quarter century has been near uniform in depicting our society's internalized view of what makes a man and what makes a woman. Below is a representative list taken from United States surveys and research:[3]

HE:	SHE:
More self-interested	More other-focused
Very competitive	Less competitive
Needs less intimacy	Needs more intimacy
Needs less approval	Needs more approval
Very active	More passive
Very objective	Very subjective
More independent	Less independent
More logical	More irrational
Often detached	Often emotional
Strong drive for power and money	Power and money less important
More manipulative	More cooperative
More machine-oriented	Less technically adept
Never cries	Cries easily
Very ambitious	Less ambitious
Talks mostly about things	Talks mostly about people
Takes things literally	Looks for hidden meanings
Engages in put-downs	Engages in backbiting
Less responsive listener	More responsive listener
Less apologetic	More apologetic
Less willing to seek help	Seeks help readily
Less interested in the arts and religion	More interested in the arts and religion
Often intimidates others	Seldom intimidates others
Often seeks conflict	Tends to avoid conflict
Thrives on receiving	Thrives on giving
More polygamous	More monogamous
More sadistic	More masochistic
More sex-oriented	More love-oriented
Worries less about others	Worries more about others
More aggressive	Less aggressive
Initiates war	Does not make war

It would be easy to point out numerous exceptions to these generalizations, and many of us are angered by the gross simplifications and stereotypes in this list. Nevertheless surveys show that the composite gender traits presented above have for the most part become accepted in our society. When confronted with behavior that is overtly competitive, aggressive, dangerous, violent, insensitive, abusive, selfish, unemotional, hyperrational, or ambitious, we respond with "Just like a man!" When viewing behavior that is nurturing, selfless, overtly sensitive, passive, irrational, emotional, and intuitive, we tend not to think of men but rather of women.

Many women have of course challenged the prevalent stereotypes of modern gender consciousness. They have launched a three-decade-long assault on the "feminine mystique." Feminists have attacked stereotypes that destroy the rich diversity of feminine traits and archetypes. They have relentlessly torn down defective modern myths about women that they see as limiting women's aspirations and effectively excluding women from personal growth and an equal share of power and financial opportunity.

Unfortunately few men or women have mounted a similar assault on the "masculine mystique" of our times. There have been few "masculinists" to defend masculinity from the onslaught of the current stereotypical view of the male gender. There has been a remarkable silence about the ongoing destruction of the diversity of masculine traits and archetypes.

Yet the current masculine mystique reduces and limits male archetypes and potentialities at least as much as the feminine mystique did those of women. The wide variety of masculine ideals of numerous past cultures have all but vanished. Gone is the premodern man, whether hunter-gatherer, farmer, or craftsman, who was steeped in family, land, community, and religion. The traditional masculine traits of generativity, stewardship, generosity, teaching, husbandry, honor, and even adventure are virtually ignored. These traits have been largely replaced by self-interest, efficiency, power-seeking, promiscuity, greed, insensitivity, competition, manipulation, and the numerous other characteristics consistently listed as emblems of modern masculinity. Assuming these current characteristics to be the essence of masculinity inevitably leads to the degradation of men and an historic, if hidden, crisis in sustaining a viable and generative concept of masculinity itself.

The crisis undermining masculinity has now reached alarming proportions. Under the aegis of the masculine mystique, masculinity has become the "shadow" gender. This is especially apparent in the general view that many men and women have of male sexuality. Masculine sexuality has become routinely associated with promiscuity, rape, and violence. Phallic penetration is most often analogized to the destructive penetration of guns (bullets) and missiles. The concept of generative penetration, the phallus as seed bearer, similar to the creative penetration of planting seeds in the soil or communicating a penetrating idea, is almost never associated with masculine power in our culture but was commonplace in virtually all prior cultures. Men now hear that "the hurting of women is . . . basic to the sexual pleasure of men,"[4] as well as the hair-raising statement that "all men are rapists and that's all they are."[5]

Further, most of the world's woes, from violence and racism to war, the environmental crisis, and poverty, are seen as the direct result of masculine values. Feminist scholars and authors Daphne Patai and Noretta Koertge document how the habit of blaming masculinity and men for all the problems of women and society has become endemic in Women's Studies courses at universities around the country. "Classical psychotherapy (like traditional motherhood) is a very demanding endeavor," they write. "But a sort of 'I'm OK— you're OK, but men are horrible' variant of it is—as we have seen— very popular in the pedagogy of Women's Studies. On this model women empower themselves by realizing that all their troubles result from patriarchy."[6]

One female student interviewed by Patai and Koertge describes her experience in a Women's Studies course:

> The course was Introduction to Women's Studies. . . . The class made me think of a skit on Monty Python which involves a quiz show, except the answer to every question is "pork." And whatever the quiz show host asks—for example, "What's the capital of

Pennsylvania?"—the answer is "pork." In the class I took the answer was always "men." . . . "Who contributes to all the violence in the world?" "Men." "Who's responsible for everything we endure?" "Men." . . . I was involved with a man at the time, and I thought that he didn't fit their categories of what men were like. And I also saw him as having been pressed into stereotypes of his own.[7]

Author Sally Miller Gearhart, former chairperson of the Department of Speech and Communication at San Francisco State University, takes masculinity bashing to disturbing heights when she prescribes three "strategies . . . to create and preserve a less violent world. I) Every culture must affirm a female future. II) Species responsibility must be returned to women in every culture. III) The proportion of men must be reduced to and maintained at approximately 10 percent of the human race."[8]

Clearly we have come a long way from the traditional view of the complementary creativity of genders and seeing the phallus as the "tree" of creation. The masculine-mystique view of masculinity has led society into a general misandry, which matches the misogyny of prior generations.

Misandry is the general assumption that masculinity is the source of all our social ills. It is the sexist assumption that it is "natural" for any male person to be dominating, oppressive, violent, sexually abusive, spiritually immature, and antagonistic to nature. It assigns blame solely to men for humanity's historic evils. It naturally leads to a hatred of men and masculinity.

MEN: NATURE'S BLUNDER

Unfortunately, far from challenging the masculine mystique, misandry, and the reduction and destruction of masculinity, many are now attempting to bolster the mystique's version of masculinity by advocating that it is scientifically based. Numerous so-called gender experts, seemingly unaware of the diversity of masculine archetypes of past ages, now insist that modern masculine traits are an inevitable result of biology. They adamantly proclaim that the masculine-mystique man is the true man, the universal man. Neoconservative columnist George F. Will summarized this view. He writes that "nature blundered badly in designing males . . . because of neurochemical stuff like testosterone, males are not naturally suited to civilization."[9] Congressman Newt Gingrich, current Speaker of the House of Representatives, follows suit: "One of the things that we know historically and biologically is that males are designed to be relatively irresponsible [as compared to women]."[10]

Fellow conservative and author George Gilder is also sure that men are biologically and intrinsically selfish, violent, and sex-driven—needing women, marriage, and children to civilize their innate competitive and destructive drives. Basic to his view is the insistence that, anthropologically speaking, men are neither generative nor nurturing. According to Gilder, "fatherhood is but a frail impulse."[11] He makes the following further comparisons between the genders:

> Women's sex drive is not usually short term and copulatory; it embraces the rich physical events of maternity. The man has only one sex act, intercourse, and a more compulsive need to perform with whoever is immediately available.
>
> Women's orgasms are partly dependent on a reliable partner who will stay. Men's are not.
>
> Women want to know the father of their children. Men may be far away when their children are born.
>
> Women become pregnant, feel vulnerable, want protection. Men do not have these experiences.
>
> Women labor and bear children, nurture them, sense their terrible fragility, see the need for a stable society. The men's connection to children is more tenuous and is granted by the women. . . .
>
> Women are strikingly less interested in competition, dominance, and power than are men.[12]

Renowned Democratic-party spokesperson and former member of Congress Barbara Jordan is the political opposite of Will, Gingrich, and Gilder on most issues. However, she is in full agreement with them that masculine stereotypes are a result of men's biology. In 1991 Jordan told a gathering of women political leaders that men are "structurally" inferior to women when it comes to empathy and caring for others. Appearing as a featured speaker at the Women's Campaign Research Fund meeting in Austin, Texas, Jordan stated, "I believe that women have a capacity for understanding and compassion which a man structurally does not have, does not have it because he cannot have it. He's just incapable of it." Jordan continued, stating that "this caring, this compassion is endemic to women" and makes them good political candidates and officeholders. She also stated that "women, I believe, would be more willing to engage in compromises than men are. We recognize this value of compromise, and the reason we recognize the value of compromise is we do not delude ourselves into thinking we are always right."[13] Later, when confronted with protests over her "sexist" remarks, Jordan explained that she did not intend to offend but that her views were based on "observable fact."[14]

It is not just the political pundits who have assumed that biology determines the behavior of men in our society. Numerous respected researchers fervently believe that the central components of the masculine mystique are a product of the mix of men's biochemicals and the "circuitry" of their brains. Researchers Anne Moir and David Jessel, authors of the book *Brain Sex: The Real Difference Between Men and Women,* provide the basic cutting-edge scientific view of gender differentiation:

Until recently, behavioral differences between the sexes have been explained away by social conditioning—the expectations of parents, whose attitudes in turn reflect the expectations of society. . . . Today, there is too much new biological evidence for the sociological argument to prevail. *The argument of biology at last provides a comprehensive, and scientifically provable framework within which we can begin to understand why we are who we are. . . . It is our hormones which make us behave in specific, stereotypical ways. . . .* What makes the difference is the interplay between those hormones and the male or female brains, prewired specifically to react with them.[15] (Emphasis added.)

An increasing number of gender scientists are now joining Moir and Jessel in claiming to have discovered "proof" that men are biologically preset to become the cutthroat, power-driven, hypercompetitive, sexually promiscuous, destructive, militarist, corporate achiever.[16] These claims give rise to a chilling proposition: If men are biologically more aggressive and antisocial, why not begin to tinker with their genes and brains? If economics or culture create the hidden crisis for men, then we should change our society but if the "real" problem with men is their masculine biology, why not change that biology? Moir and Jessel give us one version of this eugenic suggestion:

Just as there is a marked gender difference in schizophrenia, it is possible that the overwhelming male bias in criminal behavior may have a similar origin—in the wiring errors liable to occur when the natural female circuitry of the embryonic brain is reconnected to the male mode. . . . If so, is it conceivable that we might, chemically, be able to abort the incidence [in men] not only of some psychiatric disorders, but of some aspects of criminality itself. . . . And should we? What eugenic implications may this new knowledge bring—what opportunities and what terrors?[17]

The implications of this view are terrifying. The scientific boosting of the masculine mystique leads almost inevitably to the prospect of the genetic engineering of men. As we will describe in a later chapter, the drugging of millions of boys to change their "antisocial" behavior is already well under way. Before long, if the new biologists have their way, the rest of the male gender may soon also be candidates for a chemical or genetic makeover.

As certain scientists contemplate the profoundly disturbing prospect of biologically altering the male, their view of men has other, less dramatic, but equally unfortunate consequences. Perhaps most importantly the biologistic view of male behavior obviates the need for political action to address the growing hidden crisis for men. Real men aren't "wired" to be nurturing parents, so society may as well accept that men are made for work, not parenting, and further legally codify the belief that mothers make better parents than fathers. Men are hormonally predisposed to crime and violence, so don't look to education, rehabilitation, or job programs to ease the epidemic of male teenage suicide or the violence of young African-American men. Since men are biologically preset for competition and ruthlessness, the unemployed, homeless, and aged men just have to get used to the fact that in every competitive activity someone loses. The scientific analysis of gender view would also not offer much comfort to veterans. After all, the destructiveness and carnage of modern mechanized warfare is just part of the "uncivilized" biology of males. Additionally the prevalence of schizophrenia, drug addiction, alcoholism, and other behavioral "abnormalities" in men is linked to the hormone-brain relationship, so attempting to solve these and other male problems through education, counseling, and other social efforts would be futile.

Fortunately the biological view of gender behavior has not won universal acceptance. Many have criticized its reductionistic view of gender and its questionable attempt to attribute a wide range of human behaviors solely to hormones, genes, and "brain wiring." Feminists such as Carol Tavris, Barbara Ehrenreich, and Katha Pollitt have cautioned that using biologically based assumptions about feminine behavior is not only scientifically unsound but also socially damaging. They make a compelling argument that the biological-determinist view is a dangerous tool used to destroy the ability of women to fully explore all the aspects of their gender. Clearly the same applies for men.

This is of course not to deny that there are differences in male and female biology and physiology. However, anthropological evidence overwhelmingly indicates that neither physiology nor biology is the determining factor in how men and women behave, but rather that cultural and social factors are the key influences in determining how any purported complex of biological predispositions are manifested in the real world.

In fact, as has been noted, the view that men are biologically or intrinsically competitive, self-centered, autonomous, promiscuous, work-obsessed, and power-driven is simply not borne out by reports on the behavior of men in other cultures and in other times. Even the earliest anthropology classics, from Bronislaw Malinowski's view of the Trobriand Islanders to Margaret Mead's voluminous research, revealed that men in different cultures were often almost the direct opposites of the supposedly biologically based modern male. Moreover, subsequent international anthropological scholarship has revealed modes of male social interaction that are remarkably diverse and often in striking contrast to nearly every element of the masculine mystique as advertised by Will, Gilder, Jordan, and the new gender scientists.[18]

These findings continue to surprise some researchers, who have been entrained to the belief that the modern masculine model was biologically based and ubiquitous throughout history. Researcher David D. Gilmore, who has studied male behavior from a wide range of societies and cultures around the globe, remarks on his own discovery of the variety of male behavior:

When I started researching . . . I was prepared to rediscover the old saw that conventional femininity is nurturing and passive and that masculinity is self-serving, egotistical, and uncaring. But I did not find this. One of my findings is that manhood ideologies always include a criterion of selfless generosity even to the point of sacrifice. Again and again we find that "real" men are those who give more than they take; they serve others. Real men are generous to a fault, like the Mehinaku fisherman, the Samburu cattle-herder, or the Sambia or Dodith Big Man. Non-men are often stigmatized as stingy and unproductive. Manhood therefore is also a nurturing concept, if we define that term as giving, subventing, or other directed. . . . What is important about all this is that it . . . [ends by] refuting the sociobiological evocation of male aggressiveness as innate.[19]

Over the last two chapters we have seen how a little-recognized crisis has engulfed modern men and how the very concept of masculinity has been distorted into a dangerous and dysfunctional image. It is important to point out that the hidden crisis for men and masculinity does not affect only men. Each member of a family is devastated by the illness or early death of a husband and father due to stress or accident. Daughters and sons are deprived of the presence of a father, whether the absence is due to the exigencies of work or to divorce. When men who have provided for their families for decades lose their jobs, marriages are destroyed and families are torn apart, resulting in increased poverty, hopelessness, violence, and illness. The suicide of a young man is an irreplaceable loss to his family, school, and community. The epidemic of male alcohol and drug abuse also affects families and society at large. And all of society pays both morally and financially for the neglect of African-American men, veterans, and the homeless.

The impacts of the masculine mystique's decimation of masculinity are also shared by all. Under the masculine mystique both boys and girls are brought up with a reduced and dangerously disfigured concept of the masculine. Our educational system and work system are built around this faulty image. Virtually all our marriages, parental relationships, and friendships are compromised by this dysfunctional masculine stereotype.

Most importantly the masculine mystique is the ideological underpinning for many of our current social plights. If we are to address virtually any of the pressing problems of our time—employment, health, deteriorating families and communities, violence and crime, or the environment—we can only succeed if we recognize and address the masculine mystique and its disfigurement of masculinity.

Unfortunately little progress has been made toward this goal. While impressive strides have been made over the last decades in analyzing and confronting psychological attitudes and social structures that result in the demeaning and oppression of women and the feminine, we are long overdue for the same kind of examination for men and the masculine.

Therefore an understanding of the genesis and spread of the masculine mystique is of key relevance for men and the men's movement. For men cannot counter the biologistic view of masculine behavior, and the frightening proposals to remake male biology, without an adequate analysis of the cultural and historic basis of current gender stereotypes. Men cannot fully address the structural ills responsible for the hidden crisis without first understanding how those toxic psychic and social structures were created. Men cannot recover from the pathology and denial spawned by the masculine mystique until they have revisited the extraordinary historical trauma that initiated it, centuries ago.

3

THE ENCLOSURE OF MEN

The regime of industrial economics crushed gender.   —Ivan Illich[1]

It is impossible to imagine the scope and impact of the process of enclosure.   —Robert L. Heilbroner[2]

On December 23, 1988, the assassination of Francisco "Chico" Mendes was headline news around the world. Prior to his death Mendes, who lived in the state of Acre in western Brazil, had become a folk hero to the people of his region. A tireless labor leader and a self-taught environmentalist, Mendes had also become an international symbol of the attempt to save the rain forests of Brazil from ever-encroaching development.

Mendes originally made his livelihood as a rubber tapper in the rain forests of Acre. He and others who tapped the rubber trees practiced a form of agriculture that had remained a constant for generations. They lived off the forest but did little permanent harm to that unique and fragile ecosystem.

In the late 1960s Mendes began to see the invasion of his beloved forests by cattle ranchers who were cutting down and burning the rain forest for grazing land. As the cattle ranchers became more numerous, they needed to acquire and raze ever more of the forest and transform it into pasture. As part of their land grab, the ranchers routinely terrorized local rubber tappers in order to force them off their traditional lands. They often used hired gunmen (*pistoleiros*) to commit the necessary violence. By the mid-1980s over 100,000 tappers had lost their homes and had been effectively expelled from the region.

The ranchers destroyed the Brazilian rain forest at an alarming rate. By the late 1980s over 20 percent of the forest had been burned. In the summer of 1988 world attention became focused on the magnitude of this ecological disaster when the *The New York Times* published a stunning composite nighttime photograph taken by satellite showing thousands of fires burning throughout the Amazon rain forest.

Unlike many others who were too frightened or discouraged to fight the ranchers, Mendes was a tenacious defender of the rain forest and his way of life. He became a leader in the rubber tappers' union and led a powerful grass-roots movement of several hundred thousand workers. For over a decade he fought countless local battles to halt the ranchers' onslaught. Mendes was also innovative in his approach to preserving the forest. He invented new regulatory approaches that allowed the government to protect the forest while still permitting the tappers their traditional work.

Mendes's efforts put his life in constant danger. By 1988 he had survived five assassination attempts. In the prior year eighty-eight union leaders had been killed by the ranchers and their *pistoleiros*. In the 1980s, land conflicts in the Amazon had led to over one thousand murders (and only two convictions). Chico was too dedicated an activist to seek the role of martyr. "Public gestures and a well-attended funeral will not save Amazonia," he said in one of his last interviews. "I want to live."[3] Chico kept on organizing despite the risk, but he was ever vigilant for his own safety and that of his wife and two young children. In the last months of his life, as he saw other union leaders cut down, Chico repeatedly asked the police and the local and national governments for protection. But the authorities and politicians, often themselves little more than mouthpieces for the ranchers, let his pleas go unanswered.

Two days before Christmas 1988 the inevitable occurred. Mendes was assassinated by order of the cattle interests as he stepped out of his backyard headed for the outdoor shower. A single shotgun blast ripped through his chest. After he was shot, Chico stumbled back into his home and died on his bedroom floor while his four-year-old daughter, Elenira, looked on. After a lengthy investigation and a publicized trial a local rancher and his son were convicted of the murder. However, many felt that the conspiracy surrounding the Mendes murder went far beyond the immediate defendants to include national politicians and transnational business interests. In February 1993 Chico's murderers escaped from prison. They remain at large.

Though he did not seek the role, Mendes became a true martyr for environmental protection. The outrage over his murder led to even greater pressure on the Brazilian government, the multinational beef cartel, and other international companies to halt the destruction of the rain forest.

Of equal importance, however, Mendes was and remains a powerful symbol of resistance to another social ill, one far less discussed than the ecological crisis but of key relevance for men. Mendes is part of a long tradition of men—farmers, peasants, and craftsmen—who over the last centuries have fought and died rather than relinquish their land, independence, and traditional way of life.

The historical process by which a people are separated from their ancestral work and land, as happened to Mendes and the rubber tappers of the Brazilian rain forest, is termed *enclosure*. The land-enclosure process is not just a recent phenomenon for indigenous peoples and local communities in the Third World. Rather it began in Europe over half a millennium ago at the dawn of the industrial age. This slow revolution in taking land from those who for generations have lived and worked on it, to free it for the mass production of valuable export crops, has now spread to nearly every area of the planet.

The land-enclosure phenomenon is not a mere historic curiosity. It has played a key role in shaping modern life. Whether practiced in late-medieval Europe or late-twentieth-century South America, enclosure caused the most traumatic changes in the lives of working men and their families in modern history. It shattered traditional communities, created untold millions of economic refugees, and disrupted virtually every element of the lives of the people on whom it descended.

Given its crucial role in spawning modern economic and social life, and its continuing toll on humanity and the environment, it is surprising that the land-enclosure phenomenon has received so little academic or media attention. It is either ignored or only lightly reviewed in our history texts. Popular literature and the media are devoid of tales about the heroes and villains that have for centuries populated this blood-soaked social battlefield. Yet in order to understand the origins of the masculine mystique and some of the most egregious problems that currently beset men, we will have to review this epochal change in human history. For the enclosure revolution that permanently altered landownership and economic production in Europe and America, and that killed Chico Mendes and destroyed so much of the rain forest in Brazil, has had a special impact on all men. For generations this social transformation has slipped a physical and psychic harness over men from which they have not yet escaped.

THE ENCLOSURE REVOLUTION

In 1595, in the waning years of her life, Queen Elizabeth returned greatly perturbed from what was supposed to be a triumphal tour of her realm. "Paupers are everywhere!" she exclaimed repeatedly. The queen's surprise and chagrin were understandable. Only a generation before, the English agriculture system had been a source of great national pride. The yeomen of England were viewed as the "largest body of independent, free and prosperous citizens in the world."[4] Now paupers were everywhere, choking the roads and filling up the parishes. What catastrophe had occurred?

What Queen Elizabeth was seeing were the first casualties of a revolution in landownership and land use in England. For centuries during the Middle Ages the village commons were the primary social units in England. The commons system of organizing agricultural life has origins going back to the Holy Roman Empire. In this system the peasantry comprised a village community of shareholders who utilized the majority of land on a collective basis. The commons system varied in each particular area of England, but it generally involved peasants pooling their individual holdings into open fields that were jointly cultivated. While the commons system involved a class system, it also allowed for upward mobility, and most decisions about the use of the commons were made democratically.

Agricultural life and work in medieval England as elsewhere in Europe was "gendered." That is, certain tools and tasks were generally used by men, others by women. In certain areas only men were allowed to plant and women to harvest, in other areas the reverse. While each gender had absolute control of its milieu, the society still depended on the close complementary relationship of gender work. Researcher Yvonne Verdier describes how French customs in gendered agriculture work extended to even the most mundane of tasks, such as the slaughtering of pigs. According to Verdier, only the women chose which animal was to be slaughtered. The men, however, set the day of slaughter. Both then went through dozens of interactions in the slaughtering process, ending with the women preparing the sausage while the men salted the lard. Historians of medieval Europe find that the relationship between men and women of the period is governed much less by the couple unit and far more on the "matched interdependence of men's and women's hands" in the household and field. As such, medieval society was grouped not just by family but by gender. The rhythms of society and work were a counterpoint between male and female.[5]

To be sure, medieval England was no Eden. Over centuries plagues and famines decimated many agrarian communities. Moreover tyranny in the shape of an overbearing squire or parson often visited the village commons, and despite widespread, if primitive, democratic rule making, disputes over lands and rights of the commons occurred frequently. Finally family strife was widespread, though violence in the home was quickly punished by the community. Still, as noted by an historian of the period, "Whatever the troubles within, it remains true that the common-field system formed a world in which the villagers lived their own lives and cultivated the soil on the basis of independence."[6]

By the early 1500s a social upheaval was initiated in England that began to undermine the commons and that created the pauperization witnessed by Queen Elizabeth. Spurred on by new economic forces, a cynical appropriation of village commons began, an appropriation that became the first "enclosure." The term *enclosure* is literally defined as "surrounding a piece of land with hedges, ditches, or other barriers to the free passage of men and animals."[7] In the early decades of enclosure wealthy landowners threw up fences around the formerly commonly owned fields, permanently cutting off tens of thousands of peasants from the land their families had used for hundreds of years. The enclosing of the commons of England was accomplished primarily through acts of Parliament, though private agreements between landowners were also routine. Through these public and private acts the agricultural land in the village was allowed to be bought up by the lords and large landowners, who would then claim all rights to the common meadows and pastures. The peasants and serfs were left without land or subsistence. Enclosure has often been referred to as the "revolution of the rich against the poor."

The initial wave of enclosures in the sixteenth century was spurred by the need to make more and more land available for sheep. Wool had become a new and profitable commodity that was gaining high export prices. Wool producers needed ever-larger tracts of land for grazing sheep. Land that had for generations been used by the people for subsistence farming and as a source for wood was enclosed by the wool entrepreneurs and transformed into grazing land for sheep. The fight that Mendes waged in the rain forests of Brazil in the late twentieth century against the enclosure of the forest by the cattle industry was fought by his predecessors in the fields and forests of late-medieval England over sheep. Numerous insurrections occurred.

Under considerable public pressure (the phrase "sheep devour people" had become a household adage throughout England), the government did enact some restrictions on the sale and transfer of land. However, enclosures continued throughout the next centuries. The impact of these enclosures on the farmers and small shareholders of the English commons was catastrophic. Historians J. L. Hammond and Barbara Hammond eloquently contrast the lives of the peasants and the state of their villages before and after enclosure:

> In an unenclosed village, . . . the normal laborer did not depend on wages. His livelihood was made up of various sources. His firing he took from the waste, he had a cow or a pig wandering on the common pasture, perhaps he raised a little crop on a strip in the common fields . . . he maintained himself as a producer. . . . In an enclosed village at the end of the eighteenth century the position of the agricultural laborer was very different. All his auxiliary resources were taken from him, and he was now a wage earner and nothing more. Enclosure had robbed him of the strip that he tilled, of the cow that he kept on the village pasture, of the fuel he picked up in the woods, and of the turf of the commons. . . . They had lost their gardens, they had ceased to brew beer in their cottages. In their work they had no sense of ownership or interests . . . their wives and children were starving before their eyes, their homes were squalid. . . . The sense of sympathy and comradeship, which had been mixed with rude and unskillful government, in the old village had been destroyed . . . the total effect of the changes was to destroy their [the peasants'] independence.[8]

The peasants of England and Europe did not give up their old way of life without a fight. The enclosures were bitterly resisted. As early as the middle of the sixteenth century, riots broke out against the enclosers, resulting in over 3,500 people being killed. Uprisings continued over the centuries. In the early years of the nineteenth century England witnessed the most serious riots and revolts, finally leading to the great revolt of 1830, during which entire towns were overrun and "taken back" by the peasants. Within a few months the revolt was crushed, and dozens of men who led the uprisings were tried and then imprisoned or hung.

While the enclosure revolution impoverished and suppressed the peasants, large fortunes were made by the manor lords and other large landowners. The new financial elite based its growing wealth on export crops and the greater productivity of the postcommons agriculture. Most importantly, large profits gained from the expanded export in wool and other agricultural commodities provided the capital necessary for England's pioneering investment in the great machines and factories of the industrial age.

Industrialization completed the enclosure process. The millions of peasants dislodged from the commons were forced by circumstance to migrate to the newly industrialized cities. There they began to "sell" their labor in the market system. The dispossessed, desperate peasants of England became the cheap and available labor required for the new mills and factories of the Industrial Revolution. Often living under execrable conditions, they became the new "proletarians." Now the factory rather than the farm became the center of social life.

Industrialization also claimed a new class of victims. By the late eighteenth century millions of craftsmen and artisans in England and throughout Europe were beginning to see the degradation of their labor and the undermining of their families through the displacement of handcrafts by machines. The earliest incursion of mechanization into Europe occurred in textiles manufacturing. This mechanization destroyed the traditional communities that survived on the premechanical production of cotton. Mechanization soon spread to other crafts, overthrowing the guild (master and apprentice) system that had been in place for generations. Displaced

craftsmen and apprentices staged numerous open revolts, but ultimately joined the peasants as economic refugees to the newly industrialized cities.

Over time, enclosure and the industrialization of work overcame
all resistance. In England a new market system, bolstered by the
profitability of exports such as wool, scored an unconditional triumph over that of the old commons system. Land was now sold at
will by the large landowners, not held in common by the peasants.
Agricultural and craft labor was no longer based on community
needs and individual subsistence but rather on a wage system. A
new economic system was in place, but the cost in human suffering
had been high. Economist Robert L. Heilbroner writes,

> The market system with its essential components of land, labor,
> and capital was thus born in agony. . . . Never was a revolution
> less well understood, less welcomed, less planned. But the great
> market-driving forces would not be denied. Insidiously they
> ripped apart the mold of custom, insolently they tore away the us-
> ages of tradition. . . . For all the breakings on the wheel . . . over
> last-ditch opposition from the Old Guard, economic land was cre-
> ated out of ancestral estates, and . . . economic labor was ground
> out of unemployed apprentices and dispossessed farm laborers.[9]

Labor became the technical market term used for human beings
in the new factory system. Humans were now defined by little more
than their place in the economic system. They no longer worked in
the interests of the community, or for family, or religious duty, but
rather for wages that barely allowed for survival. Extended families
disintegrated. Even parents and children were separated as each
member sought some location where an employer would buy his or
her labor.

The enclosure revolution that transformed England over several
centuries quickly became a global phenomenon. It first spread to
the European continent and then the United States, destroying forever the Jeffersonian dream of an American democracy of small

"yeomen," craftsmen, and businessmen. As underscored by the struggle and death of Chico Mendes, enclosure continues to this day in the ongoing annihilation of subsistence communities throughout the "underdeveloped" world. In Africa, Asia, and South America millions of peasant farmers and native peoples were and still are being forced off their ancestral land to make room for the production of various export crops. In Brazil alone, this enclosure of small farmers off their lands displaced 28.4 million people between 1960 and 1980.[10] In India, over the last two decades, twenty million people have been forced from their land so that it can be utilized for export crops or as sites of large-scale development projects.[11] These peasants become refugees to the larger cities, where they attempt to market their labor in the new industrialized marketplace. The massive urban blight currently seen in Mexico City, Brasília, or Bhopal demonstrates that the horrific conditions in the early industrial age were not isolated instances but rather a precursor of the typical impacts of enclosure and industrialization throughout the world.

THE ENCLOSURE OF MEN

The enclosure movement, and the advent of industrial work, that swept England and then the globe obviously did not affect only men. Women and children suffered the same dislocation, loss of community, starvation, and hardship as men. The new factory owners, especially the local textile operators, took full advantage of a newly uprooted and impoverished population. Thousands of destitute women and children sold their labor as a commodity and were employed in the new factories. Humans of all ages and both genders competed with one another for the scant wages being offered in the new industries. The numbing work and terrible conditions became public scandals.

Ultimately, however, men were to become the primary cogs in the growing industrial system in England and elsewhere. There were several reasons for the predominance of adult male workers during the industrial age. For one, even the early industrialists had to admit that the cruelties of child labor were too much for any society to bear. By the middle of the nineteenth century child labor had been limited by Parliament, and most industrialized countries passed similar anti–child-labor statutes. Moreover, in a time when pregnancy was frequent, and often hazardous due to poor diet and the lack of sanitation, employers felt that women were less reliable as long-term workers. Additionally, because of their physical strength, men were viewed as the ideal workers for the more hazardous jobs in mining and industry. Finally, the reformers at the end of the nineteenth century aggressively advocated laws attempting to keep women from the factories in order to protect them from the dangers of the workplace. At the same time, they sought to ensure men a "family wage" (i.e., a minimum wage capable of supporting a family). They argued that the only way to save any remnant of the preindustrial family from the disruption of enclosure and industrial labor was to relegate the male to the workplace and keep the female at home with the children.[12]

Over time, industrial work became nearly synonymous with men's work. During the first four decades of the twentieth century approximately 90 percent of adult married men in England and the United States were fully employed in the industrial system. During this same period only about 12 percent of married women were part of the industrial workforce.[13]

The industrialized male now faced a grim new reality. He had become the victim of two enclosures. First, his land had been taken from him, enclosed for use by the large landowners for export crops. This enclosure violently cut him off from his traditional life, community, and work. Next he himself had been enclosed into the foreign environment of the industrial workplace, most often for six days a week, twelve to sixteen hours a day. Virtually all of his waking hours were spent away from his family and the natural world. This dual enclosure had a devastating impact on men working in the industrial workplace. Locked into their role as primary breadwinner in the new labor market, the majority of men became fully dispossessed. They were robbed of any usable property; they lost economic independence, now depending wholly on wages given by their employers; they lost spiritual independence as their fear of starvation and joblessness made them subservient to their bosses; and they had to forsake forever home employment and self-employment.

Throughout the nineteenth and twentieth centuries the new industrial system was to create vast amounts of products and wealth, unimagined in prior times. Technologies were to be developed, both for production and for the military, that astounded (and sometimes frightened) each succeeding generation. In industrialized countries many families were able to achieve standards of living, and myriad conveniences, that dwarfed those of all but the wealthiest classes in prior societies. As industrial society progressed, fewer and fewer were nostalgic for the life of preindustrial times.

However, the cost of industrial "progress" to the lives of men was, and still is, virtually ignored. The enclosure of land and the industrial enclosure of men changed virtually every personal and social relationship a man had, changes that are with men to this day. Perhaps the most profound impact was on fatherhood.

With enclosure and the establishment of the factory system, the father was wrenched from the home and often became a virtual nonentity in the household. It is a lingering irony that the purportedly "patriarchal" industrial production system began by destroying fatherhood. By separating work from family, the modes of industrial production caused the permanent alienation of father from wife and children. Even when the father returned to the house, he was often too tired and irritable from the general tensions and tedium of work in the factory/corporate system to be teacher or counselor.

The separation of men, and men's work, from the family may well be the most significant personal and social disruption men have ever had to face. For generations industrial society has been conducting an unparalleled anthropological experiment: What is the effect of virtual father absence on the family, children, and the redefinition of men's role in society? After several generations the tragic results of this experiment are being seen in the growing crisis for men and masculinity.

One particularly ominous, though little noted, effect of structural father absence is that it has made young men especially prone to the sexual stereotyping endemic to the masculine mystique. For many generations most sons have no longer had familial images of masculinity to learn from and identify with. Boys have had to attempt to develop a masculine identity in the absence of a continuous and ongoing personal relationship with their fathers, uncles, or other male elders. Moreover they have had to develop their understanding of the masculine with mothers, other female relations, and primarily female early-grade teachers as their principal adult influences. Girls by contrast had their femininity embedded and mediated by their ongoing relationship with the mother and other female relations and teachers (though this is becoming less common as more mothers enter the workforce). Thus boys' major source of instruction about the masculine derives from cultural images of masculinity promulgated by the masculine mystique, whereas girls' concept of the feminine is rooted in family. As one feminist psychologist summarizes, "Males tend to identify with a cultural stereotype of the masculine role; whereas females tend to identify with aspects of their own mother's role specifically."[14] This is a key element in the success of the masculine mystique. For generations boys and young men faced with father absence have had no alternative but to turn to the mystique's destructive dogma as the primary teacher of what it means to be a man.

The dual enclosure of land and men separated men not only from their families but also from day-to-day interaction with the natural world. As men became the primary cogs in industrial production, they lost touch with the earth and the parts of themselves that were wedded to the earth. As enclosure forced men off the land and into the factory system, the male as agrarian steward, craftsman, and woodsman all but vanished. The ultimate results of the mass alienation of the majority of men, their identity, and their jobs from a sustainable relationship with nature can be seen in the spiraling environmental crisis, as well as in the growing influence of the masculine mystique.

Another lasting impact of the enclosure into the industrial system is that it alienated men from one another. Men long priding themselves on joint work and shared roles in society were forced into a system whose ultimate goal was to turn one man against the other in the utilitarian, competitive "jungle" of industrial production. Men no longer viewed one another as a community of elders, craftsmen, or fellow farmers on the common, but rather as a collection of competitors for scarce jobs. The change in older men's relationship to younger men was especially drastic. No longer did the older generation of men see themselves as teachers or mentors to the young. Rather they often looked on younger men primarily as threats, men who might take over their jobs and destroy their livelihoods.

As the enclosure of men destroyed the bonds of kinship and male community, it also permanently alienated men from their daily work and the product of their labor. The advance of the Industrial Revolution cost men their independence, dignity, and the sense of personal responsibility and creativity associated with individual crafts and small-scale farming. Though a man worked hard all day in the mines, mills, factories, or corporations, he produced nothing that had his individual stamp, nothing that expressed who he was or what he believed in.

Finally, the enclosure of land and men alienated the genders from one another by destroying the preindustrial complementary relationship between the genders in work and family life. Men and women no longer worked together to accomplish the daily tasks necessary for survival. Men were enclosed away at the job to perform the "productive" wage work of society. Women were relegated to the forced domesticity of the industrial-age home, where without the help of their mate or extended family they shouldered alone the tasks of child rearing, housework, cooking, and piecework.

The dual enclosures of land and men were (and in many places in the world remain) traumatic, oppressive, and violent. These enclosures established the social conditions responsible for the hidden crisis men have suffered for generations. Despite the efforts of so many resistors, including the heroic struggle of Chico Mendes, men lost their ability to determine their own mode of life and work. As summarized by historian E. P. Thompson, "To lose control over one's own labour was to surrender one's independence, security, liberty, one's birthright."[15]

The enclosure of men also represented the key first stage of the transformation of male gender identity in modernity. However, the next step for the industrial system was crucial if the new modes of work and production were to succeed. The ruling elite needed to enclose not only men's bodies but also their minds. If men were to accede to the factory system, their basic goals and desires needed to be altered. In place of the image of masculinity that was endemic to the commons system, and to most prior agrarian civilizations, a new masculine myth and mystique needed to be created. The very definition of masculinity needed to be transformed into one that corresponded to the male's new enclosed reality.

PART II

THE MASCULINE MYSTIQUE

4

THE MACHINE MAN

Men have grown mechanical in head and heart, as well as in hand.
　　　　　　　　　　　　　　　　　　　　—Thomas Carlyle[1]

The man who "feels" becomes inefficient and ineffective because he gets emotionally involved and this inevitably slows him down and distracts him. His more dehumanized competitor will then surely pass him by.
　　　　　　　　　　　　　　　　　　　　—Herb Goldberg[2]

It was called "the great artificial coition machine." The unique sex-research tool was among the proudest yet most concealed achievements of noted sexologists Drs. William H. Masters and Virginia A. Johnson. The extraordinary machine was kept well hidden in the recesses of the Masters and Johnson sex-research foundation. Only staff and volunteers who demonstrably had to see it ever saw it. Casual visitors, the press, other professionals were virtually never allowed access. There are no known photographs of the coitus machine. However, one journalist was able to provide a description for posterity:

> The business end was a clear plastic phallus, with glans optics designed by Corning, suitable for photography. It looked just like a slightly larger than normal erect penis, about 8 inches long. It

was driven by an electric motor. The apparatus was long enough to provide for attachments, and sturdy enough to do the job without wincing. The phallus was gripped by solid metal arms linked to drive mechanisms and cams. Thanks to gear springs the operators could control the phallus's thrusting to accord with any desired rhythm, from total standstill to a frenzied, pre-ejaculatory staccato. The posterior end of the phallus was open, to provide for attachments such as a camera.[3]

After an unknown number of conquests the unique coitus contraption was dismantled. The demise of the great electronic dildo was not the result of any malfunction or disappointment in its performance, but apparently due to fear of potential bad publicity it might bring to the foundation. The relegation of the motor-powered phallus to the scrap heap is unfortunate. It deserved a better fate, perhaps even a featured place in the collection of this century's technology at the Smithsonian Museum. For the Masters-and-Johnson machine is a vivid icon of the transformation and mechanization of the masculine during modern times. Without question it was the most literal rendition of the phallus symbolism of the masculine mystique ever devised.

It has become a truism that as we humans have created machines, they in turn have re-created our images of ourselves. As we cast, soldered, burned, and molded the ores and fossil fuels of the earth to fashion the great engines of the industrial age, these machines just as surely recast and remolded modern consciousness. The influence of machines and the industrial mind-set on our thinking should not surprise. The modern age continues to be the machine age. Our work time is filled with adjusting, monitoring, and using a variety of technology. Our playtime is often equally concerned with mechanical toys, be they televisions, stereo equipment, or computers. We communicate by machine—the telephone. We learn by machine—tapes, calculators, and again computers. We travel by machine—automobiles, airplanes. We even see by machine—the electric light. The machine is our modern milieu. Yet we are so used to interacting with technology that we have ceased to notice how it dominates our lives.

The incorporation of the machine mentality into modern society is evident in much of what we do and say. It is immediately apparent in the lexicon we often use to describe ourselves. We speak of our soldiers as "fighting machines." Our leaders ask us to be "mighty engines of change," and our bedroom partners call on us to be "sex machines." When we are tired, we are "worn out" and "run down," perhaps near a "breakdown."

As embodied in the Masters-and-Johnson power-driven penis, the male sex organ is a prime target for machine metaphors. Older festivals celebrating the generativity of the phallus are long forgotten. The idea of the phallus as the symbolic "tree of life" or the "primary seed bearer" seems almost comical today. Under the mechanistic paradigm we now think of the penis as a man's "tool," which he has to "get up" for "screwing" and has to keep "erect" until he "gets the job done."

Other body-part terminology has also not escaped the mechanistic onslaught. Gone are the "lion hearts" of yore, to be replaced by the current well-exercised "tickers" or "pumps." Our digestive and sex organs are called "plumbing," and our brains are viewed as "computers" busy getting "feedback," assuming of course that there is not "data overload" or "a screw loose" somewhere.

The mechanistic mind-set has gone beyond generalizations to give us very specific masculine-mystique ideals for the masculine, both in body and in mind. It has created an "ideal" male physique in its own image. The current body type that most men strive for, and most women seem to favor, is the "lean machine"—a hard, hairless, overtly muscled body (occasionally well oiled for display). Of course, this machinelike "techno-body" is not a natural one for most men, and increasing numbers of men are extremely dissatisfied with their bodies. Polls indicate that over the last fifteen years the number of men unhappy with their body image has doubled to include 34 percent of all men.[4] Many boys and men, obsessed with achieving the stereotypical male form, will undergo little less than body torture. Along with many other techniques, they pump iron (like pistons working in a motor) to gain the requisite body hardness, a mechanical trait that is glorified. Softness, the preeminent nonmechanical physical trait, is eschewed at all costs. Machine manufacturers are selling $750 million worth of muscle-building equipment annually as what one commentator calls "muscle madness" sweeps the country.[5]

Even more disturbing, hundreds of thousands of young men each year get hooked on steroids and thousands more on genetically engineered human growth hormone in order to achieve the "right" machinelike body. The side effects of these drugs can be devastating and life-threatening, including potential susceptibility to a wide range of physical and mental diseases, including aggression, depression, sterility, cancer, and leukemia.

Men are also increasingly resorting to a variety of cosmetic and surgical techniques to secure the stereotype of the male physique. There has been an explosion in chest-hair removal, liposuction, and plastic "chestplate" implants for men, and even penis implants and enhancements. Some plastic surgery doctors report a 100 percent increase in male clientele over the last five years. The American Academy of Cosmetic Surgery says that 30 percent of surveyed members' procedures are done on men, up significantly since the 1980s.[6]

As it metamorphoses the male form, the mechanistic vision has performed an equal alchemy on the minds of men. Most men carry with them a deeply ingrained machine-based psychic image of what a man should be, just as they do a body image. We all know that real men, successful men, are efficient, productive, autonomous, calculating, in control, tireless, rational, and do not easily break down. Author and psychotherapist Herb Goldberg further describes this familiar "machine man" archetype:

> The autonomous male, the independent strong achiever who can be counted on to be always in control, is still essentially the preferred male image. Success in the working world is predicated on repression of self and the display of a controlled, deliberate, cal-

culated, manipulative responsiveness. To become a leader requires that one be totally goal-oriented, undistracted by personal factors, and able to tune out extraneous "noise," human or otherwise, which is unrelated to the end goal and which might impede forward motion.[7]

Perhaps the final fantasy of the machine man, in both body and mind, is represented by numerous figures in films and television, including *Robocop*, *The Terminator*, and *The Six Million Dollar Man*. Our fantasy robots, androids, and cyborgs offer images of indestructibility, super-strength, hyperrationality, total autonomy, a virtual lack of emotion, and amazing efficiency in all tasks (especially destruction). Interestingly these fictional machine men often begin as ordinary humans whose bodies have been decimated by accident or violence. They are then "rebuilt" into physical or psychic overachievers with the help of hi-tech artificial parts. These media myths re-create, in microcosm, the decades-long social engineering of the premachine masculine into the industrial model.

Today, while we have not yet reached the stage of cyborgs or androids, nevertheless, under the aegis of the masculine mystique we now have a primary male ideal, both in body and in mind—a homogenized masculine image modeled on the machine. This dehumanized "machine man" is the sine qua non of the masculine mystique. He represents the triumph of the mechanized over the organic, of technology over men.

In various guises the machine man is present in almost all men in our culture. The male type spawned by this pathology of mechanization has been given the apt name of "robopath" by sociologist Lewis Yablonsky. Robopaths are men whose behavior "simulates machines"—creatures of a society that worships mechanical efficiency, regularity, and predictability. They are individuals who tend to be "rigidly conformist, compulsively orderly and efficient, unemotional and unspontaneous." Yablonsky and other observers see the condition of robopathology as endemic to our way of life and the "classic disease of this era." They also see things getting worse. "The twenty-first century," Yablonsky warns, "may be characterized by an epidemic of robopathology."[8]

It is important to reemphasize that despite the claims of gender "experts," the robopathic, mechanistic male is not an inevitable result of biological imperatives—genes, hormones, or "brainwiring." Rather, he is the result of a centuries-long enculturation of men, an implicit and explicit indoctrination carried on for specific economic and social reasons by our industrial system. As author Ashley Montagu points out,

> The mechanization of life could be complete only with the mechanization of man. . . . Man in effect had to be emptied out of essential humanity—in order to be restocked with artificial needs and conditioned reflexes. The dehumanization of men would be finally accomplished when the individual accepted his fate [within the machine system] . . . as long as he held out, as long as he continued to struggle, the victory was not total; the process of dehumanization would be consummated in the moment when it was no longer felt or comprehended by its victim, no longer opposed but welcomed. What was required, in short, was the unconditional surrender of self.[9]

Understanding the genealogy of the masculine mystique, and the fate of men in our culture, requires an examination of the triumph of mechanism over men. When and how did men surrender their masculinity and independence to the machine? Did they oppose or welcome the mechanization of manhood? What social forces were responsible for the triumph of the robopathic incarnation of masculinity?

TOIL AND TROUBLE

At the outset it is important to realize that the dawning of the industrial age meant an unprecedented and massive increase in work for men as they became enclosed into the factories and mines. Most of us have been led to believe that industrial technology has reduced human toil. We have been grateful that we were not born in former times and subject to the dreary, endless labor of the subsistence farmer. This central myth about our society is false. As economist Juliet B. Schor writes, "Before capitalism, most people did not work very long hours at all. The tempo of life was slow, even leisurely: the pace of work relaxed. Our ancestors may not have been rich, but they had an abundance of leisure. When capitalism raised their incomes, it also took away their time."[10]

Most researchers agree that the working hours of the nineteenth- and early-twentieth-century industrial workers constituted the most prodigious labor effort in the history of humankind. Schor estimates that medieval European peasants worked between 120 and 135 days a year for a total of only 1,500 to 1,600 hours annually—less than half the 3,650 hours worked each year by the average U.S. worker in 1850 at the dawn of the industrial age; and also less than the nearly 2,000 hours worked annually by the average U.S. worker in 1987.[11] As men spent the vast majority of their waking hours in the industrial workplace, their relationship to machines became, by necessity, a surrogate for their prior relationship to family and the natural world.

Along with a massively increased workload, the laborers of the industrial age were also faced with a new kind of work—mechanical, cacophonous, fast-paced, and repetitive. It is difficult for us today to realize the pace and quality of change faced by the average worker during enclosure and the rise of factory work. We have become so accustomed to industrial life that we forget the trauma caused by the farm-to-factory transition. For the peasant or craftsman desperately seeking to sell his labor in an industrial setting, this transfer requires a drastic adjustment. No longer does he work at his own pace, or within the cycles of the day and season, but rather at the tempo of a machine and under the dictates of the factory clock. No longer are slack times determined by the weather or natural fatigue, but by the state of the market and the need for production. The land is no longer an eternal source of sustenance close at hand; the new worker has only the industrial machine and the crowded floor of the industrial site as his daily environment. No longer does the worker craft a whole product but rather is reduced to a few endlessly repetitive motions in the division of labor in the factory or mill. As historian Sidney Pollard writes, "The worker who left his domestic workshop or peasant holding for the factory entered a new culture a well as a new sense of direction . . . the new economic order needed not men but rather 'part-humans': soulless, depersonalized, disembodied, who could become members, or little wheels rather, of a complex mechanism."[12]

The men who were the workers of choice for the factories and mines of the industrial age were remarkably ill suited for the new "culture" of industrial work. They were physically unprepared for the backbreaking schedule of the industrial workplace. Temperamentally they were nearly incapable of adjusting to the machine-paced, mind-dulling repetitive labor that awaited them after their enclosure into the factory or mine. They were almost the direct opposite of the depersonalized, emotionless, efficient, technology-oriented, workaholic machine men required by the new economic order. Like men of so many other premodern cultures, they had always worked to live, but they had never lived only to work.

When the first factories were opened in Great Britain, men vigorously resisted working in them. One owner reported with great concern, "the utmost distaste on the part of the men to any regular hours or regular habits. . . . The men themselves were considerably dissatisfied, because they could not go in and out as they pleased, and have the holidays they pleased, and go on just as they had been used to."[13] Another early factory manager reported that his men "were found ill-disposed to submit to the long confinement and regular industry that is required of them."[14] Still another said that sitting a man at a machine "is like putting a deer in the plough."[15]

In the early years of industrialization employers often resorted to hiring ex-criminals and "wanted" men because family men simply refused to enter the mills, factories, and mines. The situation for the laboring men of the eighteenth century was both desperate and paradoxical: Employers could not find laborers who were properly "disciplined," while farmers and craftsmen displaced by enclosure could not find work that allowed them their traditional masculine independence and way of life. As explained by one historian, "The lack of employment opportunities, as seen by the displaced peasant and hand worker, existed simultaneously with a labor shortage, as seen by the employer . . . this paradox is explained by the fact that the worker was averse to taking up the *type* of employment offered, and the employer was unwilling to tolerate the habits of work which the men seeking work desired."[16]

Matters worsened for the industrialists. As the industrial empires expanded around the globe, nineteenth- and twentieth-century English colonialists were horrified to see that the character of men in almost all primitive cultures was the same as that of their own peasants, one that was antithetical to the industrial ethic. Predictably the industrialists expressed the same concern about the "lazy" men they found in Asia and Africa (men who also worked far fewer hours than industrialized men) as they had the European peasant. They found these men to be as indolent, unpunctual, machine-phobic, and "irresponsible" as their own agrarian population. Numerous writers openly compared the reluctance of the European and American males to become enthusiastic industrial workers to the backwardness of the "niggers and hindoos."[17]

The nonindustrious character of men in Europe and around the world was a source of growing alarm and open disgust to the early captains of industrialism. They were vociferous in their call for a new public work ethic. They knew that the character of the average man would have to be radically transformed if a productive industrial economy was to be forged from the agrarian commons of the world. Men, and masculinity itself, had to be re-created in the machine's image if the epochal industrial enterprise was to succeed.

However sympathetic he was to the plight of the worker, even Karl Marx saw their mechanization as a vital and desirable step in industrialism. "The main difficulty [of the factory system]," he wrote, "is in training men to renounce their desultory habits of work, and to identify themselves with the unvarying regularity of the automaton."[18]

In order to break the resistance of men to the machine, the industrialists forged an active alliance with the Protestant churches sprouting up in England and throughout Europe. Everywhere churches, chapels, and Sunday schools were built and financially supported by employers to inculcate obedience in working populations and to promulgate the required work ethic. The new gospel of industrial discipline was eagerly spread by Protestant evangelical ministers, who were becoming ever more popular in the early industrial age. Pulpits across Europe resounded with the new "Protestant ethic" as the clergy loudly condemned as sinful every aspect of men's lives that did not comport with the needs of the new factory system.

All traditional aspects of masculinity, and indeed all social habits of any sort, which did not fit into the new discipline demands of industrial work were discredited as offenses against God and as hindrances to spiritual progress. Laxity, lack of ambition, indolence, consumption of alcohol, and the failure to be punctual were now presented as human flaws worthy of eternal "fire and brimstone."[19]

However, despite the best efforts of the industrialists and their religious apologists, resistance to the new labor regime remained strong. For centuries men fought their mechanization. They did not surrender to the depersonalization demanded of them. Strikes and walkouts were common. Many thousands of men were killed or imprisoned as the system attempted to enforce the new industrial rules on them. There were also mass sabotages of factory machines and clocks (the word *sabotage* is derived from the "sabot," or shoe that workers used to jam up the machines). Employers knew that the introduction of new machinery or new work rules would inevitably cause riots. Managers were turned into military officers to control their men. The state worked with the new industrial employers to subject men to the factory system. Uprisings were regularly suppressed by mass imprisonment and capital punishment.

Over generations the factory system, fostered by violence, star-vation, and relentless religious indoctrination, finally overcame all resistance and began to succeed, by attrition, in molding men to the machine. As Pollard writes, "The modern industrial proletariat was introduced to its role not so much by attraction or monetary reward, but by compulsion, force and fear . . . fear of hunger, of eviction, of prison for those who disobeyed the new industrial rules."[20]

Finally subsumed into the industrial mode, men became the "robots" demanded by the industrial system. They became condi-tioned by the factory clock and the fear of the factory manager, and ended up being virtually absorbed into the rhythms and needs of the machines with which they worked. In 1972 a British worker de-scribed this process firsthand: "Inside a factory it soon becomes ob-vious that steel brought to life by electricity takes precedence over blood and flesh. The onus is on the machines to such an extent that they appear to assume the human attributes of those who work them. Machines have become as much like people as people have become like machines. They pulsate with life, while man becomes a robot."[21]

UNIFORM MEN

As the industrialists and the new Protestant reformers force-fed the mechanistic imperative to workers, they were greatly aided and pro-foundly influenced by another impressive social force: the military. If there is one common experience that men have shared in the modern age besides work and breadwinning, it is military training. For generations we have sent our boys into the armed forces in the hope that they will come back as "men," though of course millions of these boys never returned at all.

The modern "military man" archetype is well known to all of us. Through thorough indoctrination by movies and TV we know what "Be all you can be" means for a man. Any young man joining the military knows what to expect. The young recruit is socially engineered from his original identity as a civilian to become a military machine. Recruits are dressed in identical uniforms, taught, through months of drilling, to make identical mechanical motions and sounds (including the very way they walk and talk), and billeted in standardized housing. The soldier is instructed to obey and not think, to be impervious to emotion and pain, and hopefully at the end of the training is able to kill other men with mechanical dispatch. At his best he is an efficient killing robot—the ultimate robopath.

G. Gordon Liddy, of Watergate fame and self-proclaimed soldier par excellence, remembers the satisfaction in training so hard that he knew that he could "kill efficiently and without emotion or thought." "I was satisfied: when it came my turn to go to war, I would be ready," Liddy recalls. "I could kill as I could run—like a machine."[22]

The military man was not always the wind-up warrior of today. The evolution of the new military robopath took approximately four centuries. In medieval Europe the soldier was recruited for only short periods of time and at irregular periods. He was generally part of a disorganized, ragtag fighting force that fought with little discipline or strategy. For those few trained for combat the battle was a highly ritualized affair.

Between the sixteenth and twentieth centuries the feudal knight was to disappear and the modern mechanized professional soldier was to emerge. New technologies of war, especially more sophisticated firearms and ordnance, made the feudal concept of war obsolete. The modern army required proficient soldiers trained to synchronize with the new machines of destruction.

France, under the guidance of Louis XIV, was the first country to make the full transition into a professional standing army and navy. Subsequently the French war ministry was to become the first military bureaucracy of modern times. The French were also the first to implement a military draft. Starting in 1798 all men between the ages of twenty and twenty-five were conscripted into the military for an indefinite period. Over 200,000 young men were drafted in the first year. The only way a young Frenchman could avoid the draft was by death, contagious disease, or infliction of a wound so serious that he could not walk onto the battlefield. Men now had as little choice over being subjected to the military regimen as they were to have in avoiding industrial discipline.

As conscription became common in Europe, the ranks of the military swelled. By the early nineteenth century, Berlin had a military population of twenty thousand young men in a city totaling less than ninety thousand total population. The new legions of soldiers would repeatedly make the rounds of cities, parading like so many identical automatons. The sight of large numbers of synchronized military men in the thoroughfares of Europe fired the imaginations of the new industrialists. They began to envision a mode of industrial production patterned after the exacting division of labor used in the military. As noted by author Jeremy Rifkin,

> [In the new armies] there were now infantrymen, cavalrymen, artillerymen, men who handled ordnance, men who handled transportation, and men who handled corpses. There were field and support staff—in short, there developed a complex system of division of labor that bore all the earmarks of the industrial process. *The professional army predated the professional business enterprise and provided the training ground in the art of reducing people to machine-like status.*[23] (Emphasis added.)

The modern corporation still shows its military roots. It has a top-down command structure and strict hierarchies in which, over time, one advances. It demands absolute loyalty and obedience. It involves masses of men wearing nearly identical uniforms—the business suit (women are given far more leeway in dress). Business itself is routinely analogized to the military; there is a "corporate battleground," where a company may be fighting a "hostile takeover," often employing "headhunters" to find "hired guns." We are repeatedly told that "business is war." A recent business best-seller was entitled *Waging Business Warfare*. Its jacket copy urged readers to "become a master on today's corporate killing-fields," and it reminded businessmen, "Believe it: if you're in business, you're at war."[24]

As military training, the factory system, and Protestant teachings forcefully inculcated the machine ethic into generations of men, the masculine mystique's robopathic man was also being promulgated by a more subtle, if equally influential, social force. A new scientific philosophy was being born. Starting in the seventeenth century, scientists and philosophers were busy proving that humans, along with the rest of the living world, were essentially biological machines. Over several centuries this mechanistic ideology was put forth by some of the most highly regarded thinkers in the Western tradition. These scientists were an invaluable aid in helping brand the mechanical paradigm onto the masculine psyche.

DESCARTES'S DREAM

On a November night in 1619 French philosopher René Descartes experienced a fateful dream. In his dream "the Spirit of Truth" revealed to him the "Science of Sciences"—that mechanical principles, and only such principles, underlay and illuminated all reality. Intoxicated by his vision, Descartes boasted, "Give me extension and motion, and I will construct the universe."[25] Under the influence of his nocturnal apparition Descartes wrote his famous *Discourse on Method*, in which he declared that all living organisms, even animals, were nothing more than machines. Descartes had made of nature, as one writer has put it, "a machine and nothing but a machine; purposes and spiritual significance alike had been banished."[26]

Descartes's understanding of life and nature as a machine was not his alone. Rather his views marked the initiation of over a century of thought that posited a thoroughly mechanistic view of nature. The mechanistic dogma was a central tenet of virtually all the great Enlightenment thinkers. The leading lights of the seventeenth cen-

tury—Bacon, Kepler, Galileo, Newton, Descartes, and Hobbes—
separated out all nonmechanical aspects of nature and man and held
them to be incapable of analysis and unknowable, and ultimately of
little importance. They focused on treating nature in strictly mathe-
matical and mechanical terms. Each man thought that nature's life-
forms were in essence machines. One of the greatest minds of the
Enlightenment, mathematician Gottfried Wilhelm Leibniz, maintained that "the machines of nature, that is, living bodies, are even in
the smallest of their parts, machines *ad infinitum.*"[27] Another scientist saw the organs of the body resembling "pillars, props, cross-
beams, fences, coverings; some like axes, wedges, levers, and
pullies, others like cords, presses or bellows; and others again like
sieves, strains, pipes, conduits and receivers."[28]

In subsequent decades the main objection to Descartes's theories was not that he and his fellow philosophers were too mechanical
but rather that they were not mechanical enough. French philosopher Julien Offroy de la Mettrie criticized Descartes for not including humans in the mechanistic paradigm. In his famous work
L'Homme Machine (Man a Machine, 1748), La Mettrie proposed a
startling thesis. Humans, he claimed, are not spiritual beings or en-
souled bodies. Rather, just like other animals, they are soulless machines. La Mettrie believed that mechanical laws produced bodily
motions and human thoughts. He rejected and saw no need for a
God or any other supramechanical force that provided humans with
spirit or soul. In one of his most-quoted lines La Mettrie writes,
"All scientists and competent judges confess that those proud and
vain beings, men . . . are at bottom only perpendicularly crawling
machines."[29]

It took over a century for Descartes's dream to evolve into La
Mettrie's "crawling machine." But as the eighteenth century came
to a close, the doctrine of mechanism had become the West's primary scientific paradigm. The doctrine enabled scientists to explain
life, whether the functions of organisms or the creative aspects of
the mind, in machine terms. In sum, life-forms were equated to
machines.[30]

Descartes's dream was to be further advanced and transformed in the nineteenth and twentieth centuries as the pioneer researchers into thermodynamics no longer saw the body as a simple machine but rather viewed it as analogous to the more complex modern motor. German physicist Hermann Helmholtz wrote almost a century after La Mettrie, "The animal body therefore does not differ from the steam engine as regards the manner in which it obtains heat and force." He posited that "expenditure of energy can be understood in terms of an analogy between human labor and that of machines."[31]

Historian Anson Rabinbach summarizes the new "man as motor" ideology: "During the nineteenth century, Descartes's animal machine was dramatically transformed by the advent of a modern motor, capable of transforming energy into various forms. . . . The human body and the industrial machine were both [seen as] motors that converted energy into mechanical work."[32]

There was, however, a major stumbling block in the attempt to treat the body as an industrial motor. Unlike motors or engines, humans became tired after working a short time. Researchers and scientists became increasingly dissatisfied with the "human machine's" predisposition to fatigue as compared with other motors. As one scientist noted, "The muscle is an imperfect machine . . . a machine for work that is unilateral . . . the biceps can flex the forearm above the arm, and that is all; its action is exhausted by this work."[33] Fatigue and weariness, long seen as normal, even benevolent results of hard work, were now analyzed as "problems" in the human motor. From the standpoint of workplace productivity and efficiency, human fatigue was costly, dysfunctional behavior.

By the early twentieth century an historic, if unholy, marriage was consummated as the goals of physiology and mechanistic science now merged with the ongoing attempt of employers to discipline their workers into ever-greater efficiency in production. Under the new banner of efficiency, armies of scientists supported by industry descended on workers to examine their modes of production and reduce worker fatigue. Their diagnosis was unanimous: The bodies of workers, primarily male bodies, needed to be made more efficient. Motor and man needed to be melded together ever more closely if greater amounts of industrial production were to be mass-produced.

The mechanical and social engineers eagerly accepted the challenge. Just as they tested machines for efficiency and metal fatigue, scientists began conducting detailed studies on human motion to find the most efficient ways to use the human machine. Efficiency means minimum input for maximum output in minimum time, and every detail of human motion was carefully examined, drawn, and photographed in order to arrive at perfectly efficient modes of factory work. Psychologists also became involved, conducting studies on workplace mental fatigue and stress.

The efforts to make the "human motor" as efficient as possible reached their zenith with the work of U.S. mechanical engineer Frederick Winslow Taylor. In the years prior to World War I, Taylor introduced into the United States and Europe a system of "managing" workers for maximum efficiency in the newly developed assembly-line production. Taylor was a pioneer in "time and motion" studies of workers, and his rigorous recommendations for worker efficiency, down to the smallest movements of the factory-line laborer, swept through the industrial nations over a period of several decades. Taylorism, as the efficiency movement was called, took what little control and dignity the worker had left and fully reduced him to the status of a machine. As historian C. George Benello notes, "[Under Taylorism] jobs were subdivided and simplified so that they could be performed mechanically and with as little skill as possible. The type of work that resulted was highly routinized and boring, and made machine tenders out of workers."[34]

Ultimately Taylorism and its drive for ever more efficient production would directly affect the working lives of untold millions of workers as the striving for efficiency became a daily reflex and a learned instinct for the average man. Of equal importance, Taylorism placed the ideal of efficiency above that of virtually any other ethic and made it into what philosopher Richard Weaver calls a "god term" of modernity. Economic historian Daniel Bell writes, "If any social upheaval can ever be attributed to one man, the logic of efficiency as a mode of life is due to Taylor."[35]

Workers submitted to Taylorism's new enforced efficiency discipline, just as they did to the more primitive factory clock, because they had to. In this arena as in so many others necessity is the masculine mystique's most effective tool. When the choice is between unemployment, or employment under the strict regimen of efficiency, employment still wins out.

Predictably the gospel of efficiency is now among the machine man's central imperatives. It goads men to strive for machinelike, tireless productivity as their main goal in life. A relentless drive for efficient use of time and energy in work and even play is an unquestioned trademark of the masculine mystique. Efficiency is the primary virtue of the modern male robopath.

The identification of men with machines and efficiency has also extended from the workplace to the home. There men are routinely expected to assume the role of primary caretaker of machines, whether it is the car, the lawn mower, or the garbage disposal. A man who is incapable or disinterested in being a Mr. Fix-it is looked upon as being emasculated, weak, and even comical. Countless media images have reinforced this machine-man stereotype. Women on the other hand tend to be seen as caretakers of the organic— children, food, gardening. This stereotypical division of domestic labor can be witnessed daily in millions of homes. The mother hard at work fixing Saturday lunch and scolding the kids about homework while the father tunes up the car or works on a leaky pipe. The woman planting the vegetable garden on an early-spring day while the man labors in his basement "workshop" accompanied by the continuous buzz of electric tools.

As machines have become the male's primary responsibility in the home, men have likewise become totally enclosed in the machine mentality. His toolroom or computerized study often resembles a minifactory or office. The enclosure of men into the machine milieu has meant that the capability of working with machines has become a center of male identity for generations.

BREAKDOWN

As we survey the history that fashioned the machine man out of pre-modern man, we can readily see that surprisingly little has changed for the working man as society has evolved from the industrial into the postindustrial age. Men are still wedded to machines, both phys-ically and mentally, and men still have little choice about sub-mitting themselves to efficiency-based workplace discipline. The modern man remains what author Warren Farrell calls, in his pio-neering book *The Myth of Male Power*, the No-Option Man.[36] While many married women have three life options—(a) to work full-time; (b) to be a mother full-time; or (c) to have a combination of part-time work and mothering—the modern married man still has only one acceptable option if he is to survive economically and retain his male masculine-mystique identity: (a) to work full-time.

Men are still the major breadwinners in the large majority of two-parent families with children in the United States.[37] American men still spend far more time in the workplace than do women.[38] Nor have jobs changed that much. The "information age" workplace is as mechanized as its industrial forebear. Most current white-collar and service-industry jobs offer little more than the factory jobs of yore. Currently over 75 percent of all jobs consist of repetitive mo-tions and little else.[39] As for leisure, according to recent research, the overworked American male has, on average, about seventeen hours a week of free time, 40 percent less than his father did.[40]

As men remain enclosed into the machine milieu at work and home, the robopathic man of the masculine mystique becomes ever more ubiquitous. The robopath is a profoundly dysfunctional man, suited for industrial or corporate work but made unfit for other aspects of life. The machine man's overworked, mechanized, efficiency-based life is in great part responsible for the trademark masculine-mystique characteristics of lack of emotion and caring. Erich Fromm provides a telling psychological portrait of this mod-ern machine man:

He turns his interest away from life, persons, nature, ideas—in short from everything which is alive; he transforms all life into things including himself and the manifestations of his human faculties of reason, seeing, hearing, tasting, loving. Sexuality becomes a technical skill (the "love machine"); feelings are flattened and sometimes substituted for by sentimentality; joy, the expression of intense aliveness, is replaced by "fun" or excitement; and whatever love and tenderness man has is directed towards machines and gadgets. The world becomes a sum of lifeless artifacts . . . the whole man becomes part of the total machinery that he controls and is simultaneously controlled by. He has no plan or goal in life, except doing what the logic of technique determines him to do. . . . Robots are among the greatest achievement of his technical mind, and some specialists assure us that the robot will hardly be distinguished from living men. This achievement will not seem so astonishing when man himself is hardly distinguishable from a robot.[41]

The machine man so aptly described by Fromm is crippled in his ability to be a full and present, reflective and emotional human being for himself, his spouse, children, or friends. The masculine mystique celebrates the machine man's emphasis on quick reflex action and thought (demanded by machine work) rather than reflection and use of the imagination. Thus men are often assumed to be, and celebrate themselves as, the "objective," rational gender, whereas women are seen as the intuitive, subjective, irrational gender. The reflex-oriented machine man has far less interest in, or respect for, the reflective or imaginative pursuits (arts, fiction, poetry, or religion) than do the women in his life.

The machine man is also nearly incapable of authentic emotional bonding with family, friends, or community. Generations of sons and daughters have been haunted by the lack of emotionally giving and caring fathers, fathers whose lives have been separated from their children by the necessity of work and whose minds have been steered from empathy and toward efficiency and productivity.

Machines, after all, do not feel but rather are designed for efficient production.

The cult of efficiency, the premier mechanical trait, remains at the heart of the masculine mystique's emotional impoverishment of men. A large part of our personal and social policy is still constructed around the "efficiency principle" so ably advocated by Taylor. As a society we repeatedly urge the efficient use of natural resources, efficient use of human resources (human beings), efficient government, an efficient economy, and of course an efficient and productive labor force.

Yet if we extend the efficiency principle to private life, it is quickly apparent that a pathology results. Is a father to treat his children efficiently—giving them minimum food, affection, and time for maximum loyalty and academic performance? Is a man to treat his friends based on an efficiency calculation? In reality we know that to flourish, these relationships need to be based primarily on empathy and love, not efficiency. Nevertheless men have been entrained in efficiency in order to make them more productive workers and household caretakers of technology. They have been forced into a bind, in which their lives and identity are judged on an efficiency basis, yet this very quality ensures dysfunctional relationships and an emotionally deprived existence.

The machine man is not only incapable of showing care for others, he rarely shows it toward his own physical or mental health. While the disposable machine men of the workplace are still working in high gear, they do not recognize the stress caused by their labor. They tend to apply the same standard of endurance to themselves that they do to machines. They have so internalized the efficiency mandates of Taylor and the robopathic ethic that they drive themselves into overwork and stress-related disease, refusing to recognize weariness or fatigue. Fatigue for these men is a matter of shame. This results in hundreds of thousands of work-related injuries and deaths each year. For despite the best efforts of the Taylorites, men cannot make the grade. Men are not motors. They break down far more easily. They are sensitive to stress and disease. And unlike machines they need emotional security and support.

Illness also causes shame and denial for many men. Under robopathology, illness is also seen as analogous to a machine malfunction—it is often viewed as unmanly by men and women alike. Most importantly disease can threaten a man's place in the workforce (the machine man's defining societal role). Accordingly men refuse to seek care for their bodies. From heart disease and cancer to depression and drug or alcohol addiction, studies show that men are significantly less likely than women to seek medical advice when symptoms of physical and psychic disorders are present. Most men will not seek help even when their lives are in imminent danger. If a call to a doctor is made, more often than not a man's spouse or daughter will make the initial contact.

Robopathology is so ingrained in men that physicians working in men's health find that encouraging men to seek health care is most successful if they can come up with a machine metaphor. Joey Hamilton, a doctor who specializes in men's health, observes, "I spend a lot of time on education [of men]. I tell them they need to follow a health maintenance schedule, just like the maintenance schedule for their car. It's something a lot of men seem to be able to relate to."[42]

The mechanization of men in the military has led to an equally tragic fate for the modern male. Robert Graves called the wars of this century a "holocaust of young men." The average age of the nearly 100 million soldiers who died in World Wars I and II and in Korea was just over eighteen. It was only an extreme form of robopathology that allowed world leaders to feel free to sacrifice these millions of young male bodies on the battlefield as if they were so many replaceable machines. French philosopher Jean Paul Sartre, then a young French soldier on the front in the early months of World War II, wrote, "The death of a soldier is seen as nothing more than the destruction of a tool."[43]

The military's mechanized view of men, versus the organic view of women, is evident in much of the current debate over the appropriateness of females serving in combat roles in the military. One retired officer has stated, "Men get killed in wars all the time. But she's my daughter." Former Reagan administration defense secretary Caspar Weinberger was even more direct: "I think women are too valuable to be in combat."[44] Apparently for many in our society young women's bodies have not yet descended to the same mechanized status as those of young men.

The military mechanization of men is equally responsible for the psychic scarring of so many veterans, who were trained to see themselves and the enemy as depersonalized fighting machines, only to discover their own and their opponents' humanity in the horrific context of the modern battlefield. Robopathology is also behind society's seeming inability to deal with the shattered veterans that return from the battlefield. No one is interested in broken machines; once broken, they are generally discarded.

The mechanistic view of men has also spawned an increasing separation between men and nature. The masculine-mystique glorification of technology is often made at the expense of empathy for the natural world. Unlike his male ancestors, who were defined primarily as stewards and husbandrymen of fields, forests, and family, the modern man is seen as naturally and essentially mechanical. As we have seen, even in the home, men are routinely delegated the caretaking of machines, while women deal with whatever is organic, be it children or food. It is little mystery, then, that polls taken on the public's view of environmental protection usually indicate a significant "gender gap." Far more women than men place the interests of the ecology over those of industry.

As the masculine mystique's robopathology caused a breakdown in men's relationship to work, family, their health, and nature, it created a similar trauma with male sexuality. Historian Dr. Lynn Hunt writes that "not only do some men see technology in sexual terms, they see sex in technological terms."[45]

Over the years I have spoken with many men and numerous psychologists who work with men. Not one of them regarded their sexuality as essentially generative, much less as an equivalent creative symbol to women's wombs. Nor did they know men who feel this way. Instead most men view their phalluses in mechanistic, robopathic terms. As noted in Chapter Two, for men and society in general the penetration of the phallus involved in sexual union is virtually never seen as analogous to the creativity of a penetrating idea or to that of the farmer, who penetrates the earth. Though these are natural analogies for male sexual penetration, which is, after all, biologically based in the literal planting of that paradigm of creativity, the seed (semen). Unfortunately many men now view the penis's penetration in terms of a machine that works at pistonlike motion and speed to get the "job done," the graphic embodiment of which is the Masters-and-Johnson coition machine described earlier. Men may also view their penises as machines analogous to pleasure toys—joysticks—or as guns or missiles that shoot or penetrate to destroy rather than create.

Numerous psychologists have become so enamored of the "penis as machine" concept that they claim that men's obsession with machines and technology is based on their penises—"men play with gadgets because they've played with their penises . . . tools are kind of an extension of the penis."[46] In reality of course the penis is among the least mechanistic of body parts. Its ability to change shape, grow, and accomplish a key role in procreation, as well as its reliance on the mind to provide the incentive for its alteration in shape and function, are all traits antithetical to those of the machine.

The reduction of the penis to "gadget" status, and its complete loss of deep generative symbolic power, was obvious in the media treatment of the highly publicized case of John and Lorena Bobbitt, which involved Lorena amputating her husband's penis. The amputation was more often than not treated semihumorously. Late-night comedians had a field day with the amputation, and national magazines competed with one another for the cleverest titles for their stories on the case.[47] It is clear that the same humor would not have been present had a husband, badly abused by his wife, cut off her breast and thrown it out his car window. While women's breasts have been turned into sexual objects of desire, they have not yet fully lost their generative symbolism. The penis, however, has been totally mechanized and banalized.

The reduction of the penis to tool status has also been accompanied by the "Taylorization" of sex. Starting with the work of Krafft-Ebing in the early decades of this century (which was contemporary with the rise of Taylorism) extending through Kinsey, Masters and Johnson, and now a growing horde of sex researchers, we have been inundated with scientific research on sex and with how-to manuals on achieving orgasm in the most pleasurable and efficient ways. Each possible sexual position and act has been analyzed. The reactions of each sexual component—penis, scrotum, clitoris, labia, vagina—have been scrutinized and measured. Sex, like work, has become depersonalized and given over to efficiency-based expertise.

This revolution in men's and women's perception of sexuality no doubt has an impact on the growth of pornography, violence, and rape. As one historian of pornography suggests, "Pornography is about cataloguing all the [sexual desire] variations, treating bodies as interchangeable parts in machines."[48] Men who see themselves as little more than machines in the production process and their penises as yet another tool to get the job done will also begin to see their female partners in similar mechanical terms. If men are viewed, and view themselves, as mere objects of production, they will turn women into objects of desire.

Finally, the machine-man myth has yet one more devastating impact on men and society. The masculine mystique promulgates the social prejudice that mothers are more nurturing and caring than fathers. Men face this discrimination in courts around the country every day as they consistently lose in custody cases because the mother is viewed as generative while the father is seen in terms of his ability to work with technology and be productive. This means that, tragically, millions of fathers are regularly deprived of one of the few relationships that could redeem them and society from robopathology.

Industrial labor and military life, aided by the chief scientific teachings of the modern age, finally succeeded in changing how men felt and thought about themselves, including the most intimate aspect of their sexuality and masculinity. As we have seen, the masculine mystique's mechanistic reduction of masculinity was a disaster for men. However, the masculine mystique was also at work on other fronts, including drastically altering men's fundamental relationship to one another.

5

THE COMPETITION MAN

There is no room for second place. I have finished second twice . . . and I never want to finish second again. . . . It is and always has been an American zeal to be first in anything we do and to win and to win and to win. —Vince Lombardi[1]

Men constantly compare successes and accomplishments. When two men get together for the first time, the question "What do you do?" comes up immediately. Men measure everything from the size of their bank accounts to the size of their sex organ. —Cris Evatt[2]

It was without question the high point of President Bill Clinton's first years in office. On November 17, 1993, after weeks of bitter debate and a last-minute flurry of wheeling and dealing, the House of Representatives approved the historic North American Free Trade Agreement (NAFTA). The president had made passage of the trade agreement with Canada and Mexico a key test of his presidency. The night of his victory, standing in the crowded Grand Foyer at the White House, Clinton addressed the country. Flushed with triumph, he declaimed a paean to the glories of economic competition—the fundamental virtue embodied in the free-trade agreement. "Tonight's vote is a defining moment for our nation. At a time when many of our people are hurting from the strains of this tough global economy, we chose to compete, not to retreat." The president continued, "In an economy where competition is global and change is the only constant, our only chance is to take this new world head on, to compete and to win." Throughout his brief remarks the president kept closely to his "compete and win" theme, closing with yet a final rallying call: "Tonight, I am proud to say, we have not flinched. . . . Our people are winners. And I believe we tonight are ready together to compete and to win to shape the world of the 21st century."[3]

The president achieved his free-trade victory despite tenacious opposition. Many had harshly criticized the free-trade concept and viewed the president's "compete and win" stance as overly simplistic and potentially dangerous. Labor unions had repeatedly pointed out that to freely compete with Mexico, as mandated in the NAFTA accord, might well require lowering U.S. wages and safety regulations to Mexican standards. Similarly environmentalists argued that competing with countries who had few environmental regulations could only lead to a degradation of the hard-fought limits to pollution and resource depletion achieved in the United States. Further, some economists saw NAFTA as "Victorian economics," a throwback to the late-nineteenth-century glorification of a laissez-faire free market, when there was little concern for those who lost in the unfettered competition for economic survival. They also questioned what "winning" against other countries in the global economy really meant. Was it right to enthusiastically herald victory over other nations in the international economic struggle, a "win" that would subject "losing" countries to unemployment, poverty, and social unrest?

Though controversy remained, most commentators in the media and the financial markets praised the president for definitively reasserting the credo of economic competition as the basis of American public and political life. They congratulated the Clinton administration for backing free trade despite the opposition of traditional Democratic-party constituents, including labor unions and environmentalists. By his actions, they opined, the president affirmed that the United States was not afraid to compete in the global economy, whatever the cost.

There was also a wave of public approval for the president on a more personal basis. The NAFTA vote was an important defining moment for Clinton and his vice president Al Gore, as men. On that November night they seemed to finalize an ersatz, highly public manhood-initiation rite. With their blunt dealing to get the NAFTA agreement passed, as well as their gung-ho advocacy of the competition ethic, they let it be known that they had aligned themselves with the deeply ingrained, masculine-mystique teaching that the drive for competition and victory is the very essence of manhood.

There had been suspicions about Clinton's "toughness." This discomfort with the president was based in part on his avoidance of the draft as a young man, as well as his perceived "soft" approach to social-justice issues. But now it was clear, and cause for relief, that the competition mantle had passed to a new generation. Clinton and Gore reaffirmed, as the new generation of American leadership, that competition was still to be the central ethic of America, and victory still the country's primary goal. Social justice, worker welfare, and the environment, however important, finished second.

The perception that Clinton and Gore had somehow become "men" during the struggle for their NAFTA victory should not be surprising. Competition is, after all, at the very heart of our culture's teaching about what masculinity is all about. According to author Perry Garfinkel, "The competition credo is accepted as the unspoken, unwritten and mostly unconscious contract that at once binds and divides men."[4] And competition permeates virtually every action a man takes. Educator Alfie Kohn writes, "From the time the alarm clock rings until sleep overtakes us again, from the time we are toddlers until the day we die, we are busy struggling to outdo others. This is our posture at work and at school, on the playing field and back at home. It is the common denominator of American life."[5]

The vast majority of today's men were raised to believe that they have a natural inclination for cutthroat competition, and that they are innately suited to the dog-eat-dog atmosphere of the national and international marketplace. Real men are said to awake each morning with the insatiable urge to beat out other men in the battle of the marketplace and thereby achieve wealth, power, and social esteem. We are told that real men don't ask for help but only the "opportunity to compete."

While the president and others champion the ethic of competition as a supreme value, many who have studied the psychology of competition see it as profoundly dysfunctional. Psychologist Nathan Ackerman gives a telling description of the competition man's pathology: "The strife of competition reduces empathetic sympathy, distorts communication, and impairs the mutuality of support and sharing."[6] Morton Deutsch, perhaps the most well known researcher into the psychology of competition, describes the mind-set required of men mired in constant competition: "In a competitive relationship, one is disposed to . . . have a suspicious, hostile, exploitative attitude towards the other, to be psychologically closed to the other, to be aggressive and defensive toward the other, to seek advantage and superiority for self and disadvantage and inferiority for the other."[7]

As competition becomes the male's main avenue of self-validation, fear of losing in competition remains the single greatest anxiety for many men. For boys and men, loss in competition can equal psychic annihilation. The renowned psychoanalyst Rollo May, in his pioneering study on anxiety, came to the conclusion that competition is "the most pervasive occasion for anxiety" in our culture. Ironically most men, when faced with the endless anxiety of a life of competition, attempt to solve the problem by devoting themselves ever more fervently to the competitive struggle to win. In this fashion the anxiety and loss of self-esteem caused by competition actually lead men to ever-more-intense competition. May explains:

> The culturally accepted method of allaying [competition] anxiety is redoubling one's efforts to achieve success . . . so the anxious individual increases his competitive striving. But the more com-

petitive, aggressive striving, the more isolation, hostility and anxiety. This vicious circle may be graphed as follows: competitive individual striving → intrasocial hostility → isolation → anxiety → increased competitive striving. Thus the methods most generally used to dispel anxiety in such a constellation actually increase anxiety in the long run.[8]

Men who yearn to escape the competition–anxiety–competition treadmill or who complain about the dehumanizing elements of the marketplace are often viewed as unmanly "wimps." They are dismissed with familiar bromides—"If you can't stand the heat get out of the kitchen." Worse, they are viewed as somehow unnatural. It is important to note (as was described in Chapter Two) that virtually every modern comparison of gender behavior asserts that men are the naturally more competitive gender, whereas women are seen as inherently more cooperative. Researchers further argue that aggressiveness and competition are actually encoded in the male physiology as an inevitable result of male hormones. Whatever the pathology of competition, we are told it is endemic to the masculine and cannot be avoided.

When confronted with the ubiquitous hypercompetitive American male, it is easy to understand why it is believed that men are biologically predisposed toward competition. Competition is, as Kohn suggests, the common denominator among modern men. Yet despite conventional wisdom and masculine-mystique indoctrination, the omnipresent "competition man" is of recent origin. He is a cultural, not a biological, construct.

THE GREAT TRANSFORMATION

Most assume that men have always been the competitive creatures they are today, vying with each other for survival and prestige. We even envision cavemen clubbing one another in the competition for food or for the right to drag a particular female around by the hair.

These stereotypes are of course fallacious. Historian Marshall Sahlins reminds us that cooperation and not competition was the credo that bound early men and women to one another: "The emerging human primate, in a life-and-death struggle with nature, could not afford the luxury of a social struggle. Cooperation not competition was essential. . . . Hobbes's famous fantasy of a war of 'all against all' in the natural state could not be further from the truth."[9]

Sahlins's observation is backed by anthropological research from societies as diverse as the American Indian, African, and premodern European societies. Competition was never the way in which these communities allocated scarce resources among their members. In primitive societies men cooperated with one another to fight against the hardships and exigencies of nature. In good times they survived well. If there was drought or famine, they starved together. They did not vie against one another for work or the basics of life. As we have seen, European medieval society was typical in this regard. It consisted of a mixture of freemen, apprentices, serfs, and journeymen. No matter how exploitative their labor, they never entered a market in which they competed to sell their labor and never competed against one another for survival. The conclusion from our past is clear: Competition is neither an inescapable part of human survival nor an ineluctable aspect of masculinity.[10] What, then, happened to men? How were they changed into today's pathologically competitive males?

While competition among men is part of many traditional societies (often in the form of sports, "macho" posing, or warfare), the industrial world initiated a new kind of competition between men, one that no other culture had ever engaged in—namely, the competition for jobs and livelihood. This unprecedented economic "blood" sport was the key cultural force shaping the new competition man of the masculine mystique.

With the enclosure of men into the factory system, the very definition of labor changed. The land, community, and traditional crafts no longer provided men with a living based on cooperation. Instead the division of labor and the need for new workers in the industrialized cities created a job market based on competition. Human labor was suddenly transformed from a communal effort into a commodity to be sold to an employer. Each man became a desperate salesman of his labor, seeking to prevail against the other in the fight to sell himself. This change in the very definition of human labor was what economist Karl Polanyi called "the great transformation." In just a few generations men stopped viewing themselves as a community of allies bonded in the struggle for mutual livelihood and began instead to see themselves as a collection of fierce competitors—with the stakes being survival itself. The sale of each man's labor as a commodity in the competitive free market permanently alienated men from one another.

Today we take selling ourselves in the labor market so much for granted that it is difficult to conceptualize labor as not being for sale. We think society must always have involved a vast network of job seekers attempting to sell their services to the highest bidder. But again there was no competition for jobs and livelihood in preindustrialist society. As one historian notes, "Nowhere in the uninfluenced primitive society do we find labor associated with the idea of competition or payment."[11]

The competition for labor in the modern age was based on the market theory. Competition would determine wages on a supply-and-demand basis. In market terms workers are the human "supply" that moves to the labor "demand." Human work is treated like any other commodity in the marketplace. Of course, this is an economic fiction. Human labor is not a product, nor is it manufactured for sale. Work is a normal function of all humans. It is not simply the abstract energy of a worker that has been separated out and sold in packaged form. Clearly, by selling their labor, humans sell themselves. When an employer purchases labor for his workplace, he has bought a worker's life, or at least a significant and indivisible portion of the life, thoughts, and creativity of the worker.

The competition to sell labor involves not only the life of the worker but also that of the laborer's family. For generations workers and their families have been forced to move to wherever labor is being sought. Being mobile and willing to relocate in response to the fluctuations of the labor market was, and remains, a key to being a successful competitor in the job marketplace.

Though it made the industrial economy an extraordinary success, the sale of labor was a disaster for workers, and especially for men, who were to become the vast majority of humans selling their lives. Primary among the dislocations created by the sale of labor was the dehumanization involved in viewing all other men as competitors. This alienation of man from man was exacerbated by the frequent mobility required in finding work. As workers competed for work and moved to find jobs, many key aspects of their former lives were lost. Community, family, kinship, and any other relationship based on cooperation, location, or rootedness were undermined.[12]

As the commodification and sale of labor caused an unprecedented transformation of men and society, it also fostered the earliest and most profound crisis for the industrial system. In the early days of the Industrial Revolution, losing in the market system's job competition meant destitution and often death for the wave of dispossessed peasants and craftspeople desperately seeking a livelihood. The hardships of the early industrial workplace also resulted in epidemics of disease and injuries to those competing to stay employed. Fourteen-to-sixteen-hour days were common. The life expectancy of workers in these years rarely exceeded fifty years of age. We still see many of these conditions in South America, Asia, and Africa as the new refugees of enclosure struggle for subsistence in the overpopulated cities of the Third World.

In Europe and America the mass exploitation of workers brought both revolution and reform. By the last decades of the nineteenth century, labor "unions" had begun to be formed as men and women broke the individualistic competition ethic to fight as a community of workers for change. Moreover, an angry anti-industrial populist movement swept the United States calling for a return to agrarian values. On the European continent Karl Marx had developed his theories of a work ers' state, and mass revolt and uprisings were common. The market's primary ethic—competition—was being attacked on many fronts.

However, at this crucial moment of crisis and doubt an extraordinarily influential scientific theory emerged that once again bolstered the ethic of competition. This pseudoscientific creed was to leave an indelible mark on American society, and especially on its men.

"ROOT, HOG, OR DIE"

In all of modern history there have only been a handful of scientific doctrines that have changed our very perception of ourselves and society. We have witnessed the profound influence of "Descartes's dream" and the cult of mechanism and efficiency. Of equal importance was Charles Darwin's *Origin of Species*, published in 1859, and his theory of evolution. Today, when at least the outlines of evolutionary science are often accepted, it is difficult to imagine the immense jolt that the "discovery" of evolution gave Western society. At first the primary impact was in scientific circles and on those in the religious community, who felt that the new theory challenged their beliefs. However, soon a wide range of thinkers of the Darwinian era were attempting to understand the implications of the theory of evolution for their discipline.

Social philosophers quickly transposed Darwin's "survival of the fittest" biology into a strong defense of unlimited competition for labor and livelihood in the market system. They found the evolutionary theory especially useful in dismissing the human suffering of those who lost in the economic struggle for survival. As articulated by thinkers such as Herbert Spencer, Darwin's theories clearly demonstrated that competition for survival was not an aberration of the market system but rather a basic operating principle of the natural world. They applied the purported mechanism of "natural selection" to market society and came to the conclusion that those men who were winning in the capitalist race for survival and wealth were equivalent to the superior species who were selected for survival in nature; those men who lost—the unemployed or the poor—were equivalent to the inferior species, justifiably doomed to extinction. This doctrine has been termed "Social Darwinism."[13]

Social Darwinism was especially influential in the United States. The leading U.S. spokesman for the dogma was William Graham Sumner. Born in New Jersey in 1840, Sumner became a professor at Yale in 1872 and, through numerous books, articles, and lectures, evangelized the gospel of Social Darwinism. One commentator likened Sumner to a "latter-day Calvin, who came to preach the predestination of the social order and the salvation of the economically elect through the survival of the fittest."[14] Sumner believed that all progress in civilization depended on unrestricted competition. He wrote, "Competition is a law of nature which can no more be done away with than gravitation."[15]

Sumner and his followers were firm believers that the state should not interfere with the "natural" results of market competition. They were adamantly opposed to "any device whose aim was to save individuals from any of the difficulties or hardships of the struggle for existence and the competition of life."[16] For Sumner this included competition for his own job, as reflected in a memorable exchange with a student dissenter during one of his Yale lectures in 1870:

> STUDENT: Professor [Sumner], don't you believe in any government aid to industries?
> SUMNER: No! It's root, hog, or die.
> STUDENT: Yes, but hasn't the hog got a right to root?
> SUMNER: There are no rights. The world owes nobody a living.
> STUDENT: You believe then, Professor, in only one system, the contract-competitive system?
> SUMNER: That's the only sound economic system. All others are fallacies.
> STUDENT: Well, suppose some professor of political economy came along and took your job away from you. Wouldn't you be sore?
> SUMNER: Any other professor is welcome to try. If he gets my job, it is my fault.[17]

For Sumner and the Social Darwinists millionaires are the ultimate in natural selection, the "bloom" of competitive civilization: "The millionaires are a product of natural selection. . . . It is because they are thus selected that wealth—both their own and that entrusted to them—aggregates under their hands."[18]

Sumner understood that a society based on the Darwinian view of competition for survival was a radical change from the past. He realized that the revolution of competition undermined all human relations except those based on contracts for work and services, that it exterminated "sentimental or emotional ties." Yet he saw no other path if humanity was to "progress":

In the Middle Ages men were united by custom and prescription into associations, ranks, guilds, and communities of various kinds. These ties endured as long as life lasted. Consequently society was dependent on . . . the tie, or bond [which] was sentimental. In our modern state, and in the United States more than anywhere else, the social structure is based on contract. . . . It is realistic, cold, and matter of fact. . . . In a state based on contract sentiment is out of place in any public or common affairs. . . . It is out of the question to go back to the sentimental relations which once united baron and retainer, teacher and pupil, comrade and comrade. That we have lost some grace and elegance is undeniable. That life once held more poetry and romance is true enough. But it seems impossible that any one who has studied the matter should doubt that we have gained immeasurably, and that our further gain lies in going forward, not in going backward.[19]

There were of course many dissenters to the wave of social Darwinism that was so powerful in late-nineteenth- and early-twentieth-century America. Critic Henry Demarest wrote prophetically that the Darwinian competitive ethic, like the ethic of efficiency, would be a disaster if men applied it to their personal and family relationships:

"The weakest must go first," is the golden rule of business. There is no other field of human association in which any such rule of action is allowed. The man who should apply in his family or in his citizenship this "survival of the fittest" theory as it is practically professed and operated in business would be a monster.[20]

Evolutionary scientists also debunked the Social Darwinists and their misuse of evolutionary theory to support economic competition. They pointed out that "survival of the fittest," far from mandating competitive behavior, often means the survival of those who do not compete. Noted biologist Stephen Jay Gould states, "The equation of competition with success in natural selection is merely a cultural prejudice." He notes that natural selection often means the survival of those who cooperate.[21]

Though Social Darwinism was eventually formally abandoned by academia under the force of a growing group of critics, its central teaching survived the death of the dogma. The elevation of competition to the highest value in American life did not cease with the popularity of Spencer or Sumner. It lives today in the consciousness of America and its men. Competitiveness, like efficiency, remains a "god term" for our society. Many still warn of dire results should local or federal governments interfere with the individual or corporate competition for economic survival. As we saw with President Clinton, our leaders continue to rally the population by reminding us that our public purpose is to compete successfully in the "global marketplace." On the family level we repeatedly urge our children to study, achieve high marks, and get an advanced education, not primarily to become fuller, more rounded people but rather so that they can better compete in the job market.

THE CARNAGE OF CONTEST

Sumner's Social Darwinist creed remains an essential part of the masculine mystique. As breadwinner and worker the "no-option" male has little choice but to base his life and identity on how successfully he competes in the job market. For the vast majority of men the competition ethic becomes, by necessity, the fundamental ethic of their existence.

As with the machine man, the competition man tends to become profoundly dysfunctional in all of life's arenas save the workplace. The competition man thrives as an autonomous economic combatant. He therefore has difficulty honestly sharing thoughts or emotions. Most importantly he is incapable of balancing cooperation with his main activity, competition.

Perhaps the most tragic consequence of the competition-man dysfunction is that it profoundly undermines male friendship and bonding. Psychologist Herb Goldberg writes, "The drive for financial survival typically has a tendency to erode friendships between men, producing deep distrust and progressively alienating them from each other."[22] The competition ethic is without doubt the ethic of isolation—it turns men permanently against one another in the tooth-and-claw world of competing to make a living. As the successful stock trader in the movie *Wall Street* tells his young apprentice, "If you need a friend, get a dog."

The deep antagonism between men born of competition is reflected not only in our highly combative daily business practices, but also in the degrading, hostile, homoerotic terms with which businessmen routinely describe one another. They often speak of each other as "assholes" and "pricks," as having each other "by the balls" or giving it to each other "up the ass," and of course "being screwed" by their competitor. Our media's representation of men's relationships with one another also reflects the neurotic hatred and violence among men spawned by the necessity of competition. The vast majority of the murder, mayhem, and destruction that proliferate on television and in the movies is violence perpetrated by men against men.

The isolation, hostility, and suspicion with which men view one another in the competition market system acts as a powerful disincentive for men to organize and cooperate around gender issues, including the myriad problems identified and described earlier as "the hidden crisis." After years of indoctrination in the masculine mystique's competition ethic, men instinctively hide their hurt or emotion so that their competitors will not see or sense their weakness. This deeply entrained denial in men is evident as many men, especially in public, will call those who are working on men's issues "unmanly" or "whiners." While these same men might admit to their own and other men's despair in private, they feel that public exposure of their "weaknesses" could disarm them and fatally compromise their ability to be successful competitors. In this pernicious manner the masculine mystique actively works against those forces attempting to break it. The urgent task of building community among men therefore directly confronts the competition pathology and is in direct conflict with the primary ethic among men in our society.

The competition pathology also disfigures and ultimately destroys men's ability to play. In his classic work *Homo Ludens* ("Man at Play"), Johan Huizinga describes how play is central to a healthy culture. Play at once allows us to express our freedom and creativity. Huizinga writes that play is "free activity standing quite consciously outside of 'ordinary' life as being 'not serious' but at the same time absorbing the player intensely and utterly."[23] However, under the competition ethic boys, especially as they get older, are forced into a variety of organized sports that have little to do with play but more often than not imitate the competitive intensity and brutality of professional sports. The young male learns early on that winning is, as Vince Lombardi suggested, the only thing. Moreover, the boy's running, swimming, and jumping are all heavily performance oriented, timed down to the second. A combination of the cult of efficiency and the obsession with competition drains all the joy, improvisation, and spontaneity out of the play activity itself, making it merely the most efficient means to the end of "winning." Each boy's performance, as judged by the clock and the score, are seen as portents of how he will perform in the future in the all-important job competition in the "real" world.[24]

Many young athletes "burn out" under the competition pressure. Others withdraw from the permanent psychological trauma of losing or being left out of the competition. Still others pay an even higher price in the sports competition. Almost one-third of all high school football players receive injuries each year. That translates into over 550,000 injuries annually. With all high school sports added together, over one million boys are injured each year.[25] Each year dozens of young athletes die. One trainer commented on the charnel house of high school and collegiate football: "The fans like the hitting in football. So do the coaches, who love to hear the pop. But it's the trainer who hears the other sound—the break."

The competition pathology also leads hundreds of thousands of young men to become hooked on steroids each year in the hopes that their chemically improved bodies will give them the competitive edge to make it onto a team and then be a successful athlete. Athletes are among the most common users of anabolic steroids among high school and college students. One high school study found that 84 percent of anabolic-steroid users participated in sports. According to a one-year study of college students at five universities, between 15 and 20 percent of college athletes reported using steroids.[26]

Once they are beyond the competition of high school or college sports, men also fall victim to the injuries inherent in competing for jobs in the labor market. Over 90 percent of those involved in the nation's most dangerous professions are men. Additionally, though men comprise just over 55 percent of the workforce, 93 percent of those killed in the workplace are men.[27] To these casualties must be added the unemployed men, who are the losers in the labor competition and who are prey to despair, hopelessness, and high rates of suicide.

Over the last few years we have seen a whole new generation of male workers, millions of men, who have lost their jobs in the factories, mills, and mines and other manufacturing sectors, as well as in the middle-manager ranks of America's corporations. These generally middle-aged men cannot compete for the sophisticated new jobs being offered in the hi-tech service economy. For many of the millions of men who became unemployed in the last decade, the competition is over. They are being discarded along with the machines they worked. They now face poverty and loss of family, dignity, and masculine identity.

Along with the growing numbers of the unemployed, there are other groups of men, including the homeless and many veterans—men being shunned not just because they are poor or disabled but also because they have committed the greatest crime against the masculine mystique: They have become dependent and can no longer compete.

6

THE PROFIT MAN

What is a man, anyway? Everything I see around me in life tells me a man is he who makes money.
—Narrator of *The Women's Room* by Marilyn French[1]

For what shall it profit a man, if he shall gain the whole world and lose his soul? Or what shall a man give in exchange for his soul?
—Mark 8:36, 37[2]

You cannot miss the successful ones. They bustle through airports in well-tailored suits, clutching leather briefcases. They rush down busy city streets, cellular phone in hand. They sit conversing at the corner tables of the best downtown restaurants, downing their business lunches. We recognize them in their luxury cars on the expressway. We can even identify them by their conspicuous winter tans, gained no doubt at faraway beach resorts. They are the envy of most men, the epitome of the American way of life: the successful businessman.

The businessman has been, and remains, America's primary social icon. For generations the businessman has been the figure of leadership in our communities. A recent magazine headline even referred to America's entrepreneurs as its "romantic heroes." By the end of the nineteenth century the hegemony of the businessman in American life was visible for the world to see. The vast fortunes of men such as Andrew Carnegie, John D. Rockefeller, J. P. Morgan, and Edward Harriman gave gaudy proof of the benefits of the relentless pursuit of profit. By the turn of the century these men had been accorded top status by their own countrymen and had become the stuff of legends for Europeans.

Since the early days of the tycoons, the deification of the businessman and his profit philosophy has gone virtually unchallenged in the United States. Over the last several decades we have questioned every secular and sacred institution in our society, from the Pentagon to marriage, from Congress to the churches, yet the gospel of the pursuit of profit and its leading shamans, the businessmen, have gone unscathed. The profit ethic remains the central axiom of our culture.

The absolute dominance of the business ethic in our culture has led many to aptly term the pursuit of profit our civil religion. Our banks have the same authoritative ambience, and often imposing architecture, that was once given over to our churches. It is well to recall that *trust, bond, save, goods, incorporation, service, full faith,* and *credit* are no longer primarily religious or moral terms but rather financial. In place of the sacred and all other traditional masculine values, our culture has set men only one primary goal and ideal: the accumulation of profit. Historian Max Lerner accurately proclaims, "The persona of the American civilization has been the businessman; where other civilization types have pursued wisdom, beauty, sanctity, military glory, predacity, asceticism, the businessman pursues the magnitudes of profit with a similar singleminded drive."[3]

We are surrounded with the business mentality wherever we turn. How-to books on profiting in the economy regularly top our best-seller lists. Most of our newspapers contain both headline business news and large separate business sections. Business information and discussion flood our radio and TV reports and talk shows. The media is replete with information and analysis about the stock market, price fluctuations, inflation, the deficit, employment, interest rates, the gross national product, investment strategies, CDs, IRAs, mortgage rates, and retirement funds.

But most men do not need the print or electronic media to know that their business is business. Men's everyday lives are utterly dominated by the unending struggle for profit. The prevailing masculine-mystique ethic demands that men constantly attempt to make more money and work every angle toward their own self-interest. "Making the deal," "getting the contract," and "bottom-line thinking" are as American as apple pie.

The businessman's general job description is straightforward. Sell insurance, real estate, bonds, legal services, food, drugs, or bicycles; just keep selling, and if it doesn't sell, try something else. Most importantly of course sell yourself and your talent to the highest bidder. One historian summarizes the hegemony of the salesman in our society: "Selling has achieved dominion over the world in our time, not only determining the economic spirit of the nation but deeply affecting its social, political, cultural, and moral life."[4]

The profit man is not only an essential element of our society, but also performs an ever more vital role in our economy. The legions of businessmen and salesmen have to ensure that every time technology increases the pace of production, the pace of consumption is increased accordingly. In recent decades the profit man's task has become increasingly important and difficult. As technology has rapidly expanded production of goods, the profit man has had to frenetically ratchet-up sales to keep up, lest the economy collapse overburdened with too much supply and too little demand.

Advertising executive and author Earl Shorris has aptly described the unique pathology of the salesman (whom he dubs "Homo Vendens")—a pathology caused by the daily requirement for endless and quick sales. Shorris notes that Homo Venden's bottom line has to be the transaction, the contract, the sale; the profit man is therefore isolated and alienated. He is isolated from other men because they are the omnipresent competing salesmen against whom he must succeed to make a living. He is isolated from the rest of humanity because collectively and individually they are studied and treated as targets for the sale. He is isolated from the product he sells. The morality, value, or destructiveness of that which is sold is irrelevant. Whether a product is good for people or the environment is beside the point, unless, of course, it can be a selling point.

The profit man is ultimately alienated from himself. Whatever his own nature, it must be changed nearly instantaneously to the demeanor required by the transaction. There is no room for dignity or integrity. The salesman is a thespian by necessity, shifting easily and skillfully into whatever character is required to make the deal. The greatest psychological fear of Homo Vendens is not loss of a sense of self, it is the loss of a sale. Shorris sums up the tragic human consequences of the life of the profit man, "To do his business Homo Vendens must deny all that is authentic, intrinsic and meaningful. Once he has rid himself of those impediments, he can proceed to achieve the velocity required of a salesman in a nation of salesmen."[5]

The business world, still somewhat dominated by men, allows no exception to the unfortunate profit man model. The road to success means constantly staying busy doing business, moving inexorably and relentlessly toward the goal of increasing profits, material success, and upward mobility (material not spiritual). Author Richard M. Huber comments on this understanding of what it means to be successful: "In America, success has always meant making money. . . . Success was not earned by being a loyal friend or good husband. It was a reward for performance on the job."[6]

When confronted with the social phenomenon of Homo Vendens and the business culture, most commentators predictably claim that men are predisposed toward selling and profiteering, and are innately wedded to material things. As we have seen, the gender-behavior lists are unanimous: The masculine prefers to receive; the feminine, to give. The masculine loves material things; the feminine, spiritual goals. Men, according to one leading feminist, are consumed with furthering their own careers and are "hostile, to any alternative to the kind of aggressive, competitive, radically individualistic, profit oriented values and activities that have always represented the 'American Way.' "[7]

Moreover book after book, author after author, insist that the most important difference between the genders is that men are more self-seeking and selfish in virtually all aspects of life than women. Dr. John Gray, in *Men, Women and Relationships*, writes, "A man's biggest difficulty is to overcome his tendency to be self-absorbed."[8] One feminist author summarizes the stereotypical view of the selfish man and selfless woman:

> Women see themselves primarily in relation to the people around them and their sense of self comes from relatedness. Women habitually focus outward and have a virtually inexhaustible fascination with, and concern for, others and their needs. It's what makes women such good mothers, mates and friends. . . . On the other hand, men tend to think, act, and feel in ways that show the self is primary and others are secondary. . . . Therefore to be close to others, men must travel a greater psychological distance than women.[9]

Commentators credit this masculine selfishness with fostering America's "patriarchal," profit-driven economic system. Adding insult to injury, many believe that men's selfishness, as well as their purported penchant for material goods, salesmanship, and profit, is intrinsic to their biology. We recall that such well-known political thinkers as George Gilder and Barbara Jordan, as well as many research scientists, are convinced that men are "structurally" built for self-interest, that their genes and "brainwiring" naturally incline them toward profiting off others and disincline them to feel compassion or care for others. Feminist ideologue Andrea Dworkin goes further and suggests that the pursuit of profit is an inevitable result of the male sex drive. According to Dworkin, "Wealth of any kind, to any degree, is an expression of male sexual power."[10]

If we are to understand and address this powerful and destructive masculine-mystique stereotype of men, and the misandry that it has fostered, it is necessary to trace the origins of the profit man and the process by which the self-interest profit ethic came to dominate our society and the lives of so many men. Questions must be answered: Are men innately interested in themselves and financial gain in contrast to women who are other-oriented? And if it is not primarily biological, how did the profit motive become such a powerful force among men?

THE INVISIBLE HAND

The current august place that business and profit have in our society is without precedent in human history. As with the competition ethic, the doctrine of profit and self-interest is of recent origin. Historian Marcel Mauss reminds us that "it is only our Western societies that quite recently turned man into an economic animal."[11]

Trading for gain is not a modern invention. Markets have been part of human behavior for millennia. There is evidence that the Cro-Magnon hunters of the central valleys of France obtained shells in trade from the Mediterranean. The Tablets of Tell-el-Amarna describe a lively trade in chariots and slaves between the pharaohs and the Levantine kings in 1400 B.C. But profit seeking, whether in the exchanges between primitive tribes or the elaborate traveling fairs of the Middle Ages, are not the same as our present business system. Though trading was an important adjunct to early societies, selling goods and the profit motive were never the means by which these societies solved their basic economic problems or organized their societies. Economic historian R. C. Thurnwald writes, "The characteristic feature of primitive economics is the absence of any desire to make profits from production or exchange."[12] Nor did the peoples of antiquity work in order to gain profits. They worked for subsistence, family, or their gods but not for Mammon. The anthropologist Bronislaw Malinowski reminds us that "gain, such as is often the stimulus for work in more civilized communities, never acts as an impulse to work under the original native conditions."[13]

How, then, did early societies allocate their goods if not on a profit basis? The central ethic of many prior cultures was gift giving, a practice diametrically opposed to the profit principle. Early economic historians, who often assumed that all cultures based their societies on market relations, were jolted by the publication in 1922 of Malinowski's classic *Argonauts of the Pacific*. Malinowski's work described the society of the Trobriand Islanders, one group of the Massim peoples, who occupy the South Sea islands. Though avid and courageous seamen (hence Malinowski's use of the term *argonauts*), the Trobriand society was held together not primarily by trading but rather by elaborate gift-giving rituals between peoples of various islands. Malinowski points out that this society, like so many other primitive societies, was based on reciprocity: "Most, if not all, economic acts are found to belong to some chain of reciprocal gifts and countergifts, which balance in the long run, benefiting both sides equally."[14]

Subsequent economic historians came to see that Malinowski's argonauts were not an isolated case. Gift giving had a long history of helping to organize the economic and social life of a variety of cultures. Moreover studies of preindustrial cultures around the globe found that societies based on the individualistic, self-interested struggle for gain were virtually nonexistent.[15] Economist Robert L. Heilbroner summarizes this key point about the relatively recent origin of the profit man:

> It may strike us as odd the idea that gain is a relatively modern one; we are schooled to believe that man is essentially an acquisitive creature and that left to himself he will behave as any self-respecting businessman would. The profit motive, we are constantly being told, is as old as man himself.
>
> But it is not. The profit motive as we know it is only as old as "modern man." Even today the notion of gain for gain's sake is

foreign to a large portion of the world's population, and it has been conspicuous by its absence over most of recorded history.[16]

The profit man is even absent from preindustrial European society. As described in an earlier chapter, the commons system, based on subsistence and land sharing, was the major organizing force in the growth of European society for over a millennium. The drive for profit was not a significant part of the picture for the average medieval male. Moreover medieval Christian society condemned those who attempted to gain profit from the sale of goods or the loaning and investment of money. Saint Augustine proclaimed that "business is in itself an evil." Saint Jerome reminded the faithful that "a man who is a merchant can seldom if ever please God."[17] Of all the unworthy professions, merchants and usurers shared with prostitution the lowest rank.

The Church also declared usury, the lending of money for profit over time (a central requirement of a market economy), to be a mortal sin. The Church argued that the time that the usurer "sold" for profit as part of his loan belonged to God and was not a commodity. Theologian Thomas Chobham argued that by charging interest on loans, "the usurer sells nothing to the borrower that belongs to him. He sells only time which belongs to God. He can therefore not make a profit from selling someone else's property."[18]

Historian Raymond Williams reminds us that until the seventeenth century the very word *wealth* was associated with physical and spiritual well-being and happiness and had nothing to do with the accumulation of capital or goods. In 1542 the poet Sir Thomas Wyatt writes to his beloved, "Without you have I neither joye ne welthe." Throughout the late medieval period it was also still possible for a man to work and live "for the welth of his soul."[19]

However, beginning in the late seventeenth century, society's attitude and lexicon about wealth and profit changed radically. Within two generations the concept of profit became an economic ideology upon which an entire social system was constructed. As Western culture was transformed into a market economy, the ethic of the market-place—unfettered self-interest—became central to society.

The profit ideology began as an outgrowth of the scientific discoveries of the seventeenth century. Emboldened by the technological progress made possible by findings in natural silence, the Enlightenment thinkers were committed to discovering rules of human behavior that were as scientific as the natural laws found to operate in the inanimate world. They searched for a philosophy of man that would replace the "superstitions" and religious dictates of the past. They sought to discover scientific principles for human conduct. Eighteenth-century philosopher Francis Hutcheson was a pioneer in the attempt to find a physics of the behavior of men. Hutcheson was convinced that the traditional Judeo-Christian concept of benevolence, or ancient concepts of gift giving, were outmoded and were no longer the principal movers of men. He posited another social force of even greater power: self interest. Self-interest, according to Hutcheson, was to social life what gravity was to the physical universe: "Self love . . . is as necessary to the regular State of the Whole as gravitation."[20]

The doctrine of self-interest was an immediate success. It perfectly matched the new industrial system in Europe. Suddenly the competition for jobs and the opportunity for wealth made each man into a self-seeker. Soon a world that had emphasized gift giving and reciprocity, that had condemned merchants, worried about just prices, and made usury a sin, began to vanish. Society now operated under a new set of "self-evident" principles:

> "Every man is naturally covetous of lucre."
> "No laws are prevalent against gain."
> "Gaine is the Centre of the Circle of Commerce."[21]

With this new propagandized faith as a backdrop, a new man, the profit man, emerged. Self-interest and the profit motive began their hegemony over men. Robert L. Heilbroner writes, "By the year

1700 . . . a new idea has come into being: 'economic man'—a creature who follows his adding machine brain wherever it leads him."[22]

In 1776 Adam Smith (a student of Hutcheson) published his famous work *The Wealth of Nations*. The book would become the gospel of the new reign of the profit man. Smith's work fully transformed human self-interest into a revolutionary new social doctrine. For Smith the imperative of each individual pursuing his own interest was so basic a human instinct that he was sure a foundation for a new economic order could be built on it. The Scottish philosopher propounded what came to be called the free-market doctrine. He denigrated benevolence, gift giving, and old economies in favor of his dogma of self-interest:

> It is not from the benevolence of the butcher, the brewer or the baker that we expect our dinner, but from their regard to their own interest. We address ourselves, not to their humanity but to their self-love, and never talk to them of our own necessities but of their advantages. Nobody but a beggar chuses [sic] to depend chiefly on the benevolence of his fellow citizens.[23]

Smith follows up this assumption with an even more surprising one. Namely that each individual, freely pursuing his own selfish needs, is nevertheless bound to serve the common good, whether he consciously intends to or not—that market principles are an "invisible hand" that in almost magical fashion lead to the good of all. Given the unavoidable and benevolent nature of selfishness, Smith advocates that the government that governs least, governs best. If the government keeps its hands out of economic affairs, the natural selfish order of each man will speedily flower into economic well-being for all. As each pursues his self-interest, the "laws" of supply and demand will be applied to all commodities and will govern price and production. Society will be led to a cornucopia of economic wealth.

Smith's teachings would sustain the growth of the Industrial Revolution and provide the moral basis for the development of the factory-production system. As noted by one historian, Smith's market theories "evolved into a veritable faith in man's secular salvation through a self-regulating market."[24] That faith is alive and well today. Though only a product of the last two centuries, the dogma of the free market has become a virtual substitute for the religious and cultural norms that permeated preindustrial European society and most past civilizations. Believing that men are basically egoists in pursuit of economic self-interest, Smith's doctrine subordinates all other human desires and needs to the quest for material abundance to satisfy physical needs. In his system there are no ethical choices to be made, only utilitarian judgments exercised by each individual pursuing their own material self-interest. The new divinely ordained purpose of each man is to make profit, and for society the mandate is to consume, and to produce ever more goods for consumption. The human being after Adam Smith has been dubbed "Homo Consumptor."[25]

Few men today have read Adam Smith. Yet the gospel of self-interest has become second nature to modern men and a chief element of the masculine mystique. It has totally replaced older concepts of the masculine steeped in gift giving and reciprocity. Instead individual self-interest and upward mobility, greater consumption of goods and services, and suspicion of government interference with business affairs remain unquestioned masculine values in our society. Men are expected to comport their lives to the dictates of the profit dogma. Success for men means material success, and the successful pursuit of profit is secular salvation for them and their masculinity.

As such it becomes evident that the profit ethic is not a biological fact written into men's hormones, synapses, genes, or penises. It is simply standard operating procedure in modern economic society as first propagated by Adam Smith and the propounders of the free-market doctrine. The omnipresent profit man, as with the other masculine-mystique archetypes, is a cultural construct. Other cultures did not, and do not, contain or celebrate business or the profit man. They are more likely to celebrate the "gift-giving" man. However, just as mechanism and Social Darwinism girded men into the masculine mystique's machine and competition modes, the success of Smith's self-interest ideology spawned the profit man. In viewing the extraordinary impact of the self-interest ethic on men and society, one can only admire the prescience of Edmund Burke, who commented shortly after *The Wealth of Nations* was published that, "in its ultimate result, this was probably the most important book that has ever been written."[26]

CONSUMING DESIRES

Smith's ideas, and the reign of the profit motive, remained controversial. Many prominent social thinkers objected to its materialist "commodity over everything" bent. They found its reductionist view of human behavior abhorrent, and mourned its destructive impact on all human relationships not part of the market system. Early in the twentieth century, sociologist Max Weber noted that under the market ideology the business contract became the central bond between men, forever replacing "the obligations of brotherliness or reverence, and . . . those spontaneous human relations that are sustained by personal unions." He termed the market economy the "absolute de-personalization" of men.[27]

Opposition to the market ideology was not only among intellectuals. In the century following the publication of Smith's influential theories, a coalition of social liberals, trade unionists, and religious leaders began actively fighting against the "depersonalization" of men brought about by the endless search for profit. They urged that society devote itself not to an increase in profits or consumption but an increase in time spent away from the enclosure of the workplace. Rather than the expansion of output and private expenditures, they argued for more time so that working men could care for their families and pursue education and culture. As one union leader stated, "Workers have declared their lives not to be bartered at any price, that no wage, no matter how high, can induce them to sell their birthright. The worker is not the slave of fifty years ago . . . he reads

... goes to the theater ... [and] has established his own libraries, his own educational institutions. . . . And he wants time, time, time, for all these things."[28]

As had happened many times before, men en masse resisted the new industrial definition of who they were and what they were supposed to want. In 1884 the Federation of Organized Trades and Labor Unions passed a resolution demanding an eight-hour workday. Two years later, on May 1, 1886, in one of the largest uprisings of its kind, hundreds of thousands of U.S. workers went on strike, calling for the eight-hour day. Large-scale violence ensued as police attacked striking workers, killing several of them. Similar demonstrations were held over the next several years in Europe, with the same violent results.

Massive suppression did not stop the labor movement. Between 1897 and 1904 union membership rose from 447,000 to 2,073,000.[29] With the growing strength of unions, labor unrest increased, with a shorter workweek being a central demand. In 1919 alone there were some 2,600 strikes involving more than 4 million workers.[30] The struggle for more time for workers reached a turning point in the 1920s. By that time industrial growth and automation had produced a surplus of basic goods. Moreover, there was increasing unemployment as machines began replacing men on the factory floor. These conditions caused the "free time" movement to gain in strength. A shorter workweek would allow an increase in employment without the loss of adequate amounts of needed products. The shorter-hours movement spawned numerous labor organizations. The famous 1919 Washington Eight-Hour Convention was the first project of the International Labor Organization (ILO).

William Green, president of the American Federation of Labor (AFL), and a fierce proponent of shorter hours for workers, spoke for many in the labor movement. "There must be shorter hours," he maintained, "to safeguard human nature and to lay the foundation . . . for the higher development of spiritual and intellectual powers." He noted that the ancestors of the present workers were "at liberty to rest during the day, to take moments of refreshment." Green wrote that if the modern worker is "to live at all," there must be more to his life than "pay and consumption." There must be time for family and community and to pursue education and culture.[31]

During the 1920s, worker organizations became more adamant in their call for shorter hours. Despite the fierce opposition of industry, the new coalition of labor and its supporters was instrumental in gaining the fifty- and later the forty-hour workweek. Soon workers and their adherents began calling for an even shorter workweek to assure full employment and to allow workers to have lives outside the endless pursuit of subsistence and profit. In response to the new demands, some companies actually instituted thirty-hour workweeks.

By the close of the 1920s a remarkable and revolutionary prospect opened up. Could those who worked in the factories and mines, approximately 90 percent of whom were men, begin to escape the enclosure of the workplace and the reduced lives that their mechanical enslavement necessitated? Could they reject the lure of profits and material accumulation and begin to recover family, culture, education, and a relationship to nature? One labor leader wrote,

> Will not men in the long run have greater happiness if, while enabled to have essential things as a result of a shorter number of hours of work, they are free in their spare time to engage in such activities as come from inner desires and which give spiritual satisfaction? Is it not likely that in music, art, handicraft, familiarity with nature, understanding and comprehension of the world, camaraderie in wholesomeness, inexpensive activities, there lies a pathway to greater human satisfaction than is to be found in longer hours of work to clutter homes with more furniture, more clothing, more things?[32]

The prospect of vast numbers of workers escaping the profit-man harness into leisure, education, culture, or family duties deeply concerned many old-line industrialists. As was described in an earlier chapter, employers felt that the factory labor disciplined men out of their natural indolence, and they were therefore extremely wary of men spending too much time away from work lest their natural lazy, unpunctual, and undisciplined temperaments reassert themselves. They agreed with a U.S. Steel Corporation executive who argued that a shortened workweek would create a "loose living" mass of men prone to drunkenness, lustful pursuits, and crime.[33]

More importantly, the business community understood only too well that should enough men sell less, and purchase less, opting instead for less work and more free time, the entire capitalist enterprise might fail. Technology had been harnessed to allow for a massive increase in the volume and variety of consumer goods; this was no time for men to stop selling and buying. As Frederick Allen Lewis, a chronicler of the Roaring Twenties, writes, "Business had learned the importance of the ultimate consumer. Unless he could be persuaded to buy and buy lavishly, the whole stream of six cylinder cars, radios, cigarettes, rouge compacts and electric ice boxes would be dammed up at its outlets."[34]

Business began a concerted counterattack on the shorter-hours movement. One tack was to challenge the notion that industrial work was unpleasant or dehumanizing. They spoke of work as "a wonder," "a joy," "a dignity." Patriotism was brought to bear as work was touted as "the American secret"; one industrialist stated that "any man demanding the forty-hour week should be ashamed to claim citizenship in this great country." The masculine mystique made frequent appearances in these arguments as the masculinity of those calling for less work was directly challenged. As one business spokesperson put it, "The men of our country are becoming a race of softies and mollycoddles." Finally, religion was once again called on to rally men to labor. Factory work was called "a spiritual inspiration," and workers themselves "saints of the workshop." One author even assured readers that Christ was "the first businessman" and that "great progress will be made in the world when we rid ourselves of the idea that there is a difference between work and religious work."[35]

The attempt to resurrect industrial labor as an ideal or uplifting occupation was a significant failure in the early 1920s. It did little to slow the call for shorter hours and more leisure. As their propaganda failed, the alarm of the industrialists grew.

American business soon crystallized a more effective strategy to oppose the shorter-work-hours, anticonsumption movement. They began offering a seductive alternative vision for America's working men, one that would reinvigorate the profit motive. The new cultural ethic would be one of unlimited desires. If working families could be convinced that they needed ever more goods and services, they could forever be put on a treadmill of "work and spend." If people could be turned into endlessly dissatisfied consumers, they would no longer seek fewer work hours but rather work longer to purchase more merchandise. One business consultant called the new approach "the gospel of consumption."[36]

To convert Americans to the consumption gospel, new consumer desires, and the financial capability of fulfilling those desires, had to be given to workers and their families. The plan of action was obvious: American workers would be paid enough to become purchasers, and then convinced, through the constant manufacturing of discontent about their lifestyle, to consume ever-more-unnecessary products. As explained by economist John Kenneth Galbraith, production would have to "create the wants it seeks to satisfy."[37] The treadmill of longer work hours and increasing consumption would foster ever more wealth and jobs and keep the average man working harder than ever.

Industry's drive to fashion a work-and-spend culture based on ever-increasing consumer desires required a sea change in the consciousness of workers. The populace needed to be persuaded into mass consumption, as an alternative to mass leisure. This sparked the wild growth of advertisement that was to become a trademark of the profit man. Economist Juliet Schor writes, "The 1920s was the decade for advertising. The admen went wild: everything from walnuts to household coal was being individually branded and nationally advertised."[38]

The task for advertisers was not easy. Americans were still

schooled in the ethic of thrift and had a deep affection for the "home-made." Ironically the very Protestant ethic that was used to encourage the populace to work hard but live frugally now had to be revised. Workers needed to work hard—now not for their salvation but rather for their secular ascension into the lifestyle of the rich. As 1920s ad agency head Bruce Barton told a radio audience, "The American concept of advertising is to arouse desires and stimulate wants, to make people dissatisfied with the old and out-of-date and by constant iteration to send them out to work harder to get the latest model—whether that model be an icebox or a rug, or a new home."[39]

The admen invented many now-familiar techniques to accomplish their goal. New public fears were generated in the drive to sell novel products. Without mouthwash, canned goods, boxed breakfast cereal, or a new brand of car, the consumer would be left diseased, unemployed, or without romance. The admen also realized that product consumption was an ideal way for people to express individuality in a society in which their work lives were ever more routinized and mechanized. They graphically projected social status and "personality" into products from cars to Coke. The luxuries of the rich were newly presented as necessities for the working class and the secret to upward mobility.

The admen also created a new masculine archetype, "Andy Consumer." Andy was a cartoon character used in advertisements throughout the 1920s in *Life* magazine, to promote the publication as an attractive vehicle for advertising. Andy is presented as "a regular guy" who under pressure from his family, especially his wife, is working ever more hours to spend more and more on consumer goods. A representative 1926 ad, entitled "Go Ahead and Make Us Want," pictures Andy and his spouse sitting in their living room. She has turned to him and is saying, "Andy, I want one of those electric washing machines!" In the ad copy Andy muses to himself:

Mrs. Consumer [Andy's wife] says I'm a little lazy anyway. Sometimes I get mighty mad at advertising. . . . Bath room ads gave Mrs. Consumer a bee for a fancy bath room (All foolishness!)

Gosh I had to hump myself to pay for that . . . Had to work so
hard for a spell. I was sore. Still . . . a real estate man told me I
had doubled the sales value of my house . . . I begin to see it's advertising that makes America hum. It gives ginks like me a goal.
Makes us want something. . . . Looking at the ads makes me think
I've GOT to succeed. *Every advertisement is an advertisement for
success.*

I guess one reason there's so much success in America is because
there's so much advertising—of things to want—things to work for.[40]

Along with advertising, another important weapon for those
fighting for the new consumption ethic was the concept of
consumer credit. The installment plan allowed for immediate
gratification of the consumer's desire along with the delay of responsibilities and consequences. Buying on credit swept the
country in the early 1920s, and within a few years America had
stopped saving and was eagerly buying itself into debt. By the
time of the 1929 stock-market crash, more than 60 percent of the
automobiles, radios, and furniture in U.S. homes were bought on
the installment plan.[41]

The gospel of consumption was a stunning success. Within a
short time it had galvanized workers away from the call for shorter
work hours and into a frenzy of consumption. In 1929 a committee
was set up by President Herbert Hoover to assess how Americans
were responding to the new emphasis on consumption. The committee's report to the new chief executive was glowing:

The survey has proved conclusively what has long been held
theoretically to be true, that wants are insatiable; that one want
satisfied makes way for another. The conclusion is that economically we have a boundless field before us; that there are new
wants which will make way endlessly for newer wants as fast as
they are satisfied. . . . By advertising and other promotional devices . . . a measurable pull on production has been created. . . .
Our situation is fortunate, our momentum remarkable.[42]

Critics still fought against the growing strength of the consumer frenzy. The Catholic theologian John Ryan was one of the leading dissenters against the gospel of consumption. Throughout the twenties and thirties he lamented the process by which increased consumption was substituted for increased time away from work:

> One of the most baneful assumptions of our materialistic industrial society is that all men should spend at least one third of the twenty four hour day in some productive occupation. . . . If men still have leisure, new luxuries must be created to keep them busy [at the workplace] and new wants must be stimulated to keep the industries going. Of course, the true and rational doctrine is that when men have produced sufficient necessaries and reasonable comforts and conveniences to supply all the population they should spend what time is left in the cultivation of their intellects and wills, in the pursuit of the higher life.[43]

Ryan also recommended redefining the meaning of progress away from consumption and toward increased leisure. He suggested that the "good life" be measured in terms of time with family and friends and the enjoyment of nature, not in the number of goods purchased and consumed.[44]

Ultimately, however rational their argument, those seeking more time rather than more products proved no match for the economic and political power of business. It quickly became apparent that the gospel of consumption had an unbeatable twofold power. It not only lured the public into buying what it did not need, it also had them buying these products with money consumers did not have. Once seduced into the treadmill of consumption, workers stayed there and worked ever harder in order to pay off their increasing debt.

Despite the setback of the Depression, the massive rise in U.S. consumption continued during and after World War II. The gospel of consumption became synonymous with "the American Dream" and national prosperity. Retailing analyst Victor Lebow told his

1950s readers that "our enormously productive economy ... demands that we make consumption a way of life, that we convert the buying and use of goods into rituals, that we seek our spiritual satisfaction, our ego satisfaction, in consumption. . . . We need things consumed, burned up, worn out, replaced, and discarded at an ever increasing rate."[45]

The citizens of the United States responded to the consumption call. By the sixties and seventies the work-and-spend cycle had become a dizzying upward spiral. Credit-card purchases, installment buying, car loans, and multiple mortgages had become rituals and a way of life for most Americans. Rampant consumerism locked families into ever-increasing debt, and the breadwinner, primarily the male, was strapped ever more securely into the workplace harness as he carried his increasing credit burden. Private consumer debt increased 210 percent in the 1960s and 268 percent in the 1970s.[46]

The 1980s may have been the pinnacle of the consumer culture fostered a half century before. In that decade Americans went on an unprecedented buying spree, a consumer frenzy of phenomenal proportions. From small to large products, from everyday to once-in-a-lifetime items, Americans consumed as never before. By the end of the decade consumer debt in the United States was more than $4 trillion, and it increases by an annual rate of close to $800 billion each year.[47]

ON THE TREADMILL

In recent times the disturbing costs of America's gospel of consumption, especially in terms of the degradation of the environment, have been well documented. But the consumption ethic has not only "consumed" the natural resources of the earth at an alarming rate, it has also consumed the lives of untold millions of men.

The enclosure of men that had been initiated by the industrial revolution of the nineteenth century was cemented by the consumer revolution of the twentieth. Driven by the work-and-spend cycle, men worked ever more hours. Between 1935 and 1965 disposable time for male workers fell from forty to thirty-four hours per week. By 1973 free time was down to twenty-six hours. As we have noted, by 1990 male workers had only seventeen hours of free time a week, less than half that experienced by their grandfathers. The profit man of the work-and-spend cycle becomes an even more invisible father as his leisure time continues to vanish from one generation to the next. Not surprisingly the nine-to-five dads of the fifties and sixties have all but vanished in the eighties and nineties. Currently 30 percent of men with children under fourteen report working fifty or more hours a week. Not only are these fathers working until eight or nine at night, they are often absent on weekends. Thirty percent of fathers work Saturdays and/or Sundays at their regular job, while a significant percentage of men also use the weekends to make money on a second job.[48]

The gospel of consumption also undermined fatherhood in a subtler way. Starting in the 1920s, and increasingly over the next decades, advertising represented parents, and especially fathers, as grossly out of step with current trends. The father's wisdom was held to be far inferior to that of the commodity advertiser. Advertisers told each successive generation of youth how to live, what to eat, what music to listen to, and what clothes to wear. If a parent objected to the transformation of authority, he or she simply fulfilled the stereotype of the out-of-touch parent presented in ads.

Over time, as consumption became America's primary passion, the father's social authority, already undermined by his work-related absence, disappeared altogether. He became little more than the "family's wallet." Advertising historian Stuart Ewen writes, "While women were cultivated as general purchasing managers of the household, the basic definition of *men* in advertisements was as breadwinners, wage-earners. *Man's* role was divested of all social authority, except insofar as his wages underwrote family consumption" (emphasis in the original).[49] Advertisers had ultimately succeeded in turning America's fathers and workers into Andy Consumer. As Ewen notes, by way of advertising, corporate America had defined itself as "the father of us all."

Our legal system seems equally sold on the idea that men are essentially profit-making entities. They discriminate against men in custody cases, in part due to the assumption that men's real role is in the marketplace, not in the family, whereas women are viewed as natural caretakers. "Daddy pay and go away" is still the unfortunate logic of the vast majority of current custody orders.

The profit man is not only a diminished father, he is a diminished person. As a salesman of his own labor the profit man demeans himself by selling himself as mere means to an end—profit. As a seller of goods, the profit man sees his neighbors and larger community as a mass of potential customers, again merely the means to the end of profit. All life becomes transaction. Earl Shorris sums up the results of the profit-man dysfunction on men and society:

> Under the dominion of homo vendens . . . [a] man is interchangeable with a thing; he no longer determines his own worth; a price can be put on him. Man has lost his humanity.
>
> When homo vendens, who recognizes himself as merely means, makes all men into a means for his use, he takes away their freedom. Man has lost his nobility.
>
> Under the conditions of a life dominated by homo vendens . . . the unthinking market initiates action. The world no longer begins from man; he has forfeited the autonomy of his own reason. Man has lost his mind.[50]

As consumerism accelerated the transformation of men into the profit-man mold, it also led to a novel and unfortunate new economic relationship between the genders. The new sexual division of labor had men as "passive consumers" closely bound to wage earning in order to purchase goods and pay off debt, while women were the active consumers buying goods. By the 1930s only about one in ten women held marketplace jobs, whereas about 90 percent of men did. This meant that it was primarily women who orchestrated domestic consumption. This gender relationship, which was so functional for consumer capitalism, was a dysfunctional disaster for the genders. It caused further stereotyping of the genders—the man as the profit man, the woman as the homemaker and shopper—and acted as a principal catalyst to the fostering of not only the masculine mystique but also the feminine mystique.

While many more women have now joined the workforce, the gender stereotypes brought to us by the consumption lifestyle are still with us today. Overall, women still control consumer spending by a wide margin in most consumer categories.[51] Interestingly a study of large shopping malls found that seven times as much floor space is devoted to women's personal items as to men's.[52] Men are still seen as Andy Consumer, "success objects," whose main task is to make enough profit for themselves and their family to keep up with the consumption standard.

The ultimate irony and tragedy of the profit-man ethic is that it has become a cruel hoax on American men. While the average man sacrifices family and personal goals for financial status, ardently defends the profit system, and works longer and harder for material upward mobility, his financial success becomes ever more unlikely and his masculine identity ever more threatened. America's men have not become a nation of Rockefellers but rather Willy Lomans.

Upward mobility has become a sad delusion for the profit man. Despite myths to the contrary, the gap between the haves and the have-nots in American society has been steadily increasing and is now greater than it has been in a half century. Economic inequality has been on a steep rise in the United States since the 1970s. Currently the top 1 percent of American households owns nearly 40 percent of the country's wealth, and the top 20 percent of households owns 80 percent of the wealth. This leaves the other 80 percent of the population to struggle among themselves for the remaining one-fifth of the nation's wealth. This wealth gap is the highest among any of the industrialized nations.[53]

As wealth has increased for the few, blue- and white-collar

male workers have seen a steep decline in their real wages. From 1973 to 1991, the average hourly wage for production and non-supervisory workers fell from $11.37 to $10.37 (in constant 1991 dollars). Meanwhile, average annual hours worked increased during the same time period from 1,683 hours to 1,781 hours.[54] Even worse, fewer and fewer jobs pay a living wage. According to a U.S. Census Bureau Report, 18 percent of full-time workers receive wages that are not adequate to maintain a family of four above the official poverty line ($13,091); this is up from 12 percent of full-time workers in 1979. Among younger full-time workers (aged eighteen to twenty-four) the report stated that 47 percent earned under the poverty level wage (up from 23 percent in 1979). The Census Bureau called these statistics "astounding."[55] Robert Reich, the current secretary of labor, has recently noted that the average wages of America's production workers continue to slide at a rate far greater than the wages of workers in other industrialized countries.[56]

The growing percentage of men experiencing unemployment or declining wages, including a vast army of middle-aged men formerly employed in heavy industry or as corporate middle managers, leads to a cycle of shame for men schooled in the profit myth. Should he not make enough money to be part of the consumer society, or lose his job, the profit man can no longer play his role as "provider" to the modern consuming family, and must face the full brunt of their discontent and disappointment. He cannot "keep up with the Joneses" and suffers social ostracism from his peer group and community. Many male workers, blue- and white-collar, report feeling ashamed and afraid to leave their homes after being laid off. Others dress in their work suits and spend the day in the library so that their neighbors assume they have been at work. For men whose lives have been circumscribed by the masculine mystique, failure in the profit-man role can mean psychic annihilation.

7

THE POWER MAN

Exploitative power identifies power with force. . . . It is sometimes
rationalized as the "masculine way."   —Rollo May[1]

John F. Welch, fifty-eight, is described as a "cheerfully combative" Irish American. The dapper, silver-haired executive is
widely acknowledged as "the leading master of corporate
change in our time."[2] Since 1981 he has been the chief executive officer of General Electric (GE), the massive multinational company that deals in everything from lightbulbs, appliances, and jet
engines to nuclear power plants, coal mines, and diamonds.

Welch is among the world's most powerful men. Since he took
over as CEO of GE, the market value of the company has increased
by a whopping $67.6 billion. Welch also has near-dictatorial power
over millions of people. His decisions intimately affect the lives of
GE employees and their families around the world. He has not been
shy in the use of that power. During his regime he has fired over
200,000 employees as part of his "re-engineering" of the company.[3]

As it causes massive layoffs, Welch's new "lean" production
program at GE has been controversial. The legendary CEO is un-
apologetic, however, about the toll his corporate reorganization has
taken. Welch notes that whatever the human cost, his job is to as-

sure GE's survival in the competitive, ever-changing environment of the global economy. "You've got to be on the cutting edge of change. You can't simply maintain the status quo, because somebody's coming from another country with another product, or consumer tastes change, or the cost structure does, or there's a technology breakthrough. If you're not fast and adaptable, you're vulnerable." When commenting on his laying off of hundreds of thousands of people, the CEO's only regret is "I should have done it faster. But we're all human. We don't like to face up to some of these unpleasant things. . . . GE would be better off if I had acted faster."[4]

The son of Irish immigrants, John Welch's career is a striking example of the revolution in power allocation that has occurred in the modern age. From time immemorial, power over people was allotted by birth or religious hierarchy. Royalty, castes, and priesthoods all claimed material or spiritual powers. Each claimed a "divine" right for obtaining and maintaining power over people and nations. Some even claimed a heaven-sent mandate to conquer the earth. Alexander the Great wept by a riverbank when he felt that there was no world left to conquer. Subsequent leaders—kings, queens, or generals—with more accurate maps of the earth made ever more ambitious attempts to establish empires that reached around the globe.

With the evolution of the industrial system a great transfer of power occurred in Western civilization. The idea of divinely ordained power bestowed on a single individual or elite, which in one form or another had justified power over society and nature, was usurped. By the early years of the Industrial Revolution a new elite of commercial adventurers had effectively wrested sovereignty. Power was no longer associated with a purported divination of God's will or with brute military force. Rather the pursuit of power became inexorably linked with the pursuit of profit. As men became the primary competitors in the market system, they were given the chance, if successful, to buy more and more of the means of production, including of course the labor of other men. Importantly they could also finance the development of extraordinary new technologies that allowed even greater control over men and nature. The potential for amassing power was no longer restricted to a chosen few; the mass of men now had the opportunity to gain massive powers over men and natural resources. The winners in the competition-and-profit game became the "power men" of the new order.

As successful commercial entrepreneurs gained hegemony over society, they created a new institution of power that was to replace the manor, Church, and eventually even the nation-state as society's primary wielder of power. This institution was the business corporation, primarily the "joint stock" company. Beginning in the sixteenth century various corporate entities were formed and slowly expanded their commercial reach. The British East India Company, chartered on December 31, 1600, offers a representative example of the extraordinary power wielded by early corporations. Initially the company was given an exclusive monopoly over the Indian trade by the British Crown. As the corporation's profits soared, its power expanded. In 1661 the Crown revised the company's charter to include "jurisdiction over all Englishmen in the East, and power to maintain fortifications and to raise troops for their defense." At the height of its power the East India Company ruled over virtually all of India and its 250 million inhabitants, boasted the largest professional army in the world, and deployed forty-three warships.[5]

General Electric, and today's leading transnational corporations, are worthy descendants of the East India Company. Harnessing the great technologies of our age, many multinational corporations have garnered greater economic power than most nations. Corporate behemoths control raw materials, labor pools, and primary and secondary markets and enjoy a virtual monopoly over international communications and transportation. Many have air and naval fleets that rival those of the superpowers. Companies such as GE employ hundreds of thousands of people in dozens of countries.

Controlling technologies and markets on a global scale, transnational-company CEOs such as Welch exercise a degree of power over world events that few heads of state can match. Unlike the misguided and ultimately defeated world conquerors of the past, the modern CEO has real power with a global reach. Political scientist Richard Barnet sums up the remarkable influence that the multinational CEOs have over the affairs of our civilization:

> The men who run the global corporations are the first in history with the organization, technology, money, and ideology to make a credible try at managing the world as an integrated unit. . . . The managers of firms like GM, IBM, Pepsico, GE . . . and a few hundred others are making daily business decisions which have more impact than those of sovereign governments on where people live; what work, if any, they do; what they will eat, drink, and wear; what sorts of knowledge, schools, and universities they will encourage; and what kind of society their children will inherit.[6]

Unlike the leaders of the past who represented national interests, the power of the modern CEO is magnified because he has no necessary attachment to any country. For him there are no petty nationalist motives, only the logic of international capital. There are no boundaries; the whole world is a potential source of supply and demand. The modern computer makes the corporation's abstract global power real as electronic computation and telecommunications can transmit millions of pieces of information virtually instantaneously around the world.

Wielding the power of the multinational corporation, the CEO has reached the epitome of power in the modern world. He is the optimal result of the machine-, competition-, and profit-man mentality. Under the banner of efficiency he has successfully reached preeminence in the corporate jungle and has now, in the name of profit, attained power over untold legions of his fellows. Remarkably, even as Welch and his fellow Fortune 500 CEOs downsize by firing millions of employees, their economic power increases. From 1980 to 1993, the Fortune 500 companies shed more than one quarter (4.4 million) of all the jobs they had previously provided. Meanwhile, during that same period, their companies increased their assets by 2.3 times, and their sales by 1.4 times. As for the major CEOs themselves, their average annual compensation increased 6.1 times to $3.8 million.[7]

Welch and other CEOs wield a specific kind of power—the power to dominate and coerce others into actions and behavior. Corporations are not democracies, and the CEO is expected to set policy and ensure obedience throughout the corporation. A former head of strategic planning for GE states that the modern corporation is a "virtual dictatorship." Regardless of the politics of the country in which they live, corporate executives and employees spend the majority of their waking hours in a "totally autocratic state."

The corporation's power is also primarily the power to exploit. Its mission is to expropriate and fully utilize resources and markets. Its guiding principles are those of efficiency and profit. "Working through great corporations that straddle the earth," says George Ball, former undersecretary of state, "men are able for the first time to utilize world resources with an efficiency dictated by the objective logic of profit."[8]

The dominating, controlling, and manipulative power exercised by CEOs and corporations is the favored form of power in our society. The exercise of such power is what our society teaches men to strive for and women to admire. We are told that "power is an aphrodisiac" and that the gaining of power is the crowning accomplishment, the ultimate achievement, of masculinity. The power to dominate, exploit, and control is the final prize for the machine, competition, and profit man. It is the ticket to manhood, freedom, and respect. Suzanne Gordon succinctly states the primary status we place on power in our culture: "In this society productivity, creativity and initiative are channeled toward very specific aims: the accumulation of wealth, status, and ultimately power."[9]

The drive for dominance and power is of course a fundamental aspect of the masculine mystique. The mystique teaches that men are at heart power seekers, that the need to have power over vast amounts of capital, resources, and labor is an inevitable product of masculinity. This stereotype of masculinity has many outspoken purveyors. Gender researcher Anne Moir says, "Men will make the most extraordinary sacrifices of personal happiness, health, time, friendships, and relationships in the pursuit and maintenance of power . . . women won't; most of them are simply not made that way."[10] One feminist insists that for women "power is viewed in much the same way as love. It is limitless, and when it is shared it regenerates and expands. There is no need to hoard it because it only increases when it is given away." For men, however, power is dominance and force; "men tend to see power as limited; the question is power over whom. Either you have it over them or the other guy has it over you."[11]

As described in an earlier chapter, awesome power both generative and destructive has always been associated with gender, both masculine and feminine. However, we now define power almost solely as the use of force to dominate or control, and associate this definition and use of power solely with the masculine. But whether exercised by men or women, force and coercion are only the shadow aspects of power. By contrast the ancient Greek philosophers defined power as "fullness of being." We still speak of power in this generative way when we refer to an individual as having the power—the capability—of great thought or action. Power is also used to denote creativity, as in the power of nature. Power can also mean the ability to influence, teach, or change individuals. We refer to certain people as powerful teachers and routinely talk of powerful ideas or concepts. Rollo May speaks of the power that creates or teaches as "nutrient" power.[12] Nutrient power is exercised for the individual but also for the benefit of others; it does not attempt to exploit or control.

Through the masculine mystique the definition of power has been genderized. Men are no longer associated with nutrient power but rather are seen as permanently embodying the shadow definition of power. Rape, harassment, destruction of the earth, crime, violence, exploitation of workers—all are seen as results of masculine power. Creative, nurturing, and teaching powers are most often associated with women. The story of how masculinity lost its identification with nutrient power and came instead to be associated almost entirely with power as force, violence, and coercion brings us to the final denouement of the inculcation of the masculine mystique.

OF LIONS AND FOXES

Political scientist James Burnham, a leading twentieth-century analyst of political power and its uses, was fond of quoting a brief snippet from a Pericles play:

> THIRD FISHERMAN: Master, How do the fishes live in the sea?
> FIRST FISHERMAN: Why, as men do on land; the great ones eat up
>   the little ones.

Burnham felt that this quote represented an accurate picture of the real power relationship among men in society. He advocated the view that the drive for power of some over the many was the key dynamic in history. He regarded those who claimed that they sought political power to help people or further the public good to be at best wishful thinkers and at worst hypocrites. He is straightforward in his view: "The primary real goal of every ruling group is the maintenance of its own power and privilege."[13]

One of Burnham's most noted predecessors in the analysis of modern political power was Gaetano Mosca, an early twentieth-century Italian thinker, who formulated the theory of the ruling class. Mosca felt that both Adam Smith and the Social Darwinists were wrong in their view of what motivates men. For Mosca, as for Burnham, the main drive in the life of men is not a Darwinian struggle for existence nor a mere accumulation of wealth but rather power over other men:

> If we consider . . . the inner ferment that goes on within the body
> of every society, we see at once that the struggle for pre-eminence
> is far more conspicuous there than the struggle for existence.
> Competition between individuals of every social unit is focused

upon higher position, wealth, authority, control of the means and instruments that enable a person to direct many human activities, many human wills, as he sees fit. The losers, who are of course the majority in that sort of struggle, are not devoured, destroyed or even kept from reproducing their kind, as is basically characteristic of the struggle for life. They merely enjoy fewer material satisfactions and, especially, less freedom and independence.[14]

Both Burnham and Mosca were self-proclaimed disciples of the man who centuries ago was the first "scientist of power." Their views on the nature of power and politics are directly descended from Niccolò Machiavelli. Writing at the end of the fifteenth century, Machiavelli was the first to break away from the great Aristotelian tradition, which viewed power as an expression of God's will on earth—"Thy will be done on earth as it is in heaven." Instead Machiavelli advocated a new vision of power, one not based on divine will or natural law but rather based on mastering the craft of force and coercion. As such, Machiavelli was a world splitter. He self-consciously removed the definition and analysis of power from any basis in ethics. He had little interest in power wielded to "save men's souls" or power deemed to be in the interest of the people. Rather Machiavelli was only interested in "scientifically" analyzing how a ruler could gain and maintain power by the most efficacious means. Machiavelli was inspired to construct this analysis of power by his desire to see Italy, at the time violence-torn and fragmented, united under one ruler. Machiavelli's most famous work, *The Prince*, was a sort of how-to manual by which a leader could seize power, unite Italy's many warring factions, and make it a world power.

Machiavelli's prescription for all princes was simple: "Power is secure only on the basis of force." To be sure, Machiavelli also noted that fraud and wiliness are key attributes for a prince who is to gain and maintain power. The combination of force and fraud is picturesquely described in a famous passage in *The Prince*, which portrays the successful ruler as both Lion and Fox: "Seeing, therefore, it is of such importance to a Prince to take upon him the nature and disposition of a beast, of all the animal flock, he ought to imitate the Lion and the Fox; for the Lion is in danger of toils and snares, and the Fox of the Wolf: so he must be a Fox to find out the snares, and a Lion to fright away the Wolves."[15]

Machiavelli's view of the men over which a prince must gain power was remarkably dim for his time and was a striking precursor to similar descriptions by Thomas Hobbes and Adam Smith. "In the general," Machiavelli finds, "men are ungrateful, inconsistent, hypocritical, fearful of danger, and covetous of gain."[16] For the prince to succeed against such men, he must dominate them and understand that "government is nothing but keeping subjects in such a posture as that they may have no will, or power to offend you."[17]

Machiavelli's revolutionary view of power was to be enormously influential. Oliver Cromwell was said to keep a copy of *The Prince* in his pocket at all times. Dictators including Napoleon and Mussolini credited Machiavelli with helping them gain and maintain power. Writing nearly five centuries after Machiavelli, Burnham credited the entire corporate-managerial revolution of the later part of the twentieth century to the power politics of Machiavelli. Burnham like so many moderns was to become a true believer in one kind of political power, and it was that proclaimed by Machiavelli:

> The Machiavellians are the only ones who have told us the truth about power. . . . The Machiavellians present the complete record: the primary object, in practice, of all rulers is to serve their own interest, to maintain their own power and privilege. There are no exceptions, no amount of good will, no religion will restrain power. . . . Only power restrains power.[18]

Of course, Machiavelli is still with us today. Numerous articles and books seek to apply his message and tactics to the modern corporate situation. Titles such as *The Machiavellian Manager* are a frequent sight in the libraries of CEOs. Certainly if Machiavelli were to survey the careers of men such as Welch and the world's other CEOs, he would feel that his lessons had been well learned.

More importantly Machiavelli's shadow view of power is now fully shared by most men in politics or business. Machiavelli and his followers continue to give us our vision of political power over men, one divorced from ethics and based in force, cleverness, manipulation, and control. Just as the views of Descartes, Darwin, and Adam Smith "trickled down" into society to contribute to so much of the masculine mystique, Machiavelli's concept of power has become the power image for the masculine mystique. Men who can gain and maintain control over other men are admired and envied. While the majority hate their bosses, each would like to become one.

Machiavelli's science of power, however, is only half of the arsenal required by today's power man. To be successful, he needs to do more than become a prince over men. His economic clout and his power to produce are equally dependent on technologies for the expropriation of natural resources. It is not enough to have power over men; the power man must also control nature.

SUBDUING THE HARLOT

Humanity has always been at the mercy of the power of nature. While we celebrate the generativity of nature, we also recognize its devastating destructive power. No matter how powerful the potentate or the high priest of the past, his or her relationship to nature was as a supplicant, pleading for benevolence from the nature gods. Droughts, floods, fires, and disease were all seen as signs that required an alteration in human behavior. Humility and the promise of obedience was the only way to approach the grandeur of the created order.

By the seventeenth century this all was to change. In 1620 Francis Bacon, the "father of modern science," published his revolutionary tract *Novum Organum*. In this tome Bacon challenged the traditional wisdom of both the ancient Greeks and the medievals. He dismissed the Socratic method, which was concerned with the "why" of nature, as useless. Bacon was equally dismissive of the medieval Christian concept of nature that was full of "superstitions" and prohibitions. Bacon wanted to know the "how" of nature and then, using that knowledge, to harness the natural order to improve man's lot.

Just as Machiavelli analyzed power in a thoroughly instrumental manner in order to help a prince gain power over men, Bacon attempted to articulate a method of gaining power over nature that allowed for the fullest exploitation of its resources. As such, Bacon was among the first to view the natural world solely as an exploitable medium. He excised any purported sacred value from nature, reducing all earthly phenomena to quantifiable standards that could easily be manipulated to serve human needs and economic interest, and to greatly extend the power of men. Bacon's theories transformed nature from an enormous animated community of subjects into a large assortment of exploitable objects. "The goal of all scientific study," said Bacon, "is to enlarge the bounds of the human empire, to the effecting of all things Possible . . . to establish and extend the power of the human race itself over the universe."[19]

Bacon's theories had an enormous influence on his contemporaries. He successfully evangelized them into putting all their energies into subduing, conquering, and enslaving nature, which he often referred to as a "harlot."[20] By a thoroughgoing practice of the scientific method, he assured them, nature could be forced out of her natural state and squeezed and molded by human will. There is often an undeniable sexual overtone in Bacon's passion for the domination of and (nongenerative) penetration into nature: "For you have but to follow and as it were hound nature in her wanderings, and you will be able when you like to lead her and drive her. . . . For the further disclosing of the secrets of nature [you should make no] scruple of entering and penetrating into these holes and corners, when the inquisition of truth is his whole object."[21]

For Bacon, then, "knowledge is power," as he wrote in his most famous dictum. This not only disfigured Western culture's definition of knowledge but also revolutionized its concept of power. Traditionally power, however brutal, was exercised directly, whether it be over people or over nature. Power in all its nutrient or destructive forms was intimate. Bacon brought to Western civilization a new power, one based on separation, detachment, and withdrawal. Steeped in the newly devised scientific method, the new power was rational and analytical. The prior passion for direct engagement with men or nature was replaced with technological coercion from a distance. The new power man was the removed observer of nature or men, a man capable of erecting an "objective" separation between himself and the world. With the myth of objectivity and neutrality, man could act on the world without having to participate in it or be vulnerable to it.

As with Machiavelli's theories of political power, Bacon's method for gaining power over nature worked. Over the next centuries, using the scientific method, scientists and technologists were able to fashion the great engines and machines of the modern age. Science became nearly synonymous with the attempt to gain ever greater control of nature. One social scientist sums up the importance of Bacon's contribution:

> Any history of the development of Western science and technology is fatally skewed without the recognition that the urge to dominate nature forms the basis of the epistemological quest. Bacon's dictum "Knowledge is power" was the rationale for the desire to understand nature not in an empathetic sense, but to control it. In the process, nature was desacralized and stripped of its full reality in order that it could be quantified.[22]

The great technological changes of our times spawned by the Baconian worldview have had a greater impact on our personal and public lives than any other modern phenomenon. Our technology legislates our lives more than any laws passed by the world's legislators. But remarkably the parliaments of the world did not debate the cultural, economic, environmental, or ethical implications of the petrochemical revolution, the electronic revolution, the nuclear revolution, the television and computer revolutions, or the managerial revolution. Instead we let these technologies of domination over nature and humanity be controlled and utilized by the power men of science and politics, the descendants of Machiavelli and Bacon.

However, in the 1970s there was a significant challenge to the Baconian power technologies of our time. Confronted with environmental degradation, an energy crisis, and the trauma of the technological destruction involved in the Vietnam War, the "appropriate technology" movement was born. This movement supported technologies that consumed less energy, were friendly to the environment, and did not involve large, centralized bureaucracies. The movement championed solar energy, the use of recyclable materials, a reemphasis on nonautomotive transportation (mass transit, bicycles), and similar technologies and initiatives.

Despite a promising start, over time the movement was blunted and has had only a limited impact. The movement's failure to flourish was in large part due to years of probusiness government in Washington, which kept federal dollars from appropriate-technology projects. But the masculine mystique also played a role. Historian Dr. Carroll Pursell notes that a critical aspect in the fall of the appropriate-technology movement was that "it was perceived as less manly, more feminine, than the nation's dominant technological culture." The movement's aims were "far from the rhetoric of conquest and domination, rationality and control, that are often associated with masculine constructions of technology."[23]

Dr. Pursell also points out the irony that in actuality the appropriate-technology movement was an expression of older masculine ideals such as stewardship, generosity toward others, independence, and craftsmanship. As has been described, the enclosure of men obliterated these masculine values and substituted the other masculine myths, including that of the power man, in their place. Thus under the power-man myth solar energy was described as a "soft" energy path, and those supporting appropriate technology were seen as feminized. It is a tribute to the strength of the masculine mystique that it could so entrance a society that people could see a utility plant as masculine but the sun's energy (the very archetype of masculine strength in many cultures) as unmanly.

THE PARADOX OF POWER

From early childhood men are taught to identify with the power philosophies developed by Machiavelli, Bacon, and their many followers. Though few men have examined the intellectual or historical roots of their understanding of power, it is now accepted masculine parlance to speak of power as the use of force, coercion, or even violence in an instrumental fashion, without regard to ethics. We expect our business and political leaders to do whatever it takes to stay in power. Real men don't talk about religious or moral scruples in America's boardrooms or political backrooms.

Just as surely the masculine mystique teaches that men's view of nature should be one of scientific detachment and analysis, in the service of efficient exploitation. Real men do not worry about spotted owls, the suffering of animals in slaughterhouses, or the fate of trees. They know that progress means exploitation of natural resources to further the goals of economic power and growth.

Perhaps most importantly, many men have projected their very masculinity into the great technological achievements of the machine age. A prior chapter described how industrial society foisted a mechanized self-image on the male gender. It is important to add that the use of technology provides men not only with a new identity but also with a surrogate means by which to act out the power myth. As noted by historian Michael L. Smith, "National advertising had portrayed technological literacy as a definitive male characteristic since the turn of the century."[24]

The power man's relationship to technology is typified by the romance of American men with the automobile. The car offers him immediate access to autonomy (*auto*) and mobility (*mobile*), the new power gods of the market system and the masculine mystique. It also offers the detachment and separation from one's surroundings so prized by the Baconian worldview. The automobile allows one to master and dominate one's environment from behind closed windows and locked doors. The automobile exudes control, power, and detachment at the same time. The driver can be in the world without having to be of it. He can control events around him while retaining a sense of anonymity.

Over several generations technology's growth and increasing power seemed to justify the projection of so many men. After all, how could the strength, mind, or phallic power of any single man compare to the increasing might of industrial machines and war armaments, or the dizzying analytical abilities of computer-based information technology? Moreover, the "miracle" of automotive travel, flight, telegraph, telephone, and even the frighteningly destructive potential of the mechanized weapons of war seemed to augur the average man's increasing power through technology. The apex of this unbridled projection of masculine identity into technology may have been the 1969 landing of a spacecraft on the moon. On the day the *Eagle* landed, a *Washington Post* editorial semihysterically proclaimed (in terms eerily similar to Bacon's seventeenth-century proclamations), "The creature who had once stood blinking at the door of his Paleolithic cave has come a long way. . . . At long last, man is on the brink of mastering the Universe."[25] It is notable that several of the astronauts who landed on the moon went on to become advertising spokesmen for various car companies.

The identification of men with power and technology has, as with all aspects of the masculine mystique, made them profoundly one-sided and dysfunctional. The power-man myth has led many men to sacrifice community, family, aesthetic appreciation of nature, and ethical and religious values to the single-minded drive for power. In the name of dominance men en masse have forsaken participation and relationship with other men, women, and nature.

The ultimate irony is that, like the profit man, the power man is a ruse. All the sacrifices made by men to conform to the power image are in vain. The power that men have been taught to seek has made all but the tiniest minority of men powerless.

The vast majority of men never reach anywhere close to the top of the power pyramid. Rather they are the primary victims of the power mentality. They are not the princes but rather those whom the princes have made powerless. Worse, they are the vast majority of the untold millions whom the "princes" have sent to war to be maimed or killed fighting the modern conflicts of power. They are not the owners of the great technologies that exploit nature but rather the handservants to those machines in the workplace. They are the majority of workers who are subject to the new techniques of managerial control. They are the majority of those whose lives have been wedded to the hazardous and wearying work of machines.

Author Scott Russell Sanders writes about the surprise he felt when, upon entering college, he was told by feminists that men had the power and privilege. He describes the power men of the Tennessee and Ohio of his youth:

> When I was a boy . . . the men I knew labored with their bodies. . . . They got up before light, worked all day long whatever the weather, and when they came home at night they looked as though somebody had been whipping them. . . . The bodies of the men I knew were twisted and maimed in ways visible and invisible. The nails of the hands were black and split, the hands tattooed with scars. Some had lost fingers. Heavy lifting had given them finicky backs and guts weak with hernias. Racing against conveyor belts had given them ulcers. Their ankles and knees ached from years standing on concrete. Anyone who had worked for long around machines was hard of hearing. . . . There were times studying them I dreaded growing up. Most of them coughed, from dust or cigarettes, and most of them drank cheap wine or whiskey, so their eyes looked bloodshot and bruised. The fathers of my friends always seemed older than the mothers. Men wore out sooner. Only women lived to old age.[26]

Regardless of the general view that men as a class have "power" in our society, in reality almost all jobs in factories or the corporate workplace are highly routinized and debilitating, involving little control or power but instead a great deal of placating a superior or boss. When many feminists speak of the power of men, they are not referring to the vast majority of men but rather to the CEOs, bankers, stockbrokers, and politicians who have become successful power men. Even most corporate men live lives not primarily of power but rather of fear. Joseph Heller captures the atmosphere of corporate work in his novel *Something Happened*:

> In the office in which I work there are five people of whom I am afraid. Each of these five people is afraid of four people (excluding overlaps), for a total of twenty, and each of these twenty people is afraid of six people, making a total of one hundred and twenty people who are feared by at least one person. Each of these one hundred and twenty people is afraid of the other one hundred and nineteen, and all of the one hundred and forty-five people are afraid of the twelve men at the top who helped found and build the company and now own and direct it.[27]

Living under the masculine mystique's mandate—seek and attain power—the vast majority of men become increasingly frustrated as they remain powerless, unable to "get ahead." Our society has designed an obvious strategy, even if a tragicomic one, to deal with this pent-up anger. As men become more and more powerless, they are given simulated media images of excessive, caricatured "masculine" power with which to identify. The media managers search for resonances to the Wild West, working-class America, and mechanized war in order to convince men that power is their destiny and purpose. Over several decades these simulated masculine figures have evolved from the Western independent man—John Wayne, Gary Cooper—to the blue-collar macho type—Sylvester Stallone, Robert De Niro—and finally to a variety of military/police figures typified by the violent revelry of *Robocop*.

No matter how the power images of the male mystique evolve or are modified, men are entranced by simulated masculinity, experiencing danger, independence, success, sexual fulfillment, idealism, and adventure as "power" voyeurs. Meanwhile they lead mostly powerless lives in a servile state, frightened of losing their jobs, mortgaged to the gills, and still feeling responsible for supporting their families. The disparity between their real lives and the synthetic, public male perpetrated by the media is rarely mentioned, and thereby the myth of the power man continues.

Most intimately, the power paradox contributes to sexual confusion and dysfunction in many men. The power-man model demands that men be able to dominate women as part of their sexual role, that they penetrate women to control and conquer in true Baconian fashion. Men in our society therefore face a difficult bind. While the growth of technology, with its identification with masculine power, swells in Priapus-like fashion, the average male faces the terror of the potential failure of his all-too-human personal power machine. If he is to be validated as a power man, he has to "get it up," keep it up, and use it in tireless pumping fashion so as to dominate and subdue his partner, preferably through her exhaustion from total sexual satiation. Anything less is seen as a failure of power by many men and women alike. So-called impotence (literally lack of power) or premature ejaculation then becomes the intimate sexual corollary to unemployment or technological illiteracy for men. It stigmatizes a man as a failure—demonstrates his inability to fulfill the dictates of the machine and power mythologies. As pressure has increased on men to identify their very masculinity with penile power and performance, the number of cases of so-called impotence has soared. Currently up to thirty million American men are labeled impotent. This pressure also drives men to pornography and prostitutes as the only avenues open that can assure the domination they are told they must have in order to be men.

The stigmatizing of the failure of men to achieve or maintain erection is compounded by the medical community's buying into the masculine mystique and continuing to label this phenomenon as impotence. The diagnosis and indeed the very word *impotence* is loaded. Many are becoming increasingly concerned about the demeaning connotations of the label. One doctor writes, "The word 'impotent' is used to describe the man who does not get an erection, not just his penis. If a man is told by his doctor that he is impotent, then the man turns to his partner and says he is impotent, they are saying a lot more than that the penis cannot become erect."[28]

Clearly the persistent and increased use of the stress-inducing and demeaning label of impotence represents a significant development in the social construct of masculinity, and an important triumph for the masculine mystique as men stake their masculine identity on the power of their phalluses. Interestingly a recent survey of psychological literature found that the frequency of articles with the term *impotence* in the title has risen dramatically since 1970, in contrast to the almost total disappearance of the term *frigidity*—a term with comparable pejorative connotation for women and used with comparable frequency prior to 1970.[29]

The paradox of power, namely that the power myth and technologies of our time disempower men rather than empower them, is also at the root of much of the problem of male violence. Despite popular opinion, for most men violence is not an expression of power but rather an expression of their near-total powerlessness. It is the only way they have of expressing the repressed rage of lives spent in servility, of existences permanently frustrated by trying to gain economic or personal power or independence. It is important to remember that the masculine-mystique image of real men being powerful men is shared by many women, who often show little respect for men who have failed in the power game. Spurred by derision and rejection, men often express violence simply because they can no longer hold in their frustration. This same pattern is seen in many oppressed groups. Unfortunately and tragically violence is the only path many men can find in their fruitless at-

tempts to gain respect. As summarized by feminist Barbara Ehrenreich, "But what the marginal men . . . need most is respect. If
they can't find that in work, or in a working class lifestyle that is
no longer honored, they'll extract it from someone weaker—a girl-
friend, a random jogger, a neighbor, perhaps just any girl. They'll
find a victim."[30]

PART III

A MOVEMENT OF MEN

8

OUT OF THE WOODS

*The grief in men has been increasing steadily since the start of the
Industrial Revolution and the grief has reached a depth now that
cannot be ignored.*   —Robert Bly[1]

The men's movement is coming out of the woods and into reality.
                                                                —Warren Farrell[2]

The pictures appeared in newspapers and magazines around the
country—groups of men in wilderness settings beating drums,
tearfully hugging one another, dancing in ritualistic circles,
smearing one another's bodies with mud, or huddled around a
campfire howling. Throughout the 1980s increasing numbers of men
gathered at retreats, often called Wildman gatherings, to grieve
their current condition and to rediscover some primeval, earthier,
more emotional aspect of their masculinity that they felt they had
lost in the industrialization of masculinity generations before. Retreats lasting from a day to a week were organized in dozens of cities
around the country; tens of thousands of men participated.

The new and seemingly bizarre behavior of thousands of men
caught the American public off guard. But the media soon became
enamored of the novel phenomenon. Within a short time the images

of these gatherings were omnipresent, even becoming a popular theme for TV sitcoms.

The wilderness retreats were quickly dubbed "the men's movement," and the significance of the nascent "mythopoetic" movement was debated in numerous forums. Most commentators, whether male or female, did not know whether to be amused or chagrined. One male journalist opined, "Harken to the sounds of men made new! Whimpers, sobs, shuddering, grunts from the solar plexus, high-pitched beseeching, whines for the mom and dad that did you dirt—these are the sounds of men today."[3] Many of the earliest critics of the gatherings came from the political right. They saw the Wildman movement as a potential challenge to the American male's prized economic productivity:

> Is it possible that the men's movement can swell outward from the ranks of the balding and sodden and pudgy and sexually inept, to overtake the well-coiffed, employed, and reasonably fit middle-class American male? Could this rock on which American prosperity has been built, this hardworking, self-denying model of rectitude and enterprise at last succumb to the siren song of self-flattery and indulgence, and come to believe that he too is oppressed and wounded and desperately needful of expensive healing?[4]

Criticism from some ideological feminists was not far behind, and was no more tolerant. One feminist wrote, "How do I feel about the mythopoetic men's movement? I feel frightened, and angry, and critical, and amused. I think that anything which is so terrifically attractive to white, middle-class, heterosexual men . . . is probably very dangerous to women."[5] For feminist clinical psychologist Laura S. Brown the men's gatherings were even reminiscent of the Nazi movement in Germany:

> Don't tell me "it can't happen here," that no such terrible outcome [female exploitation and genocide] can arise from something

as apparently silly as men in a room with a drum. As a Jew, I know better; Hitler and his gang began as just a fringe-group joke to the assimilated Jews of Germany. Hitler, too, looked to myth and legend, and to what was "essentially German" to feed his murderous visions of reality; he, too, relied upon ritual, upon the special bonds between men, to build his movement. Millions of Jews and Gypsies and queers died in his attempts to make those myths real.[6]

Some critics were more empathetic. Writer Trip Gabriel, reporting on a men's gathering for *The New York Times*, wrote,

The Wildman Gathering was at an end, and for me it was ending on a note of pitched emotion and some confusion. On the one hand, there seemed a patent foolishness in the rituals we enacted—the drumming and dancing. But on the other hand who could not be moved by the stories. . . . The men around the campfire seemed at times ridiculous, but they were ridiculous and real. Many were struggling to overcome the image of a man, passed down by their fathers, as someone who is miserly with his feelings and to whom any sign of vulnerability is a sign of weakness. They had bought into this code of masculinity, and in all cases, they said, it had stunted them.[7]

In retrospect most of the comments and fears of the critics of the fledgling movement seemed both gratuitous and self-serving. The caustic right-wing opponents of the mythopoetic movement generally fell into the category of "knee-pad conservatives"—men and women who publicly genuflect to the interests of the corporate world even at the cost of fatherhood, male community, a right relationship to the earth, and the crushing of the generativity of the male gender. They will continue to fear any group that seeks to define men outside of the masculine mystique's glorification of productivity, competition, materialism, and technological power. They will also continue to insist that "real men" thrive in corporate servility, repetitive and meaningless work, and in the endless attempt to compete for survival.

While there is without doubt truth in the feminist criticism that the men's movement has been somewhat separatist, and occasionally insensitive to the plight of women, it is equally clear that this criticism can be reversed. Feminist critics of the men's movement rarely if ever show even the slightest concern, much less outrage, over the shocking destruction of untold millions of men by our socioeconomic system. One can search in vain in feminist responses to the men's movement for empathy toward the plight of young men who are committing suicide at ever-increasing rates as compared with young women. Nor is there even an attempt to understand men being decimated through the military, or at the job, or in the family courts, or through unemployment or homelessness. For the most part these feminists are so focused on the harm being done to women that they do not recognize the pain of men and therefore cannot understand the need for men to experience healing. They do not see the chains on men and therefore cannot understand the need for liberation. These opponents of the movement project their fears onto surface images of the men's movement. They are not aware of the long history of the crushing of masculine gender through the forces of industrialism and modernity. They do not comprehend the historical significance of the movement's attempt to recover and discover a sustainable masculinity.

Clearly the Wildman gatherings and other similar events were not designed to undermine American working men, nor to begin the process of the genocide of women or children. Rather these gatherings are one of the few places in our society where men can come together in numbers to break the masculine mystique and to recapture, however briefly, a relationship to the earth, to the male community, and to their own masculine identity. For a few hours these men defeat the ideologies of the marketplace and view each other as a community of comrades, not as a collection of competitors. For a fleeting moment they abolish the myth that they are productive, unfeeling machines and embrace each other as courageous yet fragile beings full of fears, daring, hopes, and needs. As Mark Gerzon writes, "Tribes of 'wild men' make sense only in the context of the real worlds in which men live. . . . *Men in the movement are doing what they do on weekends because [of] . . . the worlds in which they live during the week.*"[8] (Emphasis in original.)

RUMORS OF LIBERATION

As the Wildman gatherings galvanized thousands of men into a new sensibility about their condition, the new movement among men was also being spawned by a growing literature on men's issues. Remarkably the devastating impact of the Industrial Revolution on men, fatherhood, and masculinity went virtually unrecognized by academics and writers for generations. The first work devoted to the issue of father absence caused by the Industrial Revolution was not published until 1963 (the same year that Betty Friedan's *Feminine Mystique* was published in America). The author was a little-known German psychiatrist, Alexander Mitscherlich. The book was titled *Society Without the Father* (more accurately translated as "Toward a Fatherless Community").

Mitscherlich's book was not widely read in the United States, no doubt due in part to its unfortunate style. Mitscherlich was at one time the director of the Sigmund Freud Institute in Frankfurt, and his prose is heavily laden with psychoanalytic jargon. Nevertheless Mitscherlich was a pioneer on the issue of the disappearance of the father in the industrial world, a phenomenon he calls the invisible father.

Though he avoids any detailed discussion of history or economics, and makes no mention of a masculine mystique, Mitscherlich is aware that the destruction of fatherhood was linked to the advent of industrial society and the division of labor: "The progressive fragmentation of labour, combined with mass production and complicated administration, the separation of home from place of work, the transition from independent producer to paid employee who uses consumer goods, has led to a progressive loss of substance of the father's authority and a diminution of his power in the family."[9]

In one of his most important insights, Mitscherlich warns that the growing vacuum in the father-child relationship creates dangerous and complex psychological impacts on children and society. Children in prior cultures learned and worked alongside the father in the home and in the fields. For better or worse he was a constant physical and psychic presence for his children. Now, however, children rarely see their father at his work. They often have little or no idea what he does during the day. Nor does the father see the day-to-day life and growth of his children. According to Mitscherlich this absence can breed suspicion and alienation:

> The child does not know what his father does, and the father does not see the child daily developing its skill. . . . It is difficult for the child to find his identity because, instead of seeing and getting to know his father in his working world, too much is left to fantasy. The same situation is repeated during the pubertal crisis of identity. He cannot easily find his identity in roles performed by his father or forefathers before him. . . . All this must give him a sense of isolation, and may suggest to him that his father is weak, incompetent or not to be depended on; and the father for his part may find in his son a non-understanding reserve that makes it difficult for him to say the right thing at the right time.[10]

Too often the son (as well as the daughter) fills the void of father absence by creating what Mitscherlich calls a "bogey man"—a negative fantasy that makes up for the lack of knowledge about the father. The father's authority is thus broken as he ceases to be a teaching and generative presence in his own household and instead becomes an unknown with characteristics that vary from the threatening to the incompetent.

The father is equally alienated from his children. He is incapable of understanding their negative projections of him. He is angered by not finding them as grateful and sympathetic as he feels they should be for his labor on their behalf. Moreover, as noted by

Mitscherlich, the father, now a "wage slave" in the new labor market, is also frustrated with his working life: "It must also be borne in mind that the father, too, suffers from doing work that does not enable him to develop his own aptitudes and thus express himself. He works for pay, by time or on piece rates, but the final product shows no trace of his individuality. This keeps alive in him a permanent sense of frustration."[11]

The term *fatherlessness* is extended by Mitscherlich beyond the primary absence of teaching and nurturing fathers in the home to include the missing "fathers" in political power. The reduced father role in the family has created a model for the technocratic, non-generative, "shadow" patriarchs in power in most countries, male leaders who do not understand the people they serve and are absent to their needs. Meanwhile, as with fatherless children, the populace creates "bogey man" fantasies of the "absent" political leaders and their dirty work behind closed doors in faraway capital cities.

For all its insights, Mitscherlich's work contains no clarion call for action to address the invisible father syndrome. Nor does he offer a panacea for the seemingly terminal illness that has befallen fatherhood. Rather he looks upon the destruction of the father and mother roles as virtually inevitable. His only hope is that some new "moral" understanding of the family unit will arrive to take its place.

The first important American work on the modern enclosure of men was far different from Mitscherlich's weighty tome. The book, *The Hazards of Being Male, Surviving the Myth of Masculine Privilege*, was written in popular style by Herb Goldberg, a practicing psychotherapist in Los Angeles. The book, published in 1976, begins with the jarring sentence "Most men live in harness." Goldberg continues, through the use of compelling case studies, to describe a plethora of ills plaguing men as part of the price of their "privilege." We witness men decimated by overwork, ignoring their health problems, stricken by sexual anxiety, prone to committing suicide, trapped in unhappy marriages, and unable to express emotions.

Goldberg gives few historical or psychological insights on father absence, nor is he concerned with how men reached their present state. He was, however, among the first to describe the many binds that modernity creates for men, including the "Identity Bind":

> At work, if he is success- and achievement-oriented, he will develop a style of being dominant, aggressive, emotionally controlled and detached. At home with his family, however, he will try to be tender, empathetic, sensitive, selfless, warm, and caring.
>
> *Either way he loses:* If he tries to be an emotionally integrated, unified, whole person, he will either be too soft at work or too harsh at home. If he tries to be all things to all people, the aggressor at work and the lover at home, he will have a split personality, controlling and monitoring his responses in each setting and paying the price of being overly controlled and only partially himself in both settings.[12]

Throughout the 1980s more and more books on men's issues appeared. Men were increasingly facing the costs of the masculine role to themselves, their families, and to the earth. Clearly a new masculine purpose was needed. Many were especially concerned with redefining the masculine, and particularly the male "hero," into a more sustainable model.[13]

The most widely read book on men in recent times is Robert Bly's *Iron John*, published in 1990. The book was a national bestseller, with hundreds of thousands of copies being sold. Bly came to his writing on men as a renowned poet, translator, and lecturer. The book and Bly's lecturing around the country were also primarily responsible for the growth of the Wildman gatherings.

Among Bly's central concerns is the loss of the older-male spirit. He associates this loss with several factors in modernity, most significantly the destruction of the role of the father. As with Mitscherlich, whom he admires and openly champions, many of Bly's central teachings focus on this absence of father:

> The love unit most damaged by the Industrial Revolution has been the father-son bond. . . . The Industrial Revolution, in its

need for office and factory workers, pulled fathers away from their sons and, moreover, placed the sons in compulsory schools where the teachers are mostly women.[14]

Bly continues with a description of the modern father's central dilemma:

When a father, absent during the day, returns home at six, his children receive only his temperament, and not his teaching. If the father is working for a corporation, what is there to teach? He is reluctant to tell his son what is really going on. The fragmentation of decision-making in corporate life, the massive effort that produces the corporate willingness to destroy the environment for the sake of profit, the prudence, even cowardice, that one learns in bureaucracy—who wants to teach that?[15]

Like the mythopoetic movement that he helped to spawn, Bly became a frequent target for a variety of attacks. Author Sharon Doubiago contends that *Iron John* was at least symbolically responsible for the Persian Gulf War. Bly was of course vocally and vociferously opposed to the war and writes eloquently in his book of the evils of modern warfare. Undaunted by these facts, Doubiago writes,

Iron John is so . . . inflammatory, and of such potential and outright treachery as to have, if not exactly unleashed the barely contained Mass Murderer in us, been a statement of His validity. . . . The Shadow Robert Bly stepped forward to join those of George Bush and Saddam Hussein, a trinity figure into the mythic figure of Goliath massacring David—to the score of 100,000 to 48. *Iron John* is our Desert Storm book.[16]

However, some criticisms of recent men's books are more on target. Writer Diane Johnson, reviewing several books on men's issues for *The New York Review of Books*, points out how little time many of these books take in discussing the structural nature of the oppression of the male gender. She is especially puzzled by the failure to analyze the influences of machines and technology:

> Are men and women enemies? The Jungian men's movement writers do not think so. . . . What, then, is the enemy? Surely all these books find too little fault with the objective conditions of modern American life. Besides such major problems as drugs and poverty, and family disintegration, . . . there is another villain, whose shadowy presence in many of these texts is there but nearly unremarked by the authors who put it there. They fail to fully examine the pace and isolation of modern life and the relationships which are actually conducted with machines.[17]

MOVING ON

Despite the many works on men's issues and the growth of the mythopoetic men's movement, discussion and action on masculinist issues have been totally overshadowed by the highly visible and far more vocal feminist movement. The public perception of the men's movement—men in "crybaby," "touchy-feely" sessions, or beating their drums and chests in the woods—is neither particularly endearing nor accurate. Yet it is undoubtedly true that the mythopoetic men's movement comes up short in doing, ironically, what the masculine mystique says men do best, taking action. While activist feminists continue to garner widespread support for their cause by attacking, head-on, real-life issues involving inequality or injustice to their gender, mythopoetic men's advocates have tended to look inward and eschewed political battles. While the Wildman movement has allowed many thousands of men to mourn the lost fathers and sons of the last decades and to reestablish their relationships to one another and the earth, there is clearly too little emphasis on searching for ways to change the structures that have led to the growing hidden crisis for men. A cathartic "wildman" weekend in the woods, or intense sessions sharing tragic stories of loss of children or health, can be key experiences in self-discovery and personal empowerment. However, these experiences cannot in themselves reverse the victimization of men.

Moreover if the nascent men's movement ultimately fails to take on a larger agenda, it will almost certainly be marginalized and lost in self-absorption and narcissism. For as yet what the media has termed the men's movement is more an occasional personal and spiritual insurrection than a mass social movement. It still has the negative potential of being merely a fad, fast forgotten as the new postindustrial world remakes gender roles to fit its needs. It will not be a full-scale social movement until it fully challenges the masculine mystique and the social structures that cause male oppression. As activist Warren Farrell advocates, "The men's movement is coming out of the woods and into reality. The woods is part of the process: connecting with other men is part of the process; going inside yourself is part of the process; but don't stay there."[18]

The need for a coherent men's movement has become even more urgent. More and more men are becoming angered and alienated as they face ever increasing joblessness, economic decline, family disintegration, discrimination in custody courts, violence, spiraling health problems, gender confusion, and the myriad other problems associated with the hidden crisis. This anger spilled into the polling booths in 1994 as millions of "forgotten" men registered a "protest" vote against the status quo. The election has been aptly dubbed the "angry man" election. But anger and a protest vote every few years will not be sufficient to address the men's crisis, and may in fact be counterproductive and reactionary. Only a men's movement which has the vision and courage to take on the structural ills that beset men will be successful in ushering in male liberation.

Recently, an increasing number of men, some inside the mythopoetic men's movement and many not, have heeded the call to action. Individually and in groups these men are "out of the woods" and are channeling their anger into constructive action. They are courageously struggling against the masculine mystique and seeking to address the hidden crisis that has engulfed so many boys and men. In the chapters that follow we will see, firsthand, how the hidden crisis and the masculine mystique continue to devastate men in our culture. But we will also witness what men can do, and are doing, to liberate themselves. In their personal, legal, and social struggles, many pioneering men are showing the way for the future of the men's movement.

9

FIGHTING FATHERS

*Contemporary American culture has now fully incorporated the belief
that fatherhood as a distinctive social role is unnecessary, undesirable,
or both.* —David Blankenhorn[1]

"W hy is it automatically assumed that a child is better off with the mother?" asks a frustrated and angered Rusty Peverell. In September 1992 Rusty lost the most important legal battle of his life. A Virginia judge allowed Karen Condor, Peverell's ex-wife, to move to California and retain physical custody of their six-year-old daughter and five-year-old son. The judge denied Peverell's motion for custody, even though two therapists and a child psychiatrist testified in court that the move would be harmful to the children. Complying with the court order and letting his children go was not easy for Rusty. "I thought about refusing to give the kids up," Peverell admits, "but I probably would have ended up in jail."[2]

According to court transcripts, Ms. Condor, an Air Force officer, sought a transfer to Edwards Air Force Base in California because it would better her chances of advancement in the military. She also told the court she turned down a humanitarian deferment of the transfer, which would have allowed her to stay in the area and work at Andrews Air Force Base in Maryland. Condor's career move turned Rusty's world upside down. Only a year before his ex-wife decided to relocate, Rusty, who has been a police detective for over twenty years, purchased a house three thousand yards from hers in order to better facilitate the court-ordered joint custody of their children.

Rusty and Karen's divorce settlement had him paying much of the bill. Each week much of Rusty's salary check goes to child support for his children. Rusty notes the irony that while he moved his new family to be nearer his children, he will now be sending his check three thousand miles away. Peverell says that his wife, since moving, has filed a motion that would require him to pay airfare for the children's Christmas, Easter, and summer visits with him. "She has done everything in her power to alienate me from my children," Peverell states.[3]

Peverell vows to fight the judge's decision and to continue to see his kids. He is currently preparing his appeal. "Gender bias is alive and well," he states. "For too many courts the view is 'Daddy Pay and Go Away.' I won't go away."[4] Though resolute, he finds it difficult to be hopeful. "I had to get a court order to see my kids on Father's Day when they were right around the corner," Peverell recalled. "What can I expect now that they're across the country?"[5]

Rusty knows from past experience that filing motions and appeals to keep his case alive will cost thousands of dollars and will add to the emotional turmoil of his life. "It sucks the life out of you," Rusty says of the endless court battle. But like many other fathers Rusty cannot simply resign himself to a life without his children. For Rusty their absence is "like a hole in the heart. Your children are ripped away. They give you no say."[6]

David L. Levy, cofounder and president of the Children's Rights Council, a national nonprofit child advocacy group based in Washington, D.C., followed the Peverell case closely. "It was nothing more than a legal abduction," he states. "Courts are not focused on parenting. Laws don't reflect the fact that children need both parents."[7]

Though heartrending, Rusty's case is not unusual. According to one recent study, in a Virginia county close to Rusty's, of 232 custody cases decided between July 1, 1989, and December 31, 1990, no father was given physical custody of his children unless the mother had agreed or was a prostitute, drug addict, or child abuser. Only nineteen fathers were permitted any amount of physical custody of their children and then only with the full consent of the mother. The author of the study, attorney William Dolan, concluded, "Although the child custody law is neutral on its face, the huge disparity between fathers and mothers with respect to physical custody awards seems to indicate that the law is not being applied fairly."[8]

THE MOTHERHOOD MYSTIQUE

Across the country, it is estimated that family courts are granting mothers sole or primary custody of their children in close to 90 percent of divorce cases. Fathers get sole custody in about 8.5 percent of cases.[9] Even when divorcing fathers resist the pressures of family, job, and often the advice of their attorney and seek sole custody of their children, their chances of success are remote. A recent study of California custody suits found that when both parents wanted sole custody, mothers won 45 percent of the cases, fathers 11 percent, and the remainder resulted in joint custody (generally with mothers as the primary custodians of the children).[10]

The gross imbalance in granting custody to females over males has been confirmed in local studies such as Dolan's and by the gender-bias commissions of each state in which a report on the issue has been presented. However, legislatures and courts have done little or nothing to address the problem. The bias toward mother custody is now taken for granted and causes little controversy. After all, hasn't it always been the mother who has been seen as the primary caregiver for children? The surprising answer is no, it was not always so.

The trend toward a fatherless society now being legally codified by the courts has its roots in changes our society incurred through industrialization over a century and a half ago. As described in prior chapters, in preindustrial times, including the colonial era in the United States, fathers were more often than not primary caregivers to children. In both law and custom the father bore the primary responsibility for raising the offspring. Mothers were of course also key caretakers of children. In a time when work was done in the home, men and women reared the children together, each serving different but complementary roles. However, well into the eighteenth century child-rearing manuals were generally addressed to fathers, not mothers. Societal praise or blame for a child was placed on the father first. Moreover, throughout our history and that of numerous other nations, the law contained a strong, and discriminatory, presumption that sole custody would be awarded to the father in the event of family dissolution. In fact the historic early feminist meeting in Seneca Falls, New York, in 1848 included as a principal complaint in its Declaration of Sentiments the fact that fathers automatically received custody after divorce.

The industrialization of America fundamentally altered the custody equation. When men went to the factories and mines, they could no longer perform their duties as teaching and caring fathers. Mothers, on the other hand, now removed from agrarian society into the cities, were cut off from productive work and confined to the forced domesticity of the urban home. This social revolution described in the prior sections of this book spawned the feminization of parenting and the household.

Throughout the 1800s, as the shift from agrarian and rural life to industrial and urban life became more pronounced, the father's roles as caregiver, teacher, and "elder" continued to evaporate. As summarized by author David Blankenhorn, "The fatherhood script was radically rewritten during the course of the 19th century. Fatherhood became a far thinner, more shrunken social role. Within the home, fathers moved to the periphery—if not formally, then certainly in practice. In this period, fatherhood . . . became increasingly anchored in, and restricted to, two paternal tasks: head of the family and breadwinner for the family."[11]

As fathers disappeared, social scientists began "finding" that young children had unique nurturing needs—needs, they said, that mothers were better suited to fill than fathers. This view began to influence courts in custody matters as more and more women were granted custody of young children. This judicial view, known as the tender-years presumption, became ever more widely accepted.

In the twentieth century fatherhood, already reduced, became all but nonexistent. Over the last few decades the increase in divorce, single-parent families, and the "parental" power of television and advertising have eroded what little was left of the paternal familial role. Fatherhood has completed its dramatic two-century descent from the center of the family to its periphery, and well beyond the periphery to nearly total absence.

At the same time as fatherhood was being undermined, the tender-years presumption evolved into the more general presumption that all children, of whatever age, were better off with their mothers than with their fathers after divorce. Courts began to grant mothers custody in nearly all cases. As early as 1916 courts were holding that "mother love is a dominant trait even in the weakest of women, and as a general thing surpasses the paternal affection for the common offspring, and moreover, a child needs a mother's care even more than a father's. For these reasons, courts are loath to deprive the mother of custody of her children."[12] In 1921 another judge stated, "The mother is God's own institution for the rearing and upbringing of the child."[13] Judicial rhetoric on the tender-years presumption may have reached an apex with this phrase from a 1938 opinion: "There is but a twilight zone between a mother's love and the atmosphere of heaven."[14]

Despite occasional legislative attempts to abolish it, the tender-years presumption is still alive and well in U.S. courts. In 1978 Justice Richard Neely of West Virginia spoke for too many other judges when he wrote, "We are clearly justified in resolving certain custody questions on the basis of the prevailing cultural attitudes which give preference to the mother as custodian of young children."[15] Recently judges have shied away from openly citing the tender-years doctrine and instead rely on what is termed the primary-caretaker concept.

While the term *primary caretaker* sounds both neutral and appealing, in reality its foremost use is as a change-of-name device designed to maximize the number of cases in which a court can preserve the bias toward maternal custody.[16]

Custody expert Richard A. Warshak has called the societal view that mothers are intrinsically better parents than fathers the motherhood mystique. He is deeply disturbed by the motherhood mystique's influence in family law and sees it as no more just than the father presumption that preceded it:

> From the point of view of children's welfare, the evolution of child custody decisions leaves much to be desired. There has never been a genuine attempt to understand how children are affected by different custody arrangements. Instead, stereotypes about the nature of men, women, and children have dictated custody decisions throughout history. In earlier times it was assumed that men, by nature, are better suited to protect and provide for children. Since 1920, it has been assumed that women, by nature, are better suited to love and care for children. These assumptions, which so powerfully affect so many children's lives, are based on nothing more than folklore and sexual stereotypes.[17]

THE DADDY TRAP

In recent years men around the country have begun challenging both the motherhood mystique and the masculine mystique. They have refused to acquiesce to the stereotypical view of men that demands that they be second-class parents. They have become far more deeply involved with their children than were their fathers.

Over the last decade researchers and family therapists have noted that the involvement of fathers in child rearing is significantly increasing. Joseph Pleck has presented findings showing that young married fathers spend from 20 to 30 percent more time in child care and domestic work than did young fathers in the early 1960s. Pleck also finds that among two-earner couples nearly one mother in five reports that the father is the primary caregiver while the mother is working. The number of fathers staying home to take care of children, or modifying their work schedules to do so, has also increased significantly.[18] Recent studies show that in two-parent families "fathers spend just as much time in primary interaction [with children] as do mothers."[19] Judith Wallerstein, a noted researcher in family issues, concludes that "we have seen a major shift in the attitudes of fathers, more of whom are trying to maintain an active parenting role in their children's lives."[20]

Unfortunately their deepening commitment to their children has led millions of men into a cruel trap. These men now face the same pain and frustration that Rusty Peverell faces. Though men are challenging the masculine mystique and becoming more active in nurturing their children, courts are still clinging tenaciously to the motherhood mystique and its outdated and sexist notions that men are less suitable single parents. As men become more caring and nurturing fathers, they face a court system that has not caught up with the evolution in men's consciousness or the current reality of parenting in our society.

Though they have invested heart and soul into the raising of their children, fathers after divorce will almost certainly be deprived of the opportunity to maintain a meaningful relationship with their children. At best they will be confronted with a court granting them "regular visiting privileges"—that is, every other weekend with their children. This routine court practice uproots the devoted father from daily contact with his children and pushes his relationship with his kids into a rushed and artificial weekend usually crowded with entertainment and gifts. Fathers who object to this fate are viewed as strange or irrational and are urged by everyone to accept the inevitable. As Dr. Warshak writes, "If a father wants to see his children more than four to six days per month, he will learn that the odds of being allowed to do so are very slim. His lawyer, his ex-wife, his boss, his peers, and perhaps even his psychotherapist will discourage him from trying. The divorced father's second class status as a parent is firmly entrenched and accepted without question."[21]

If the divorced father should persist and attempt to see his children more often than allowed by the court, he can be arrested and jailed, as in fact many are each year. It is worth noting that under the due-process provisions of the United States Constitution, parents can only be separated from their children after a hearing and a showing of unfitness, usually one based on abuse. Divorced fathers are, however, an apparent exception; they can be limited to seeing their children only four or six days a month, having committed no crime except having been divorced.

The discrimination against fathers in divorce affects a huge number of America's men. Experts estimate that in 1990 there were about 6 million fathers who did not live with their children but who visited them on an occasional or a regular basis—that means one visiting father for every four married fathers in the United States.[22] As indicated by Rusty's case, the loss for these millions of men can be devastating. One father's lament is emblematic of men caught in the father trap: "My children are going to be taken from me, and I have put my heart into raising them." Another man says, "I can't even look at a little girl at about the same age as my little girl without thinking about her and feeling stress. It's almost an anger that you have to suppress. It is a constant. Not a day goes by that you don't, two or three times during the day, go in and suppress those feelings, which can't be healthy for you."[23]

Researcher and family-law expert Joyce A. Arditti confirms the reality that most men feel: "Men appear to suffer more from divorce than has been previously believed. Most relevant to many men's divorce experience is their change in parenting status from custodial to noncustodial parent . . . the decrease in parental responsibilities . . . is often a painful experience. Many [men] report feelings of guilt, anxiety, depression, and a loss of self esteem."[24] These feelings have led to a tragic increase in suicide, alcoholism, and stress diseases and disorders among noncustodial fathers. One father caught in the custody trap states, "As a noncustodial father you don't have anything to say about where your children go to school, what doctors they see, what sports they play, but you have to have a smile on your face, pretend to everyone at home, at work, and at church that everything's okay. Because if you don't meet your responsibilities, you're just another uncaring, unfeeling father."[25]

Arditti notes that the significant psychological impact of loss of custody has important implications for many fathers' postdivorce involvement with their children. She cites research indicating that "an arrangement that gives one parent (usually the mother) total control over visitation is placing the custodial parent in a position of control and power. This places the other parent (usually the father) in a position of powerlessness leading to stress and emotional withdrawal."[26] Author and social scientist Judith A. Seltzer came to a similar conclusion in a 1991 report: "Studies of nonresident fathers' relationships with their children suggest that many fathers handle the pain of trying to maintain close bonds after separation by limiting contact with children. By avoiding contact some fathers face fewer reminders of their 'lost' children."[27]

A 1992 study conducted by two University of Texas sociologists, Debra Umbertson and Christine Williams, surveyed one thousand fathers. The study found that fathers who don't live with their children exhibit poor mental health, which is directly linked to their tendency to repress feelings about their children. The researchers conclude that stress and conflict over their missing offspring is an important factor in men's withdrawing from their children. "The stereotype is that men aren't involved in the parenting role, especially after divorce," Williams states. "A lot of people assume that parenting doesn't matter to men after divorce." In interview after interview the researchers found that it was pain, not disinterest, that kept most fathers from deeper contact with their children.[28]

Along with emotional trauma a host of other barriers work to prevent even the best-intentioned of noncustodial fathers from having positive and sustained involvement with their kids. Often the demands of alimony and child support increase the amount of time men have to work, thus creating a decrease in the time they spend with their children. "It's an economic nightmare," states one father with joint custody of his children. "I'll have to take on a night job. What else can I do? I have to maintain a home for my children, buy clothes and food, and yet under the current federal guidelines I pay over half of what I make to my ex-wife. And we make about equal incomes!"[29]

Additionally, as shown in Rusty's case, distance created by the mobility of mothers with custody can be a nearly insurmountable problem for fathers who want a close relationship with their children. "Move-away moms" are becoming an ever more routine occurrence. Divorced mothers can also make visits more difficult for fathers in other ways. Many mothers simply disallow visits. A recent study found that between one-fourth and one-third of custodial mothers have on at least one occasion illegally denied the father court-ordered access to his children. Many noncustodial fathers are constantly haunted by the uncertainty that they may never see their children again. The continuous anxiety of noncustodial fathers about having their children potentially removed from them through mother mobility, new court actions, or denial by the mother can of itself cause psychological disturbance. Dr. John Jacobs calls this Involuntary Child Absence Syndrome. The syndrome is characterized by "high levels of anxiety, outrage and depression."[30]

Custody orders, move-aways, visitation denial, and the emotional trauma they create all play a part in the alarming and well-documented trend of divorced fathers not having consistent contact with their children. The disturbing diminishment of noncustodial fathers' involvement with their children gains in importance when we remember the epidemic levels of divorce in America. Divorce has tripled in the United States in the past thirty years. Between 40 and 50 percent of all children born in the 1980s and 1990s will experience parental divorce, and the majority will do so in early-childhood years. Despite views that depict an increasing rate of paternal custody, up to ten times as many children reside with a single mother as do a single father. This means massive current and future father loss. Over one-third of all children in the United States today are growing up apart from their biological fathers. By 1990 nearly 22 percent were living with only their mothers, compared with less than 8 percent in 1960. This translates into approximately 14 million children living in mother-only households. When families and stepfathers are added to this total, we find that nearly 19 million children today live in households that include their biological mothers, but not their biological fathers.[31]

Fathers are not the only ones who suffer from the current decimation of fatherhood. Father loss also has dire implications for children. It is generally accepted that fathers are a key element in fostering healthy psychological development in children and providing boys with a humanized and healthy masculine image. While some blame the problems of fatherless children on low income, studies that have examined children where income is not a factor show that father absence, not money absence, is the problem. Researcher Urie Bronfenbrenner found that

> controlling for associated factors such as low income, children growing up in such [female-headed] households are at greater risk for experiencing a variety of behavioral and educational problems, including . . . impaired academic achievement, school misbehavior, absenteeism, dropping out, involvement in socially alienated peer groups, and especially the so-called "teenage syndrome" of behaviors that tend to hang together—smoking, drinking, early and frequent sexual experience, and in the more extreme cases, drugs, suicide, vandalism, violence, and criminal acts. Most of these effects are more pronounced for boys than for girls.[32]

Numerous studies also demonstrate that the presence of a father in the home is directly linked to a child's ability to tell right from wrong, develop empathy toward others, take responsibility for his or her actions, and achieve academic excellence.

While much of the discussion of father absence centers around its impacts on boys, daughters suffer too. Irwin Garfinkel and Sara

McLanahan, in their intergenerational study on fatherless homes, found that "daughters of single parents are 53 percent more likely to marry as teenagers, 111 percent more likely to have children as teenagers, 164 percent more likely to have premarital birth, and 92 percent more likely to dissolve their own marriages."[33]

Remarkably the trauma associated with being a noncustodial father, and the impact on children of fatherless homes, have gone relatively unpublicized. No congressional hearings or government reports have examined this national family emergency. In fact about the only time noncustodial fathers are discussed in the media or by government officials is in terms of the "deadbeat dad" problem. Virtually every politician and family advocate has spoken at length about dads who do not pay, or are behind in, child-support payments. The media tends to exacerbate this skewed view of fathers by focusing on a few wealthy fathers who do not pay child support. In reality, according to custodial mothers themselves, over two-thirds of delinquent "deadbeat dads" do not pay because they are unemployed or otherwise unable to pay.[34] Further, a growing number of researchers have directly linked the increasing number of households headed by single women and the lack of child support payments to the economic pressures on young men to abandon their responsibilities as fathers. A 1995 study by the Annie E. Casey Foundation reported that from 1969 to 1993 the number of households headed by women increased at virtually the same rate as the economic fortunes of young men declined. Analyzing census bureau data, the Foundation discovered that the percentage of men (aged twenty-five to thirty-four) earning less than the amount needed to keep a family of four above the poverty line had doubled, from 13.6 percent in 1969 to 32.2 percent in 1993. Similarly, the percentage of children living in households headed by women increased from 11 percent to 23.3 percent during that period.[35] A 1995 report by the Urban Institute further documented the fact that the "deadbeat dad" problem is primarily one of economics, not unwillingness to pay. According to the report, up to 40 percent of all fathers and two-thirds of black noncustodial fathers who do not pay child support are poor. Thirty-two percent of nonpaying fathers are out of work and 42 percent have the added financial responsibility of a new family.[36] Not surprisingly, even the states that have been the most aggressive in pursuing deadbeat dads admit that the vast majority of the men who do not pay simply cannot pay because of their economic circumstances.[37]

Moreover, even in the deadbeat-dad context, little attention is paid to the emotional problems of fathers who fall behind in child-support payments. Those who have studied noncustodial fathers have little doubt that the need, on the part of these fathers, to repress thoughts and emotions concerning their children can also lead them not to pay child-support. "Repressing their feelings doesn't help the men, but it also doesn't help women or children," reports Umbertson. "The more a father remains in contact, the greater he's likely to pay child support."[38]

Recent government research confirms that the more a father is involved with his children after divorce the greater the likelihood that he will be in child-support compliance. Child-support compliance for fathers who have joint custody is over 90 percent. When a father's access to a child is protected by a visitation order, compliance is about 80 percent. When there is neither a joint custody agreement nor a visitation order child-support compliance falls below 45 percent.[39]

Among the most important lessons that can be learned from the current struggle of noncustodial fathers for their parental rights is that reliance on stereotypes about men, women, and children provides a poor basis for custody decisions. Children's real needs are bypassed, and psychologically harmful images of father and mother are developed. The solution involves not only attempting to reduce the divorce rate, but also fostering more joint-custody arrangements, greater psychological understanding of modern fathering, and greater cooperation between divorcing parents.

However, rather than encouraging more cooperation between divorcing parents, many lawyers and family-law activists are going in the opposite direction. As fathers become more involved with their children, custody fights are gaining in intensity and bitterness. Gender warfare is becoming the name of the game in family courts, and in the process even more virulent stereotypes of fathers are being promoted.

ABUSING ABUSE

When Roy Haines raised the children from his first marriage, he was a fairly traditional father. "I love all my children," he says. "But I was working so hard in those days, I didn't have that much time for them." But then Roy remarried and, with his new wife, Sandra, had a baby girl, Lucy. "I had this vision of what it would be like to have Lucy. I'm older and my business was going well. I used to dream of what it would be like when Sandra was pregnant. I'd walk Lucy to school; we'd read together. I'd be the sort of father I always wanted to be." Roy now finds himself driving over 180 miles every Saturday in order to spend an eight-hour supervised visit with Lucy.

The daydream of a new child turned into a nightmare for Roy shortly after Lucy was born. Within two months of the birth Roy and Sandra separated. When Roy filed for divorce, he sought joint custody. Sandra responded by asking for $1,300 a week in temporary alimony and child support. The judge turned her down, granting instead $100 a week.[40]

According to Roy, shortly after the judge's decision he got into an argument with his mother-in-law about Lucy during which he asserted he would eventually seek sole custody of the child. Shortly thereafter Sandra called Child Protective Services, claiming that Roy was abusing Lucy. Her original charges were that Roy was kissing their child's chest and putting medicine on her genital area. Lucy was then two and a half years old.

"That's the worst part of these allegations," says Roy. "On some level they're true. Of course I kiss my daughter; I love her dearly. And Lucy was in diapers, she had a rash, so I put Desitin on her. The mother takes things any father would do for his child and makes them ugly. How am I supposed to fight innuendo?" For over two years Roy was in court on the child-abuse charge. During that time each of his visits with Lucy was supervised. Finally all charges were dismissed, and full parenting rights were restored to Roy. The price had been high. He had paid more than $90,000 in legal fees. He'd been forced to sell his company—he couldn't run his company and spend the time necessary to fight the charges against him. Additionally he had to fight an IRS case in which his wife was a cooperative witness. He believes that Sandra instigated the tax charges, which were also eventually dismissed.[41]

But Roy's battle wasn't over yet. Within twenty-four hours after the first charges were dropped, Sandra raised new allegations, this time more serious. She claimed that Roy had held a knife to the child's mouth and chest. Roy's parental rights were promptly changed. A short while later Sandra also claimed that Roy may have ejaculated in the child's face. When questioned about the timing of the charge, she remarked that she had "forgotten" to mention it earlier.

Roy eventually got the second charge of abuse dismissed. But he knows only too well that there is nothing to stop future charges and further retribution should he attempt to gain custody of his daughter. "I don't think I'll ever be normal again," Roy states. "To be on your guard at all times because anything you might say or do could someday be twisted against you . . . How is a father supposed to have a relationship with his child if he's not allowed to bathe her, tickle her, kiss her, take care of her?"[42]

Throughout the last decade hundreds of thousands of fathers have been in Roy's situation. As the very real and compelling problem of child and spousal abuse become better recognized in our society and by the media, allegations of such abuse are being used irresponsibly by parties and lawyers in custody cases. Lawyers estimate that 30 to 40 percent of all custody cases today involve charges that a parent physically or sexually abused his or her children—in over 80 percent of these cases the allegations involve father abuse of children. An increasing number of these allegations are dropped or proven unfounded during trial. "It's becoming a well-known negotiating tool in divorce cases," says Kimberly Hart, an expert on abuse allegations. "The false allegations follow a certain pattern—at the time the man files for divorce, when he seeks a modification of custody, or if he asks for a support reduction. The allegations usually come a week later."[43] Well-known New York family lawyer Robert Dobrish agrees: "It's the latest tactic in a nasty divorce. If you wanted to hurt your ex-husband before, what would you say? He has affairs? He cheats on his income tax? He's a homosexual? Big deal. Who even cares about that stuff anymore? But this is the ultimate weapon. I don't care how liberal society gets, it will *never* be okay to molest your own children."[44] (Emphasis in original.) According to child psychologist Abraham Worenklein, there is a similar trend in Canada, with about 40 percent of custody cases now involving child abuse or molestation allegations. "In the 1960s the best way to get custody was to accuse the other parent of infidelity; in the 1970s it was homosexuality. Now it's sexual abuse."[45] Canadian social worker Nancy Di Natale says that about 95 percent of the charges of sexual abuse in custody cases that her Children's Aid Society was asked to investigate in 1988 proved unfounded.[46]

The false allegation of child abuse serves other needs besides legal. "The false allegation serves a lot of purposes—in a totally unconscious fashion," states Dr. Arthur Green, medical director of the Family Center and Therapeutic Nursery of Presbyterian Hospital in New York. "It's a way of getting even, a way of gaining control over your child at a time when you feel very out of control. It's a way of getting this guy you hate out of your life forever."[47]

Nor is the false allegation necessarily a conscious, premeditated attack on a former spouse. "There's no stronger impulse than a mother's need to protect her child," says Dr. Alan Levy, chief of forensic child psychiatry at Presbyterian Hospital. "You mix this with all the media focus on child abuse, plus poorly trained child-abuse 'experts,' and it's very possible for a mother to see dragons everywhere."[48]

The trend in false allegations hurts both children and fathers. First of all this misuse of the court system throws into doubt the growing number of real child-abuse cases being reported around the country. Second, false allegations are in themselves a form of child abuse. The often loosely trained "validators" called on in many states to interview children of alleged abuse often themselves suggest abuse scenarios to children, which the children then adopt. Additionally parents often coach their children into falsely testifying about abuse. One lawyer remarked after a particularly heinous group of charges were dismissed and proved to be false, "The real abuse in this case was the brainwashing done on this child. Imagine what it took to persuade her that her father did these terrible things."[49] Another lawyer exclaims, "Can you imagine how these children are tormented? What's going to happen when they get old enough to read about these allegations? What are they going to feel then?"[50] There are few studies that have examined the long-term psychological impact on children of parents pressuring them to report or acquiesce to false allegations of abuse, but the trauma created by such acts is correctly feared.

Fathers falsely accused are also permanently scarred. It is very difficult for them to shake the stigma of having been suspected of abuse or molestation. Roy Haines reflects back on his ordeal: "Even though I was found innocent, the damage is done. You know how people think: 'Okay, so maybe you didn't do anything as bad as they said you did. But, Roy, you must have done *something* for this to go on for two years.' "[51] (Emphasis in original.)

The damage done by the media and publicity surrounding child-abuse charges goes well beyond the parties involved. It hides the truth about child abuse and parents. One of the priorities in our society is, and should be, to address the growing child-abuse problem. Perpetrators should be punished and every effort must be made to prevent these crimes in the future. Moreover, men do commit the majority of sexual abuse of children. However, we cannot come to effective solutions to the significant child-abuse problem until we see the true dimensions of the issue. Numerous statistics, both those provided by state family-service agencies and those by private researchers, reveal that a majority, and in certain areas a growing majority, of overall child abuse is done not by fathers but by mothers, not by men but rather by women. The 1991 statistics for the state of Texas are typical of many others. According to the state's Department of Protective and Regulatory Services, 48.9 percent of all perpetrators in confirmed reports of child abuse are mothers, 23.1 percent are fathers, the remaining percentage being a mixture of aunts, uncles, grandparents, and stepparents.[52] Moreover, a 1994 Justice Department study found that a full 55 percent of offspring murders are committed by women.[53]

These figures should not be interpreted to mean that mothers are more prone to child abuse or murder than fathers. Mothers, after all, take care of children more than do fathers. However, these figures do flatly contradict the general stereotype of the father as the primary child abuser in our society. Few members of the public would ever guess from presentations of child abuse in print and the electronic media that mother child abuse exceeds father abuse by more than two to one.

The misconception that child abuse is solely, or even primarily, a male phenomenon skews public policy on the issue. The mistaken view of abuse actually heightens both the masculine mystique and the motherhood mystique. It causes judges in custody cases to have the feeling that the child is more "at risk" with a father than a mother, though statistics would indicate that this is not the case. Of equal importance, it causes policymakers to focus exclusively on men and abuse and ignores the need to address the crushing pressures on women, especially poor women and single mothers, that are responsible for a significant portion of child abuse. Moreover, by focusing solely on male abuse of children, our society gives young men an image of fatherhood as abusive and motherhood as benign that does not comport with reality and that destroys a boy's sense of respect for his own gender.

Divorcing fathers are also being victimized by false allegations of spousal abuse and our society's misperception of family violence. Domestic violence is another important priority for our society. Without question, a shocking number of women are battered and brutalized by their male partners. Men who abuse must be punished and preventive measures must be taken. Yet as with child abuse the crucial issue of domestic violence has been falsely framed in our society. Spousal abuse is thought of solely in terms of male behavior. In actuality wives assault their husbands at about the same rate as husbands assault wives. As noted by researcher Murray A. Strauss, "Surveys of married and dating couples find that women assault their male partners at about the same rate as men assault female partners. When assaults serious enough to cause death are examined, it was found that in contrast to the extreme rarity of homicide by women outside the family, women kill their male partners at a rate that approaches the rate at which men kill their female partners."[54] In fact according to a national survey, wives report that they were more likely to assault their husbands than their husbands were to assault them. Further, the incidence of domestic violence against females decreased between 1975 and 1985 by over 25 percent, while domestic violence against men increased slightly.[55]

Many have suggested that women's violence against men is primarily in self-defense. However, once again major studies show this view to be erroneous. About as many women as men attack a spouse who has not hit them during a one-year period.[56]

Others argue that while the assault rate may be equal between the genders, men are more powerful and can do more damage. Most researchers agree that men do more physical damage to women during family violence than women do to men. However, it is important to note that in domestic violence women are more likely than men to use a weapon. According to researchers R. L. McNeely and Coramae Richey Mann, "The average man's size and strength are neutralized by guns and knives, boiling water, bricks, fireplace pokers and baseball bats." A 1984 study of 6,200 cases of reported domestic assaults found that 86 percent of female-on-male violence involved weapons, contrasted with 25 percent of male-on-female violence.[57]

Certainly men themselves are to blame for some of the misperception about spousal abuse. The masculine mystique's mandate that men must be dominant, independent, in control of women, and never ask for help leads to few men reporting female-on-male violence. "Men are trained not to ask for help," notes Alvin Baroff, a counselor for men, "and a man's not being able to solve his own problem is seen as a sign of weakness." Men not only fail to report domestic violence on them, they are reluctant to report any violence done to them at all. According to a 1990 Department of Justice Survey on Criminal Victimization, men are 32 percent less likely than women to report violence that has been perpetrated against them.[58]

Society, equally entranced by the masculine mystique, has little tolerance for men who openly discuss being victims of domestic violence. "Skip," a Baltimore resident, reluctantly went on a 1991 television show featuring the domestic-violence issue. When he related how his wife repeatedly hit him and attacked him with knives and scissors, the audience's reaction was exactly what he had feared most—laughter.

As with the faulty public understanding of child abuse, the inadequate understanding of spousal abuse has serious implications for custody and other public-policy issues. As stated by domestic-violence researcher Gloria Robinson Simpson, "The danger of these misconceptions [about spousal abuse] is that social policy, legislation and the attitude of officials and the public are being shaped by erroneous information. . . . Men are increasingly defenseless when allegations of domestic violence are made."[59]

When viewing how our society views child and spousal abuse it becomes clear that the masculine mystique has played an important role in our blaming men as the violent gender. Despite the clear statistical evidence, all violence and especially family violence is seen as yet another product of male psychology or biology (i.e., testosterone). Female violence and aggression is dismissed or ignored. Author Katherine Dunn notes that "We live with a distinct double standard about male and female aggression. Women's aggression isn't considered real. It isn't dangerous, it's only cute. Or it's always in self-defense or otherwise inspired by a man. In the rare case where a woman is seen as genuinely responsible, she is branded as a monster—an 'unnatural' woman." Columnist and reporter Linda Ellerbee summarizes what should be obvious: "The truth is that women, like it or not, can be brutal too. Brutality's not sexist."[60]

Unfortunately family courts have not caught up with statistics on child and spousal abuse, or the growing consciousness that violence is a human not a gender problem. Accordingly, many fathers still feel the brunt of the negative stereotyping about violence that remains so endemic in custody courts. "The system assumes that the woman is a fair-minded, relatively sane individual," says one father. "They assume about me that I'm a drunken, pickup-driving, beer-can-littering, child-abusing wife beater."[61]

CASUAL INSEMINATORS

As married men fight to reverse the discrimination against fathers in American courts, another group of fathers are also claiming their parental rights. These are the growing ranks of unwed fathers. In the early 1980s the nation was shocked to learn that almost one in four minority children were born to unmarried parents, and that about 10 percent of nonminority children were being conceived out of wedlock. The national uproar over the statistics did little to stop the trend. During the past decade out-of-wedlock births in the United States nearly doubled. Currently 20 percent of nonminority children are born to unmarried parents, with almost half of all minority children now falling into this category. By 1990 close to a third of all births were to unmarried mothers. It is estimated that by the turn of the century half of all children born in the United States will be to unmarried parents.[62]

The massive increase in children being born outside of marriage has caught society unprepared. Over the last decade government belt tightening and across-the-board reductions in a number of social services have been implemented just as the number of out-of-wedlock births has skyrocketed. As such, support services for unmarried parents and their offspring remain grossly inadequate. The physical and psychological needs of unwed parents and their children are simply not being met. Moreover many of those attempting to help unmarried mothers are little more than adoption-referral agencies eager to use the increasing number of out-of-wedlock children to meet the growing demand for adoptable children. Adding to the problem is the fact that most unmarried parents are young and poor.

As with social policy, custody law has failed to keep up with the growth of the unmarried-parents phenomenon. This failure is especially evident in the ongoing legal disenfranchisement of unwed fathers. For years state laws on unwed fathers have been based on the outdated premise that virtually all these men are uninterested in the children they have cocreated, and unwilling to take responsibility for them. While far too many unwed fathers eschew responsibility for their offspring, many wish to be active fathers. Current laws grant the unwed mother full parental rights, yet treat the father as essentially a nonparent.[63]

In recent years this legally codified unequal treatment of unwed fathers has been challenged. Around the country there has been a spate of litigation seeking to invalidate laws restricting rights of unwed fathers as growing numbers of these men have gone to court seeking parental rights. Some of the cases, including several that have reached the Supreme Court, have succeeded in having various statutory provisions declared unconstitutional. However, the vast majority of unwed-father litigants fail to gain parental rights. Perhaps none has fought harder and longer than Rick M., an unwed father in California.[64]

In May 1988 Rick M. was anxiously awaiting the birth of the child that he had fathered. The baby had been a surprise, and something of a shock, to Rick and the child's mother, Kari. The couple were dating but not married and were confused about how to proceed. After numerous discussions they had agreed that after its birth Rick would take full responsibility for the child. Rick knew that raising the child as a single father was not going to be easy. His job as a security guard gave him only a small salary, and he still lived with his mother. Nevertheless he believed that with the help of his family he could give the child a loving and nurturing home. As Rick awaited his child in the spring of 1988, he had no suspicion that soon he would be forced into the legal trenches as yet another fighter in the battle against the discriminatory laws that target unwed fathers.

Rick was involved with his child from the very start. Kari was living with him in his mother's house, and he was an active presence in the early stages of the pregnancy. He went to the first doctor's appointments with Kari. He remembers the doctor allowing him to hear the baby's heartbeat—"Hearing the heartbeat I had feelings of love I never had before. I was proud I was going to be a father."[65]

Unfortunately life for the couple during the pregnancy became difficult. Relations between Kari and Rick's mother became especially tense. After a few weeks Kari moved out of Rick's mother's house and into a shelter for pregnant women. Rick remembers visiting Kari at the shelter about one month before the child was due. He felt the baby with his hand and "had the same feeling of love and joy that I felt when I heard the baby's heart beat."[66]

While awaiting his child's birth Rick prepared for the baby's arrival. He took out the queen-size bed in his room and put in a twin bed and a crib. Every Friday, after receiving his paycheck, he would stop at the Toys "Я" Us and buy stuffed animals or other baby toys. His drawers were filled with diapers and ointments.

On May 18, 1988, Kari gave birth to a baby boy, who was named Kelsey. Upon hearing that Kari had given birth, Rick immediately went to the hospital. However, to Rick's dismay the security guard had been given instructions not to let him into the maternity ward. He was told to return the following day. When he arrived the next morning at eight A.M., Rick was told that Kari and Kelsey had left the hospital at six A.M., though normal checkout was at noon. Concerned, Rick learned from mutual friends that Kari had decided, without his consent, to give Kelsey up for adoption to a couple, Steven and Suzanne. Rick, now frantic, knew that he had to act quickly if he wanted to keep his son. He withdrew his savings and paid a two-thousand-dollar retainer fee to an attorney to file a court action to obtain custody of Kelsey.

The court granted Rick's temporary-custody motion, and with

the court order in hand Rick quickly drove to the home of the couple who intended to adopt Kelsey. Just as he was driving up to their home, he saw the couple arrive in their driveway and rush into the house with the baby. Rick called the police to enforce his custody order. But when the police arrived, Suzanne insisted that there was no baby in the house.

On May 24 the couple filed adoption papers for Kelsey, and a week later they filed a petition to terminate all of Rick's parental rights. Rick fought the adoption. The court held a series of hearings to decide the issue. During a break in one of the court sessions, the lawyer appointed by the court to represent the baby allowed Rick to hold his son. "Rick," she said, "I'd like you to meet your son." Rick remembers, "I felt fantastic. . . . He was the most beautiful child I had ever seen. More beautiful than anything . . . I felt I would get to love him and he would have the opportunity to love me."[67] Later Rick was granted regular Saturday visitation with Kelsey pending the outcome of the trial.

On August 26 the court granted the petition of the adopting couple and stripped Rick of any parental rights over his son. According to the judge, under the laws of California Rick could not be seen as the legal father of his three-month-old son. In making its decision, the court went against the recommendation of the child's court-appointed attorney, who recommended that Rick get custody. How could this happen? How can a court legally strip a biological father of his rights without some showing that he is unfit?

The answer is that in California and several other states the law does not treat unwed fathers in the same manner as it does other biological parents. Under these laws an unwed mother is the legal parent of the child and must consent if a child is being given up for adoption. The unwed father, however, has no automatic parental rights. Instead the law distinguishes between two kinds of unwed fathers: "presumed fathers"—biological fathers who have fulfilled several broad legal requirements (including reasonable efforts to support the unwed mother emotionally and financially during pregnancy, expressing the intention of supporting the child prior to birth, and receiving the child into his home after birth); and "natural fathers"—fathers who have not fulfilled these requirements. Presumed fathers are given parental rights; natural fathers have no rights whatsoever as fathers and thus cannot stop a child from being adopted by third parties.

When an unwed father like Rick attempts to assert his parental rights, the court hears evidence in order to decide whether he has complied with the requirements for being a "presumed father." Since, despite his near-heroic efforts, Rick had not been able to bring his son into his home, he had not fulfilled one of the "presumed father" requirements. Therefore the court declared him only a "natural father" and held that he did not have parental rights over Kelsey and could not prevent the infant's adoption.

Rick was brokenhearted when he heard the news. "One Sunday after my regular Saturday visit, my lawyer telephoned me to say that the judge had ruled against me, that I would no longer have any visitation. I felt devastated. . . . My son had been yanked from me again, all of a sudden he was gone. . . . When I went to his room, I felt my world was shattered. I could hardly bear to look at his empty crib."[68]

Despite emotional turmoil and tight finances Rick appealed the lower court's decision, eventually all the way to the California Supreme Court. Rick's lawyers insisted that the law could not penalize Rick for failing to house his son, since Kari and the adopting couple had conspired to keep the child from him. Depriving Rick of rights over his son would mean that any unwed mother could deprive an unwed father of parental rights by preventing him from seeing or housing his child.[69]

As he fought his case through the court system, Rick knew that time was of the essence. Kelsey was getting older, and Rick's attorneys told him that the longer his son stayed in the custody of the adopting couple, the harder it would be for him to gain custody or even visitation.

The California Supreme Court finally ruled in February 1992. In its opinion the court held that certain provisions of the California law on unwed fathers were unconstitutional, including that part of the statute that required unwed fathers to house a child before being recognized as "presumed fathers." The court stressed that the law violated equal-protection assurances in the Constitution by treating unwed fathers in a radically different manner than unwed mothers:

> A mother's decision to place her newborn child for adoption may be excruciating and altogether altruistic. . . . As a legal matter, however, the mother seeks to sever all ties with her child. The natural father, by contrast, has come forward to assume the legal and practical burdens of being a parent. . . . Clearly [by denying him the possibility of parenting] the father is treated unfairly.[70]

Rick was elated by the decision. "When the supreme court ruled in my favor, I felt a sense of relief that finally someone was recognizing that I was a father. I was excited that I would be able to see him, how much he has grown and what he looks like. I was excited that he would be coming home where he belonged."[71]

Rick's relief was premature. The California Supreme Court had removed some of the most egregious elements from the law on unwed fathers but unfortunately had left the basic structure in place. The court left standing the idea that an unwed biological father, unlike an unwed biological mother, still had to fulfill numerous vague requirements prior to a determination on whether he could be a "presumed father" with legal rights over his offspring. Under the decision courts were required to examine a wide range of an unwed father's conduct both before and after the pregnancy to determine whether to grant parental rights. In sum the court had failed to abolish the invidious discrimination at the heart of the statute.

When Rick's case went back to the lower court for adjudication, in compliance with the supreme-court order, it was expected that he would finally get custody or at least be able to negotiate an arrangement with the adopting couple. But the couple refused to cooperate. And in September 1992 the same judge who terminated Rick's parental rights over four years before did it again. He declared that though Rick had spent years trying to get his son, though he had been there during the pregnancy and expressed a desire for his child at birth, though he had spent years fighting in the courts, his behavior still was not sufficient to meet the "presumed father" standards required by the law. According to the openly hostile judge, Rick had done a lot but not enough to be called a father in the state of California.

Noted family-law attorney Sharon Huddle, who worked on Rick's case, was highly critical of the court's decision:

> The law, and the judges who apply it, view unwed fathers as little more than casual inseminators. The law in this state and many others flatly discriminates against unwed fathers. Behind the unequal treatment in the law is a stereotypical view that fathers are not equal parents with mothers, and that adopting couples are better parents than unwed fathers. We not only have to change the law, we have to change our way of thinking about these fathers.[72]

Rick, disappointed yet again, continues his fight for his son. He has appealed the lower court's ruling. Short on funds, relying on the work of attorneys volunteering their time, Rick is attempting to get the case back to the California Supreme Court, where he hopes that, once and for all, unwed fathers will get equal protection under the laws of California.

A CUSTODY REVOLUTION

A major focus of any masculinist movement, and a central aspect of any comprehensive "father policy" in the United States, is the struggle to reform divorce and custody practices. As a society we can no longer ignore the court-sanctioned discrimination against fathers that is causing so much havoc among divorcing families and unwed parents. Failure to deal with this masculine-mystique–based prejudice will continue to take a heavy toll on men and children. "These men face enormous barriers in maintaining relationships with their children," writes researcher Umbertson. "The state should not constitute an additional one."[73]

The aim of a masculinist custody revolution is not to promote sole custody for fathers but rather to better protect children by establishing a child's right to continued active involvement with both parents. Changing custody decisions in this way will require a fundamental rethinking of how we legally treat divorce. Our current litigation system is based on the court's deciding winners and losers. This model may be functional for controversies involving commercial law, but it is a disaster in family law. When there is a winning parent and a losing parent in custody, it means that the courts have effectively accomplished a "parentectomy." And in the vast majority of cases the parent who has been removed from the child's life is the father. It is striking that while many commentators have criticized the masculine-mystique competition model in business or sports, we have seen little criticism of its disastrous use in the divorce setting.

Fortunately things may be changing. Now, after many years of debate, there is general agreement across the political spectrum, from liberal to conservative, that the winner-take-all system that we have developed in the domestic-relations courts simply is not working. Consider: We take two loving parents, we walk them into court at their most emotionally distraught and weakest moment, and we say to them, "Here are some weapons, fight it out, the last one left standing owns the child." In the end the loser, usually the father, not only loses the companionship of the child but is also ordered to make payment for services that the loser wanted to provide in his or her own home.

Therefore the first priority of the men's movement in addressing the custody crisis is to fight for laws that demilitarize divorce. This aim can be accomplished by several means. First states should require alternate dispute resolution (ADR) for any divorcing couple. Surveys show that a significant number of couples might have worked far harder to preserve their marriages if they had realized the magnitude of the personal, psychological, and financial costs of divorce and a custody battle. Mediation and other ADR approaches could play a key role in helping to inform couples about alternatives to divorce.

Even when couples proceed on to divorce, much can be done. All states should require the submission of a "parenting plan" prior to the entry of a divorce decree. The state of Washington has a highly developed parenting-plan requirement. The state requires that at the outset of the divorce proceeding each couple work out a detailed parenting plan covering the full range of the child's physical, emotional, and financial needs. If the parties are unable to agree upon a single plan, each parent submits a plan, and both plans are available for the court's review in determining the custody arrangement that will serve the best interests of the child. This exercise in preparing detailed parenting plans tends to make parents more realistic about their respective capabilities in providing for the needs of their children after divorce. Often it creates awareness in divorcing parents of the benefits that will accrue if they share the parenting burden with the other. The plans also aid the judge in obtaining vital information on the actual capabilities of the parties.

When neither mediation nor an agreeable parenting plan is successful, courts need to base custody not on the motherhood mystique but rather on the basic understanding that children need interaction with both parents. We need to remember that, above all, children are born with two parents and that they want, love, and need two parents. In all but the vanishingly small number of pathological cases, the courts should strive to maximize the involvement of both parents. If distance or other factors prevent a substantially equal relationship with both parents, the preference should go to that parent who shows the greater willingness and ability to cooperate and nurture the other parent's relationship with the child.

As an insurance policy against the continuing judicial policy of granting virtually automatic custody to mothers, states also need to pass minimum-access guidelines. Just as states have enacted child-support guidelines in an effort to limit idiosyncrasies and assure the adequacy of awards, minimum-access guidelines would assure that the noncustodial parent has enough time with the children to assure a lasting parent-child bond.

The demilitarization of divorce must also deal with the controversial area of child and spousal abuse. Dealing with abuse remains an important priority for our society and legal system. However, society at large will profit from a better understanding that domestic violence is very much a two-way street. Clearly addressing the important crisis of domestic violence will not be solved until the full scope of the phenomenon is examined and addressed. Further, divorce law must contain significant disincentives, including criminal and civil remedies, for those who falsely accuse a spouse of abuse.

Perhaps no man has fought harder to demilitarize divorce and assure children maximum contact with both parents than Richard Woods, director of Fathers for Equal Rights, Inc., in Des Moines, Iowa. In the early 1980s Woods fought a long, difficult, and ultimately successful custody battle for his then three-year-old daughter, Katie. Woods was the first father in Polk County, Iowa, ever to gain custody of an infant child. Despite his victory Woods's experience taught him the dangers that divorce presented to children and fathers. In 1983 Woods, an experienced state-government professional, formally created his organization. Over the next decade his group was key in the passage of laws in Iowa favoring joint custody and fostering the legal presumption that maximum contact with both parents was in the child's best interest.[74]

Woods's most lasting contribution, however, may be his pioneering of "access counseling." No issue creates more problems among divorced parents than disputes over visitation. As we have described, denial of visitation is a frequent tool used in the post-divorce situation. Often couples spend considerable time and money fighting each other in court to assure or deny visitation. Woods realized that this endless litigation over visitation did little to assure the noncustodial parent access to the child or children in question. "The courts are not the appropriate place to resolve most child custody problems," Woods states. "In fact litigation can be counterproductive."[75] Instead Woods found that counseling noncustodial parents on how to resolve visitation disputes was highly successful. In 1991 Woods received a federal grant to continue his counseling program. Independent examiners reported that 98.8 percent of those counseled by Woods found the sessions somewhat or very helpful in gaining access to their children. Woods and his organization have now counseled close to four thousand parents. He has still found time to raise Katie, who is currently a successful, motivated high school student who maintains a good relationship with her mother.

As men struggle to demilitarize divorce, they must also address the growing phenomenon of unwed fathers who wish to be active parents to their children. The tragedies for men like Rick M. and other unwed fathers could be avoided if we were to ensure that all states give unwed fathers presumed rights as fathers. It is shocking that biological fathers can be denied fatherhood status without any showing that they are unfit parents. State laws depriving them of fatherhood and forcing these men to provide extensive services to mothers prior to the birth of the children even to qualify as fathers serves the interests neither of children nor of society.

As men come together to accomplish the promulgation of a national father policy, it is well to remember that at least as important as changes in the laws and public policy are the ongoing efforts to change our culture's view of men and fatherhood. Laws will be enacted hand in hand with the personal and public defeat of the masculine-mystique teaching that men are productive, emotionless, competitive machines, not generative, caring fathers. As such the masculinist revolution's primary goal is the recovery of the nurturing and teaching father.

10

OUT OF THE HARNESS

Most men live in harness.   —Herb Goldberg[1]

Our dignity as men lies not in exhausting ourselves in work but in
discovering our vocation.   —Sam Keen[2]

In 1989 when the aircraft carrier USS *America* was about to depart on a six-month cruise, Ensign Ronnie Wayne Waldrop was facing a difficult dilemma. Waldrop, then thirty-five, was a "gung ho" career navy man. He was one of only a small group of seamen who would rise to the officer corps despite not having had a college education. In twelve years of service the ensign had compiled a spotless record. After joining the navy in 1976 he was trained as an aviation electrician's mate. Subsequently, while assigned to Miramar Naval Station in San Diego, he received two citations as Sailor of the Month for being his base's top electronics technician. His record of achievement resulted in an appointment to the celebrated Blue Angels demonstration squadron. Later he was transferred to the Norfolk Naval Air Station, where he was named Sailor of the Year. Waldrop was promoted to chief petty officer and was assigned duty aboard the USS *America*.

In 1985 Waldrop's wife, Linda, gave birth to a daughter, Cara

Renee. Unfortunately the infant was born with a severe malformation of the heart. After birth she developed a "failure to thrive" syndrome—gaining an average of only one pound a year. This small growth rate meant that Cara was simply not strong enough to face critically needed heart surgery. Ronnie and Linda had many difficult days attempting to get their child to grow. "I was going crazy," Linda Waldrop remembers. She recalls the frustration of trying to get Cara to eat and keep down her food. "We both would sit and cry. I hated feeding that child. Ronnie was forceful; he'd say, 'Eat, Cara,' and she would."[3]

While Waldrop was on his first cruise aboard the *America*, Cara suffered a severe setback, losing two pounds in two months. After hearing of her condition Waldrop had himself flown back to his home in Virginia from Norway, where the carrier was docked. In 1989, as the *America* was once again set for a lengthy cruise, Ronnie realized that "it was coming down to a choice between career and family." Despite his distinguished career Waldrop "was prepared to choose the family." Reluctantly he told his superior aboard the *America*, Cmdr. Martin W. Reagan, that he was going to quit the navy. Reagan suggested that instead of resigning, Waldrop should apply for a humanitarian transfer to shore duty. Cara's pediatric cardiologist wrote a letter to the navy confirming that it was "very much in Cara's best interest that her father be assigned to shore duty." Waldrop was given his humanitarian transfer—a three-year, shore-duty assignment at the Norfolk base.[4]

Back on shore duty Waldrop received an "automatic" advancement to lieutenant, junior grade, and continued to compile a record of excellence. Soon, however, he realized that something was wrong. Over a period of two years he consistently failed to win the almost automatic promotion to full lieutenant. (Waldrop was one of only five lieutenants, junior grade, among the seventy-five eligible, passed over for promotion in 1991; he was one of six among ninety-four who failed to be promoted in 1992.)

Cmdr. George Walker, Waldrop's superior in his shore assignment, was stunned by the development. "He probably ranks number one among his contemporaries. I'm dumbfounded that he didn't pick it [the promotion] up." Cmdr. Cheryl Fitzgerald, also a superior to Waldrop, recommended him for a Navy Commendation medal in 1992. She was also shocked by the treatment Waldrop received. "He's everything you ever wanted in an officer: totally responsible, family values, on the ball. I'm anguished. I've never seen anyone in my career I'd rather see get a promotion. I don't know what they looked at."[5]

Waldrop thinks that he has solved the mystery of what kept him from his promotion. After the humanitarian transfer was granted to Waldrop, Cmdr. Reagan wrote a fitness report on Waldrop. While the report generally praised Waldrop, it also contained what could be seen as a negative assessment of Waldrop based on his decision to leave his ship and return to his daughter's side. Waldrop believes this negative fitness report was in large part responsible for what was to happen to his career.

After his failure to be promoted Ronnie faces some painful career choices. He can revert to his enlisted rank of chief petty officer, which will mean loss of respect and a pay cut, or he can leave the navy after fifteen years "with nothing to show for it," because qualifying for a pension requires twenty years of service. Linda, angered by the destruction of her husband's career, thinks that the "humanitarian transfer" should be renamed. "It's like having car insurance, and when you have an accident, they cancel your policy," she says.

Reagan, Waldrop's former commander, when reminded of the words in his fitness report—words that may have doomed the officer's navy career—commented that he was "sorry it turned out like this," but noted that Waldrop was aware that "being an officer entails going to sea. . . . If he knew the child's illness existed, why take the commission?"[6]

While Ronnie's career suffered, Cara, with her father nearby, got better. By June 1992 doctors decided she had become strong enough to withstand surgery. A successful open-heart operation was performed, and Cara is recovering.

As was described in Chapter Three, the first casualty of the purportedly "patriarchal" industrial system was fatherhood. For over two centuries societies around the world have been engaged in the structural denial of fatherhood to men and children as men's work was divorced from home. This extraordinary and unprecedented anthropological transformation toward a fatherless society continues to this day. As such, even if the custody and divorce discrimination described in the prior chapter is resolved, fatherlessness will be with us as long as our work lives remain unaltered.

And there is no crueler bind for men than that created by their need to balance the necessity of employment outside the home with their need to be fathers. Recent surveys show that almost three-quarters of men report being "torn" between the demands of their jobs and those of their families.[7] While this dilemma for men is increasing, the masculine mystique's view that "fatherhood is but a frail impulse" has made our society extremely reluctant to acknowledge it. And men are reluctant to admit it to anyone. Denied by society and repressed by many men, the clash between fatherhood and work remains "the invisible dilemma."

There is good reason for men to keep quiet about this central conflict in their lives. Our society, still entranced by the masculine mystique, glorifies the successful professional man, frowns upon the man who picks family over work, and virtually dismisses any man who would choose to be unemployed or a "househusband" in order to be a better father. Men know their place. They know that their principal defining role is to be the breadwinner, that their primary identity is their work, not being caring fathers. They know from early childhood that their lives, far more than those of their female counterparts, will be circumscribed and judged by their success in selling their labor in the job market. They know that in the eyes of society they bear the success burden. To be seen as adequate men, they must be "productive" citizens, able to support themselves and their families. They know that they must compete successfully and gain wealth and power if they are to be validated as men. And they know that failure in this central task, whether in the form of unemployment or low-level jobs (a near-certain fate for millions upon millions of men) will spell disaster both economically and for their masculine identity.

Men like Ronnie Waldrop who are courageous enough to fight the mystique and place family over job often pay a steep price, and conflicts for fathers like Waldrop are becoming routine. Steven Shorkey, who is a bond trader, was told by his superiors to hide his intention to take a formal "paternity leave" for the birth of his child and to call it a "vacation" instead. As Shorkey remembers, "The traditional perception in senior management is that . . . any man who would want to take time to take paternal leave, and take time out from their job to take paternal leave, can't really be serious about their career."[8] The message in corporate America is clear: Men who make their invisible dilemma visible, who do not hide their need to balance work with family, continue to suffer the job consequences.

In fall 1990 Jeff Coulter was fired from a lucrative sales job at Microsoft, one of the hottest computer companies in the world. Coulter says he always worked at least fifty hours a week. But he also felt he needed to balance time at work with time with his young son and daughter. He especially wanted to be home to put them to bed. Coulter recalls, "It was really a perception of time. . . . I got in early and I was typically the first or second one in the office. And not everybody's around to see you when you come in early, but they're all there to see you when you leave, like at 5:00 to 5:30."[9]

Coulter's idea of balancing family with work apparently did not sit well with the managers at Microsoft. His immediate superior, Leanne Boyle, seemed especially antagonistic to the idea. According to Coulter, she suggested to him that survivors at the company are not the married ones. Coulter secretly taped his boss discussing the company ethic, and her comments are revealing:

LEANNE BOYLE (Microsoft): Microsoft hires everybody who's killing themselves. So everybody who's killing themselves is competing against other people killing themselves and it's like the survival of the fittest. . . . You picked a company where it's a disadvantage to be married. It's a disadvantage to have any other priority than work.

COULTER: Clearly.

BOYLE: I mean there isn't one person in this company who's spending time with their family.[10]

After being fired Coulter sued Microsoft. In his suit he made the unique claim that he was discriminated against based on his marital, and implicitly his parental, status. His is the pioneer lawsuit in what will undoubtedly become a growing litigation area—men suing to have the right to work and be fathers at the same time.

Current economic realities will undoubtedly further intensify the frustration of men caught in the invisible dilemma. In an era of economic decline and increased competition for scarce jobs, there is less and less tolerance for men who attempt to balance the demands of family and work. Employment expert and executive recruiter Lester Korn explains the bottom line for men attempting to work less and take more time for family:

> The fact is that American corporations have not geared up to provide it [family time for men], and if you decide that you want to spend time with your children, you are going to lose your place in your peer group and you're going to hurt your career. . . . Most people running corporations are trying to . . . maximize the profits and get a continuous stream of productivity going out of their executives. That's in conflict with taking time off or reducing the hours each week that you put in.[11]

Breaking with the dictates of the masculine mystique, more and more men want to spend more time with their families even though they know that it will cost them in career advancement. A 1990 survey showed a surprising 70 percent of men saying that they would accept a slower career path in exchange for more family time. As one attorney said, "It's your child, and it makes you think of your children first in the morning and last at night, and you sort of build in your work in between."[12]

THE DISPOSABLE MEN

As men fight the uphill battle to confront the masculine mystique, and seek to conserve some aspect of fatherhood from their enclosure into work, they are also becoming ever more aware of what their work lives and the machine-man mentality are doing to their physical and mental health. Each year men are dying and becoming seriously injured in the workplace at rates far higher than women.

Earl Harrell was a foundry worker. A handsome African American, Earl was married and getting by financially. He was a strongly built man capable of the heavy work demanded by his job. But one Friday afternoon in the fall of 1989, Earl became one of the untold millions of men who have become casualties of the workplace:

It was a perfect autumn Friday. As I arrived for the second shift at the foundry . . . about halfway through the shift, my supervisor came over and asked me to spend the rest of the evening operating a drill press in the maintenance department. The machine was very old, made in the early 1900s. I was reluctant to run it because I had no training on it. The supervisor showed me the on-off switch, demonstrated how the machine worked, and told me to start. I was to clean out car parts.

As I began to grind out the hole in the center of the first part, the drill bit fell out of the chuck. I stopped to locate my supervisor to tell him about the problem. He came over and put the drill bit back in. "It will be all right. Just keep running the machine," he said.

I returned to my grinding. The problem repeated itself over and over again as I ground out about a thousand or more parts in the next couple of hours. Every four or five parts, the bit fell out and I had to stop and reinsert it.

It was about seven o'clock when the bit fell only halfway out of the chuck and just hung to the side at an angle. As I had been doing repeatedly, I began to put it back into the chuck. But this time the bit caught my glove. It happened quickly, yet I remember every detail as if it had taken an hour. The glove started to pull me forward to the machine until my chest and face were pressed snug against the motor. My hand was being twisted and twisted. A warm sensation flowed over me. I was squeezed so tightly against the motor that I could hardly breathe.

I was alone in the maintenance room and beginning to panic. The doors were closed. Others were working just outside, not more than twenty yards away, but with all the machinery noise they might as well have been a mile away.

My hand was being twisted continuously, as if something were wringing out a wet towel. Every time the drill bit turned, there was more pain. I tried to hit the stop button but I couldn't reach that far. I was completely helpless.

It was over within five seconds. I heard a sudden loud noise, like lightning when it strikes a tree, and I was instantly released. I stumbled backward about ten feet and fell to the floor. I was aware of my arm feeling strangely lighter. Dreading what I might see, I raised my arm to look at it.

My hand was gone. The machine had twisted it completely off about three inches above the wrist. A feeling of uselessness swept over me. Bleeding heavily and racked with pain, I got up and started to run. Instinctively, I raised my arm and started to head toward the door, moving as quickly as I dared. . . . At times it seemed that my accident, which had undeniably happened, couldn't really have happened. I was 28. What would the rest of my life be like?[13]

Despite his horrific experience Earl was relatively lucky. Surgery was performed that reattached his hand. And after a long and difficult rehabilitation Earl regained about 50 percent of its use. However, annually over 6,000 people in the United States are killed on the job, and 2.3 million suffer serious work-related injuries or diseases. Sixty thousand are permanently disabled. The vast majority of those suffering deaths and disabling injuries are men.[14] Currently, though men represent 55 percent of the workforce, over 93 percent of all those who die in the workplace are male.[15] As noted, each day almost as many men die at work as died during an average day in the battlefields of Vietnam. This situation is unlikely to improve. As of this writing, over 90 percent of all employees in the ten most dangerous professions are men.[16]

The lack of priority that the U.S. government gives the lives of working men can be seen by the fact that over the last twelve years the federal government has consistently cut funds for workplace safety inspections. Overall the Occupational Safety and Health Administration's programs for worker safety have lost over 25 percent of their appropriations in the last decade. Workers, and especially male workers, are apparently viewed as disposable.

While deaths and injuries in the industrial sector continue to mount, another more subtle workplace health problem stalks employees: stress. The dizzy spells for Mike Warren began after twenty-five years as a lawyer with the federal government in Los Angeles. "They started out twice a week," Mike recalls. "Later it was two and three times a day. They were so bad, I had to grab a solid object and hold on for dear life." Mike consulted doctors, but they could find nothing physical to explain his symptoms. Soon Mike began to realize that his spells were job related. They only occurred when he was at work. Mike had only one way of protecting his physical and mental health. He left his job and has had to scrape by on a modest pension. Yet, he says, "since retiring, I have never had another spell."[17]

American workers have become more pressured in recent years, and the strain is making millions sick. While U.S. workers are not yet dropping dead at their desks (as are ten thousand Japanese men each year—victims of the publicized "karoshi," or overwork syndrome), stress complaints now account for 10 percent of all occupational disease claims, up from virtually zero a decade ago. In California, mental-stress claims made under the state workers' compensation system jumped over 500 percent in the 1980s. A 1990 nationwide survey found that half of those questioned said that their lives are more stressful now than five years ago, and the primary reason was greater pressure at work.[18]

The sense that there is more stress in the workplace is not simply subjective. Important changes in the workplace have created greater pressure at work. Though the American economy grew in the 1980s, much of the boom was unrelated to greater productivity and instead came by way of companies merging, reengineering, downsizing, outsourcing, cutting staff, and going overseas. The primary victims were male workers. Some three million middle managers lost their jobs in the 1980s, as did three million well-paid blue-collar workers. These workers found that available jobs in the market were far less desirable than the ones they had left. More than half the jobs created in the past decade pay less than $12,000 per year—below the poverty level for a family of four. One result of this dislocation is that more and more workers are "moonlighting" (working more than one job). Currently over seven million Americans have two or more jobs. Men forced to work a full-time job plus a second part-time or full-time job outnumber women over two to one.[19]

This greater workload has changed home lives as well as work lives. Less and less time is available for leisure, family, and stress reduction. Since 1973, according to a Louis Harris poll, the amount of leisure time available to the average American has shrunk from twenty-six hours to seventeen hours per week, while the time spent working, commuting, and doing chores has increased 20 percent.[20]

Many of America's older male workers, men like Mike, simply cannot stand the pace and are forced to leave the workplace altogether. Researchers Jean M. Mitchell and Kathryn H. Anderson document the increasing mental-health damage that the workplace is delivering to older male workers. In the 1960s they say more than 90 percent of men aged fifty-five to sixty-four were working. Today fewer than 75 percent hold jobs. The reason, according to the researchers, is poor mental health caused primarily by job-related stress. Mitchell, an economist at Florida State University, says that the more stress symptoms workers show, "the more likely they are to withdraw from the labor force at an early age."[21]

For many men the cost of stress and of an increased workload is greater than just the loss of jobs. A 1990 study of working men in New York City strongly suggests that workplace pressure is responsible for the high percentage of heart disease found in working-age men, a rate over twice that found in women. The researchers found that workers in high-strain jobs are three times more likely than their low-strain counterparts to suffer from high blood pressure. They were also significantly more likely to have enlarged hearts, a predictor for heart disease.[22] Subsequent research has shown that middle-aged men are especially vulnerable to higher blood pressure due to job stress.[23]

Many of the hundreds of thousands of men who die each year from heart disease, hypertension, alcoholism, peptic ulcers, and other diseases are dying prematurely as a direct result of the pressure of being in the harness. And though women's presence in the workplace is increasing, as are their rates of stress-related disease, men continue to represent the vast majority of those routinely destroying their health through overwork. Francis Baumli, editor of an admirable anthology on men's issues, *Men Freeing Men*, notes the tragedy of the "machine man" life of male workers: "Many men who are defined as successful by society resemble machines . . . that function impressively for a while. But like powerful engines, racing at high speed without oil, they will soon burn out."[24]

Beyond the extraordinary array of death, injury, stress, and disease that men face in the workplace, there are other more hidden costs. Some studies show that as many as 80 percent of male workers in our society feel that their work is both meaningless and oppressive. Polls taken in the 1970s and 1980s show that the single job characteristic that males want most is "important and meaningful work." Respondents felt that this characteristic was over twice as important to them as any other job factor, including "high income," "chance of advancement," or "no danger of being fired."[25] The desire of men for more meaningful work is not surprising. Despite the general view that men as a class have "power" in our society, the power-man myth is an illusion. Most jobs in corporations or the factory are highly routinized, involving little control or power, but rather a great deal of placating a superior or boss.

A life in the harness of meaningless work creates a final bind— a painful reality that psychologist Herb Goldberg calls the growth bind.[26] Men have the need to grow intellectually and spiritually. As they grow older, they search for meaning and for new ways of fulfilling their potential. Yet at the same time they are locked into routinized, demeaning work. As primary family providers they are trapped, responsible for mortgage or rent, college tuition, support of their children, and numerous other basic family expenses. Pursuit of goals outside of work is nearly impossible. Psychologist Aaron Kipnis writes,

> Most men cannot even entertain the fantasy of pursuing their . . . dreams and are locked into the binding necessity of providing the daily survival for themselves and their families. . . . Additionally, many men have forgotten how to play in their leisure time. . . . Instead we often fill our off-work hours with . . . pursuits designed to deaden the pain of work. A dreary numbness permeates the lives of many men.[27]

Either path a man chooses in order to escape the growth bind brings unacceptable losses. If he allows himself to grow by concentrating on personal or spiritual goals rather than bringing in a good salary, he is often viewed by his family and friends as selfish, irresponsible, and unmanly. If his growth search should lead to a return to college, or the need to get away to a spiritual retreat or the wilderness, it inevitably means reduced employment and income or even unemployment. Thus to go on such a personal-growth journey means that a man must risk losing economic security, his marriage, the respect of his children and community, even the mental health he is searching for. If, on the other hand, he denies his needs for growth and stays with an exhausting and stultifying job, he feels stagnant and trapped. He becomes developmentally arrested and is more susceptible to stress, disease, and alcohol or drug abuse as he attempts to repress the reality of his life. Adding insult to injury, his boring, routinized life often becomes an object of ridicule to his children and spouse. Goldberg summarizes,

> The male in our culture is at a growth impasse. He won't move—not because he is protecting his cherished central place in the sun, but because he *can't* move. He is a cardboard Goliath precariously balanced and on the verge of toppling over if he is pushed even ever so slightly out of his well worn path. The male is rigidly caught in his masculine pose and, in many subtle and direct ways, he is severely punished when he steps out of it. . . . [He only feels] comfortable when he is functioning well in harness, and not when he lives for joy and for personal growth.[28] (Emphasis in original.)

THE LOSING CLASS

As men struggle with the perils, stress, and meaninglessness of a life in harness, and with the invisible dilemma of trying to be fathers and workers at the same time, they share one more overriding work-related bind. No matter how many problems are related to their work, they know that there is a fate far worse, one that they fear far more than loss of family time, stress, or even serious disease: unemployment.

Loss of work is among the worst traumas a man currently has to face. Under the mandates of the masculine mystique it means loss of manhood and identity. The mystique teaches that it is natural for a man to compete for work, and to work his entire life to support his family. This accepted norm for men leaves them totally unprepared for unemployment. Psychologically it shakes them to the core of their identity and being. Economically it means the inability to maintain a family and home, and a life spent in a desperate search for mere subsistence.

In the recent recession and even in the current so-called jobless recovery, millions of Americans have lost their jobs. A total of 15.3 million workers lost jobs from January 1987 to January 1992. Of these workers 5.6 million had been with their employers at least three years—close to two-thirds of these laid-off workers were men. By August 1992 less than half of these long-term workers had found full-time reemployment. Of those able to find full-time work, nearly one-third took pay cuts of 20 percent or more.[29] Moreover, from 1989 to 1994 there was an increase of more than 1.1 million prime-age male workers to the ranks of the permanently unemployed. These men, no longer on the unemployment rolls, are not even counted in assessing the national unemployment rate.[30]

The recent job losses are part of a continuing two-decade trend of dramatic increases in overall male unemployment. "There's been a huge decline in work for prime-age men," notes Lawrence F. Katz, a labor economist at Harvard. In the 1970s almost 80 percent of men from 22 to 58 worked full-time, year-round. In the 1980s this had dropped to 70 percent.[31] By 1991 the number of men working full-time, year-round (fifty to fifty-two weeks) was declining by 1.2 million each year, while the number of women working full-time was increasing by 800,000. This period also witnessed a dramatic drop in real wages for the average working man—over 20 percent for men in the unskilled labor market.[32]

Increased male joblessness has had a disproportionate impact on lower- and middle-income wage workers and on older workers. "Traditional" American industries, such as steel production, automobile manufacturing, and mining have been especially hard hit, often suffering annual unemployment at three to four times the unemployment rate of nonmanufacturing industries. Altogether there were close to 20 percent fewer workers employed in manufacturing in 1992 than there were in 1979, and over 50 percent fewer in other blue-collar areas, such as mining. By contrast there was an over 40 percent increase in service jobs over the same period.[33]

The millions of men laid off from these manufacturing jobs often have nowhere to turn. Older workers have a more difficult time being retrained and becoming candidates for scarce, well-paying service-industry or high-technology jobs. They are most often the losers in the fast-paced world of the modern postindustrial economy.

Fred Kruck is one of the new displaced workers. For years he was "the keeper"—the top worker in a blast furnace. Each working day he could be heard hollering orders to dozens of other workers at the most dangerous furnace in the steel mill. His huge frame was eminently visible silhouetted against the huge furnace as he continuously deployed equipment the size of buildings. In March 1991, at age fifty, after nineteen years on the job, Fred was laid off along with two thousand other workers as USX Corporation closed most of its massive Fairless Works steel mills, just north of Philadelphia.

Soon Fred had lost not just his job but also his house. It was seized as a result of unpaid taxes. The family was next to go. Fred and his wife, Gabriela, just couldn't stop arguing, especially about money. Fred's unemployment check and Gabriela's salary as a part-time caterer were just not enough. "I guess the next step is welfare," Gabriela predicted. The tension became too much. Fred, jobless for a year, drove to Florida alone, hauling his beach trailer. No longer able to face his family, he was hoping to find work as a maintenance man. Gabriela took an apartment in Philadelphia. Fred reflects sadly on what unemployment has done to his family. "In the last year," he states, "we have gone straight backwards as a family. Not stepping. Flying."[34]

Fred had tried to stop his personal and familial free fall. A few months after being let go he enrolled in truck-driving school, courtesy of a federal program to train laid-off workers in new skills. But he panicked in the first week of training when an instructor called on him to read from a text and it became apparent to the class that Fred, though fifty, could scarcely read or write. After that embarrassment Fred never went back to the class.

Fred's job loss not only cost him his home and his spouse, it has created a shattering personal identity crisis. He so identified himself with his work that he now suffers from a near-obsessive thought. He knows it is preposterous. He knows that the steelworks are closed for good. And yet he cannot bring himself to accept that reality. "The thing I can't get out of my mind," he said, "is I'm still hoping they call me back. That's what I know how to do. I'm a steelworker. I would work anywhere for U.S. Steel. I would even go to the moon. I am worse than unemployed. I am a displaced person."[35]

There is an irony in Fred's obsession with returning to the mills. As described earlier, the very workplaces that men yearn to return to are often deadly. Fred's former work environment, the Fairless Works, was a classic example of the toxic workplace. In 1989 the Occupational Safety and Health Administration (OSHA) fined USX Corporation $6.1 million for violations at the Fairless Works, calling it "one of the most dangerous workplaces in the nation." (The fine was cut to $3.2 million in 1990.)[36]

One social-service worker describes working with men like Fred: "It's so hard to see forty- to fifty-year-old men sit there with tears in their eyes. We're talking about people who thought of themselves as the American Dream, and it's falling apart before their eyes. Their unemployment doesn't pay their bills, but it's too much to qualify them for public assistance. More and more are going to lose their houses. They have nowhere to turn."[37]

Reporter Dale Russakoff, who has chronicled the plight of the now unemployed industrial worker, notes how these men are discarded as easily as the machines that have so dominated their lives: "[They] must cope not only with a grinding national recession but also a post-industrial society that often treats laid-off industrial workers as if they were factory rejects. They are made to the wrong specifications. They do not fit. Like steel that came out wrong at the mill, there is not much of a market for them."[38]

CORPORATE FAILURES

The surge of unemployment over the last decade has hit not only blue-collar workers but also America's white-collar male workers. Forty percent of the unemployed in the recent recession were white collar, up from 22 percent in the late 1980s. The vast majority of these newly unemployed are white men in their forties and fifties who have spent many years with a corporation. As firms continue to reorganize themselves, more and more middle managers are being laid off and fewer job openings become available. More than 1.5 million midlevel management jobs were eliminated in the 1980s. (In the parlance of the white-collar unemployed, these men were "shot," "riffed," "whacked," or "excessed.") In former times these white-collar achievers were the epitome of the American "work and spend" lifestyle. Expensive homes, the best cars, and top schools for the kids were the norm. Suddenly the treadmill has stopped, and there's simply no place for these white-collar jobless to go.

Unemployment for well-to-do male management workers can be every bit as difficult as for blue-collar workers. "A lot of men here are going through a sort of death," says the pastor of a Bryn Mawr Protestant church that has witnessed a recent flood of white-collar layoffs. "They thought they were guaranteed success because they went to the right schools, married the right women, joined the right companies and clubs. When it all goes wrong, they can't cope."[39]

John Parker was a typical victim of the massive corporate cutbacks in white-collar workers. He had worked for fourteen years at IBM. His work had allowed him and his family to live the good life. Good schools for the kids, new cars, a six-bedroom colonial in an affluent suburb of Philadelphia. After IBM fired him as part of a company reorganization, Parker did not know how to proceed with his life. For a time he stayed indoors, ashamed that his neighbors would see him home during business hours. His voluntary seclusion ended one day when workers paving the road outside his home created a loud crash that had him rushing outdoors to see what had happened. He looked up to see two other neighborhood men who had come out of their homes curious about the explosion. "We gawked at each other," Parker remembers, "as if to say, 'so it's two in the afternoon and you aren't in the office either!' "[40]

After a time John turned his guest bedroom into an office and turned out a flood of resumes and cover letters in a frantic search for work. He also went to a job fair for "displaced computer professionals," only to find "the line going out the door. Everybody was my age, wearing the same clothes as me and carrying the same laser-printed resume." His initial job search landed Parker a job as a sales representative for a phone company at a far lower wage than IBM had provided him; even at that the company laid him off a few months later as part of a cost-cutting program.

Predictably John's unemployment changed his relationship to his family. His wife notes that unemployment erodes children's respect for fathers. During one of the increasingly frequent discussions about family finances, Parker's son turned, exasperated, toward his father and remarked, "You don't work, Dad. It's not *your* money."[41]

Parker did finally find employment with a small computer company. While happy to be back at work, Parker paradoxically misses his time with his family: "Watching my son play sports or my daughter dance ballet—all those things will fall out of my life again because I'm working such long hours."[42]

Other formerly successful men facing unemployment have not coped as well as Parker. George Wilkinson, forty-seven, lost his job as the manager of a tool-manufacturing company. Wilkinson knew that a man is supposed to fight for success, hold down a steady job, and bring home the bacon. "Men leave in the morning and come back at night with a paycheck in their hand." Wilkinson knew that work was how he gained status at home and that gainful employment was the rationale for a man's life. "Either you work every day in a normal nine-to-five job with a couple of weeks' vacation, or you're dead! There's no in-between. . . . Working is breathing. . . . When you stop, you die." A year after speaking those words Wilkinson, still unemployed, killed himself with a shotgun.[43]

THE WORK TRAP

The millions of men who are currently losing their jobs in the mid-management and industrial sector have been caught in a difficult dilemma born of the masculine mystique. From their earliest years they have been enculturated to see their identity as synonymous with being a worker, being a provider, and being independent. But the economy has passed them by. Employment was the rock on which their families and identities were built, but that rock has now disintegrated, and the men blame themselves.

Unemployment then leads to shame. Clinical psychologist Thomas J. Cottle, who has spent years working with the unemployed, describes these men who can no longer fulfill their stereotyped gender role: "Their masculinity and strength sapped, they [the unemployed men] appeared shameful, childlike as if they deserved to be the invisible, reclusive people they had in fact become. Covering their faces, their tracks, their own life stories, they acted out the parts of men ashamed of themselves and the utter mess they insisted they had made of their lives."[44]

One unemployed man joked that shame and guilt were his middle names. Like most men he blamed himself for his unemployment: "I'm the captain of the ship, right? I drown, it's my fault. That woman and those two kids upstairs . . . they drown, that's also my fault."[45]

Researchers Sara S. McLanahan and Jennifer L. Glass believe that a primary factor in the current men's mental-health crisis is the conflict created in men by unemployment. They note that there has been a "sharp decline in the psychological well-being of men" over the last two decades. And they believe that increasing joblessness is a major culprit: "The breadwinner role is viewed as a principle component of male identity. Loss of, or poor performance in, the employment role means loss of identification and self-esteem." They also point out that men use work as a buffer against marital or parental stress. The researchers conclude that the unemployed man is doubly vulnerable: when he loses employment he loses the major source of his identity and self-esteem, and he is also deprived of a vital buffer against other threats to his psychological well-being.[46]

The stress of unemployment also significantly increases the incidence of several deadly diseases in men. Numerous studies have shown that unemployed men are more likely to die of cardiovascular disease and cirrhosis of the liver than men who are working.[47] A 1992 report prepared by the Economic Policy Institute found that increased unemployment resulted in a shocking "trickle-down" increase in disease, violence, and crime. According to the report just a one-percentage-point increase in unemployment led to the following increases:

- Deaths due to heart disease: 5.6 percent
- Deaths due to stroke: 3.1 percent
- Homicides: 6.7 percent
- Violent crimes: 3.4 percent
- Property crimes: 2.4 percent

For a major metropolitan area this means that the 2 percent increase in unemployment from mid-1990 to mid-1992 resulted in:[48]

- Deaths due to heart disease: 35,307
- Deaths due to stroke: 2,771
- Homicides: 1,459
- Violent crimes (including burglary, aggravated assault, and murder): 62,607
- Property crimes (including robbery, larceny, and motor vehicle theft): 223,500

There is little hope that the future will bring any relief from the work-trap syndrome for men. The near-inevitable further erosion of employment will lead to significant increased physical, social, and psychic destruction for tens of millions of men. To understand how and why the future for men is so grim requires consideration of the unique set of economic and social forces that are currently shaping the world economy.

Chapter Three described how the process of enclosure—the forcing of millions of people off their traditional lands in order to make way for the production of export crops or large industrial development projects—had become global. As nations throughout the Third World, often using loans from the International Monetary Fund or the World Bank, continue to enclose land for development, more and more economic refugees flood into the cities and become a cheap and exploitable labor force for multinational corporations. As a result the United States and other industrialized countries have witnessed significant "job flight" over the last several years. Corporations have closed down factories and plants in the United States and moved them to other countries where the labor is far cheaper and where environmental and workplace health and safety standards are weak or nonexistent.

Manufacturing jobs, the employment staple of America's men, have been a major casualty of job flight. America's five hundred largest industrial companies failed to create a single net new job between 1975 and 1990. During that time period, their share of the civilian labor force dropped from 17 percent to less than 10 percent.[49] Meanwhile, American corporations have been employing a growing army of foreign workers. By 1990, for example, Whirlpool had cut its American workforce by 10 percent and shifted much of its production to Mexico. Now the company employs 43,500 people in forty-five countries—most of them non-Americans. Or consider the California-based company Seagate Technology, one of the world's leaders in hard-disk drive production. In 1990, the company employed 40,000 people, 27,000 of whom worked in Southeast Asia. By the early 1990s, more than 20 percent of the total output of American-owned firms was being produced by foreign workers outside the United States—and aided by the implementation of international trade agreements such as NAFTA and GATT. The percentage continues to rapidly increase with each passing year.[50]

The vanishing male worker is not only a casualty of job flight but also a victim of new technology. The modern age has been an era of unparalleled technological innovation. New technologies have quickened the pace of production and provided new employment opportunities, while at the same time making various forms of human labor all but obsolete. This was the case in the early years of the twentieth century, when automation replaced the agricultural worker in the United States. Millions of farmers and field workers flooded into the new industrial cities, where they were absorbed by the manufacturing industries looking for workers.

Mass automation of the manufacturing sector began in the 1950s. Along with the more recent overseas exodus of American companies searching for cheaper labor, automation forced a second major employment dislocation—this time of blue-collar workers. As we have seen, over the last dozen years unemployment in this area has skyrocketed. This time the safety net was smaller. While service-industry jobs were growing in number and able to absorb some of the new unemployed, albeit at lower wages, most older male workers were not seen as attractive candidates for these jobs. In fact women garnered over 60 percent of the new jobs created in the 1980s.

Things are only getting worse. Technology never stands still. Now the service-sector jobs are beginning to disappear due to advances in automation. In 1992 the U.S. Postal Service announced its plans to cut forty-seven thousand workers by 1995 as a result of new high-technology innovations. The postmaster general predicted that even more jobs would become expendable as computers were designed to sort mail by zip code. Other government and private service industries have announced similar cuts.[51]

The "data superhighway" and the rest of the high-technology electronic culture of the twenty-first century being planned by government and private corporations will increasingly replace service jobs as millions of people electronically carry on their day-to-day lives—from working and shopping to medical checkups—over the computer infrastructure. Automated tellers, self-service gasoline pumps, automated telephone operators, and computerized shopping are merely the first wave of the new displacement technologies. Voice and signature recognition, robotics, and artificial intelligence may soon provide substitutes for millions of jobs.

In the 1980s Nobel Laureate Wassily Leontief and his colleagues at the Institute for Economic Analysis concluded that the demand for service and clerical workers as well as semiskilled and unskilled workers will rapidly diminish in the wake of the new technological innovations. Leontief predicted that "the role of humans as the most important factor of production is bound to diminish in the same way that the role of horses in agricultural productions was first diminished then eliminated by the introduction of tractors."[52]

If these predictions are correct, then the millions of men currently being displaced in manufacturing have a dim future and are merely the forerunners of untold numbers of American workers in the service and clerical areas who will be replaced in the coming decades. And unlike the past, no mass-employment sectors are emerging to absorb these new labor refugees. According to Dr. Dennis Chamot of the AFL-CIO, "We used to assume that advances in technology increased productivity and growth, would mean more jobs. This is no longer the case."[53]

The only increases in employment opportunities expected in the new postindustrial high-technology era are among the professional class, particularly scientists, engineers, and highly trained computer specialists. While "knowledge" workers will be needed to design, build, program, and supervise the intelligent machines of these new high-technology industries, their numbers will be small in comparison to the millions of blue-collar and service workers who may be permanently displaced by the technological onslaught of the coming decades. Male workers, especially those in the blue-collar field, are not traditionally favored in many of the new jobs. Currently close to 60 percent of personnel and business managers in the new economy are women, as are over 70 percent of all elementary and high school teachers.[54]

OUT OF THE HARNESS

The potential impacts of the new unemployment dislocation become even more tragic when we remember the profiles of many of America's workers, men like Fred Kruck. While current Secretary of Labor Robert Reich speaks of the need to retrain workers for the more sophisticated skills of the high-technology age, it is well to remember Fred's embarrassment at the public discovery that though he was a successful worker in the steel industry, he was functionally illiterate. Studies show that Fred is not an exception. One out of every three adults in the United States today is marginally, functionally, or completely illiterate. Currently 25 million Americans are either unable to read or have less than an eighth-grade reading level. An additional 35 million adults read at less than a ninth-grade level.[55] It is difficult to see how government-assisted retraining programs will retrain the newly unemployed to be scientists, engineers, computer specialists, teachers, or high-level managers. And even in the unlikely event that reeducation and retraining are possible, the openings for high-tech jobs in the automated economy of the twenty-first century will never be enough to absorb even a fraction of the legions of displaced workers.

BREAKING FREE

Work remains at the center of the hidden crisis for men and the propagation of the masculine mystique. Whether the issue is fatherhood, health, personal growth, violence, or poverty, men's relationship to work is key. Though custody reform is important for the recovery of fatherhood, no fatherhood policy will be effective until men restructure their work lives so that they can have more time with their children. No health initiative for men will be successful until men deal with the accidents and stress-related diseases and disorders caused by their work and the self-destruction, violence, and illness spawned by unemployment. Men will never break free from the machine-, competition-, profit-, and power-man mandates until they have begun to free themselves from the enclosure of work, an enclosure that itself was the principal agent in fostering the masculine mystique.

The central challenge for the men's movement must be to lighten the work burden on men while at the same time addressing the problems of unemployment and lack of meaningful work. These urgent issues for men can be addressed, in part, by a single important strategy; a remedy advocated by men for decades, but one that is in urgent need of revitalization.

As was described in Chapter Six, starting in the nineteenth century, workers fought to reduce the workweek. Over several decades the workweek was shortened from over sixty hours to forty by the mid-1920s. Unfortunately since the 1920s the shorter-workweek movement has been all but moribund. The last serious attempt to reduce hours arose during the Kennedy administration, when a thirty-five-hour workweek was proposed but defeated.

It is time for men once again to take up the struggle against the enclosure of work and to advocate actively for a thirty-hour workweek. Reducing work hours must become the centerpiece in any strategy to undo the masculine mystique and reverse the trend toward a fatherlessness that is endemic to every industrialized country. The thirty-hour workweek would alleviate unemployment while at the same time giving men time for personal growth, family, and community and other meaningful volunteer activities. To be effective, proposals for the shorter workweek must also include provisions, such as tax incentives for employers and other devices, that would help workers maintain existing incomes.

The call for shorter hours to revive fatherhood is an increasingly urgent one. It is important to recall that in 1973 the centuries-long trend toward shorter work hours began to reverse. Since that time America's workers, and especially America's men, began working ever-longer hours. According to one recent poll, since 1973 the average American weekly workload went from 40.6 to 48.8 hours. This increase, in concert with the growing number of women joining the workforce, continues to devastate both fatherhood and motherhood. The current increase in work and decrease in leisure have created an unprecedented crisis for our children. The "latchkey" kid has become ever more evident in America as more than 7 million children are home alone during parts of the day. Surveys indicate that at any given time up to one-third of America's children are caring for themselves. Psychologists report a growing epidemic of the "abandonment syndrome" in children as they become traumatized by the absence of parental presence. The parenting crisis involves not only absence but also lack of real time with kids. Over the last three decades the amount of time parents spend with children has declined by 10 hours a week for white families and 12 hours for African Americans.[56]

Because it allows men to have the time to be parents, the thirty-hour workweek would also have a significant impact on male psychology and the masculine mystique. With an increase in free time men could begin the process of separating masculine identity from work and instead associate masculinity with fatherhood and with shared work on the local and community level. The reduced workweek could permit this and future generations of men to partially extricate themselves from the "growth bind" described earlier in this chapter. This bind ensures that men become intellectually and emotionally arrested when they enter the workforce, since the long hours spent working and commuting allow them little time for reeducation or cultural or community activities. Yet they cannot leave their jobs due to the necessity of their role as breadwinner.

Most directly a thirty-hour week would drastically cut unemployment and alleviate the extraordinary economic, social, and emotional impacts of joblessness. In combination with a significant cut in overtime the thirty-hour workweek would allow tens of millions of men and women to recover jobs but still have time for family and self. In a time when high deficits reduce the likelihood of significant government-sponsored job creation, the thirty-hour week emerges as one of the few options for addressing the growing unemployment problem in the United States and Europe.

Finally, the thirty-hour week could have an enormous impact on the consumer culture. By stressing free time rather than more consumer items as the main goal in people's lives, a blow will be struck against the invidious work-and-spend cycle that has imprisoned so many men in the work harness. The deemphasis on consumption and the greater amount of time fathers and mothers will have with children could also help restore parents as the central authorities in their children's lives, rather than the commodity advertiser.

The fate of the thirty-hour-workweek proposal depends on influencing three major social institutions: labor, government, and business. Over the last decades none of the three monoliths has shown any interest in reducing work hours. But there are important signs of change. For one, labor once again appears to be on the verge of embracing shorter hours as a key demand. In October 1993 during an AFL-CIO convention the shorter-work-hours concept garnered more attention and support than it had for years. Several prominent labor leaders noted that the question of reduced work hours was climbing higher and higher on labor's agenda as the alleged economic recovery unfolded as a jobless recovery. Thomas R. Donahue, secretary-treasurer of the AFL-CIO, stated that "there is no question that the long-term salvation of work lies in reducing hours."[57]

Internationally labor has been both aggressive and somewhat successful in getting shorter work hours. In Germany about 4 million workers in the metalworking industry won a thirty-six-hour week as of April 1993. The Metal Workers Union estimates that without the shorter hours an additional 800,000 to 3 million workers would be unemployed in Germany.[58]

As labor begins to embrace the shorter workweek, governments around the world are also looking at the proposal. In March 1994 the world's leading industrial nations, the so-called Group of Seven (G-7), had their first-ever meeting on job creation. The G-7 has learned that even with the recent "recovery," the number of high-wage jobs is continuing to decrease. "We used to think that jobs and the economy were the same thing," says U.S. Labor Secretary Robert Reich, "but we have learned in recent years that the paper economy and the people's economy are not always the same thing."[59]

Both the French and the Japanese have accepted shorter workweeks as a basic aspect of their long-term economic plans. However, the U.S. government remains cool to the idea, as it has been since the New Deal. This despite the fact that studies show that a reduced-hour week increases productivity and saves the government hundreds of millions annually in decreased unemployment payments.

However, there is a glimmer of hope that the government's stance may be changing. In February 1993 a breakthrough in work reduction and federal policy on parenting was achieved. After eight years of delay, and despite the active opposition of the business lobby and several vetoes by the Bush administration, the Family Leave Bill cleared the House and Senate and was signed into law by President Clinton. The fifty-seven-page measure is straightforward in intent. "It is important for the development of children and the family unit that fathers and mothers be able to participate in early childbearing and the care of family members who have serious health conditions."[60] The bill provides that workers can take up to twelve weeks of unpaid leave during any twelve-month period for the birth of a child or an adoption; the need to care for a child, a spouse, or a parent with a serious health condition; or their own serious health condition that makes them unable to perform their job. Employers are required to give employees who take advantage of the family leave their old job or an equivalent position when they return to work.[61]

There are exemptions. The bill only covers companies with fifty workers or more. It also applies only to workers who have been employed for at least one year and for at least 1,250 hours. It also allows companies to deny benefits to salaried employees within the highest-paid 10 percent of their workforce, if letting such workers take leave would create "substantial injury" to the business operation. Altogether about 95 percent of employers and about half of all workers are exempted.[62]

The large number of Americans not covered by the bill is only one of its shortfalls. In that the law provides only unpaid leave, many families cannot afford to partake of it. And since fathers are the primary breadwinners in most two-parent families, it is likely that they will be the ones working while mothers will be utilizing the leave provisions. Additionally the bill's requirements that an employer return a worker to an "equivalent" job are fuzzy at best. They will do little to comfort men who feel that taking the leave will put them on the "daddy track" of demotion.

Whatever its failings, the Family Leave Bill is an important precedent in pushing through legislation that establishes the value of family over that of work. Some U.S. politicians are looking to extend this precedent to include the shorter-workweek option. In 1994 Congressman Lucien E. Blackwell introduced a bill that would mandate a thirty-hour week; though the bill did not pass, it did garner some support.[63]

The most recalcitrant social force on shorter work hours is the American business community. While there are some defectors, U.S. business is generally opposed to any proposal that would grant more paid time off to U.S. workers. In 1989 shorter-work-hours advocate William McGaughey did a mailing to more than three hundred corporate CEOs and other business leaders inviting them to attend a meeting to discuss the formation of a business committee that would develop proposals to reduce work hours. There was not a single favorable response. One Fortune 500 CEO commented in typical masculine-mystique form, "My view of the world, our country and our country's needs is diametrically opposite of yours. I cannot imagine a shorter workweek. I can imagine a longer workweek both in school and at work if America is to be competitive in the first half of the next century."[64]

Some companies are changing. In 1993 in Germany, Volkswagen, the continent's biggest automaker, became the first major multinational company to adopt a thirty-hour week. Volkswagen made the move to avoid laying off more than thirty-one thousand workers. The workers accepted a 20 percent pay cut, but tax breaks and bonuses are expected to reduce the impact of the cut. Hewlett-Packard's plant in Grenoble, France, has opted for a four-day workweek as part of a new program to keep the factory running twenty-four hours a day. Night-shift workers are offered a twenty-six-hour-fifty-minute workweek, while morning and evening workers have a thirty-four-hour workweek. Under the new flexible-hour arrangement production has tripled at the plant. Digital Computers has initiated a different approach. The company has given its workers an option of a four-day workweek with a 7 percent loss in their wages. Hundreds of workers chose the shorter workweek. A spokesperson for Digital commented, "A larger number of people . . . want to divide their lives differently and have more leisure time."[65]

There is also a growing group of economists and thinkers who are embracing the shorter-workweek concept. Former presidential candidate Senator Eugene McCarthy, Harvard economist Juliet Schor, and social activist Jeremy Rifkin have recently published influential books advocating reducing work hours. Feminist and author Betty Friedan has also become a strong advocate for a shorter workweek. In December 1994, Friedan wrote President Clinton calling for congressional hearings on the issue. In the letter she cites "disturbing data that reveal a drastic decline in income among white, college-educated, middle-management men, in addition to previously affected blue-collar and minority workers." She continues, "A shorter workweek and flexible job structures . . . would meet the needs of both women and men in the childbearing and childrearing years. Such flexibility would also help young and old who need to combine education and training with jobs, throughout the life cycle."[66]

Few men or women have advocated the reduction of human labor more eloquently than Benjamin K. Hunnicutt. Hunnicutt, a professor at the University of Iowa, has written numerous influential articles and books calling for a shorter workweek. He is also coeditor of the newsletter of the International Society for the Reduction of Human Labor. His ideas have been influential in the United States and around the world. Hunnicutt, whose awareness of the men's movement came through one of his sons, has often spoken of the influence of modern stereotypes of gender on the shorter-hours debate. He notes that "leisure has been genderized in our society. Too often men are associated with work out of the home, and women with the forced leisure found in staying in the home." He believes that a vital task for the future is that men "break the mental and physical enclosure of the workplace and become active advocates for the reduction of work hours." According to Hunnicutt, men need to question whether progress for them "means anything if there is no time for family, care-giving, personal growth, and leisure." He notes that men constantly speak of the importance of free markets, and competitiveness for political democracy, but Hunnicutt asks whether "liberty means anything if the future means nothing but increasing and meaningless work for men, who surely can take little comfort if their children have nothing to look forward to but increased work time or unemployment." Finally Hunnicutt quotes a telling remark by William Green, former president of the AFL: "Free time will come. The only choice is unemployment or leisure." Says Hunnicutt, men need to internalize the economic realities of our time, that job flight, technology, and reengineering of corporations have made many of their jobs obsolete. Either they will face the psychological and economic disaster of unemployment or work actively for a new culture of shorter work hours, leisure, and family and community commitments.[67]

While a thirty-hour week should be the major goal of a masculinist work policy, there are several less ambitious steps toward that goal that men can take. Men collectively need to work inside corporations, small businesses, and local and state governments to establish policies allowing greater freedom to take family leave and spend time with their families. These include:

- Developing family-leave policies geared to the unique fears and concerns of male employees
- Making available flextime arrangements
- Encouraging job sharing
- Offering sick-child care
- Offering time off to attend teacher conferences
- Making home-based employment possible for those employees whose jobs lend themselves to such arrangements

Men must also vigorously support other men who are pioneering these policies. For, as we witnessed earlier in this chapter, fathers who pick family over work have often paid the price in loss of job or career advancement. Ultimately men must make employers understand that many of today's men have a set of very different concerns than prior generations, ones far more geared to fatherhood and civic involvement.

A profather policy in the United States should also help families with children stay together. Most importantly tax policies need to be altered to help families who are raising children. Since men are still the majority of primary breadwinners in two-parent homes, any reduction of their financial burden could lead to fewer hours at work and more time with the family. Currently America is the only country among the eighteen most prosperous industrialized democracies that does not have a family allowance or some other government subsidy per child. This should change.

A masculinist work policy must also advocate the rejection of international trade agreements such as the North American Free Trade Agreement (NAFTA) and the General Agreement on Tariffs and Trade (GATT). In the name of global competition these agreements cost untold thousands of American jobs. They also further undercut worker well-being and safety, as well as environmental protection, as the United States is forced to compete with countries that have lower wages and fewer safety and environmental regulations. They also undermine local crafts, businesses, and agriculture, which simply cannot compete with the mass production capability of global corporations. Of equal importance, these agreements encourage so-called developing countries to accelerate the process of enclosure (described in Chapter Three), by which people are removed from their traditional lands, which are then used by transnational corporations for export crops or development projects. The former farmers and craftspeople then become economic refugees to crowded urban areas where they are easily exploitable by corporate employers and often work under poor conditions and low wages.

Additionally men need to come together to massively increase the commitment of federal and local agencies toward worker safety. The statistics are clear: Men are the ones primarily at risk from death and injury in the workplace. They remain the vast majority of workers in America's most dangerous professions. They should be recognized and protected.

Finally, as the government and private sector look to find solutions to the structural unemployment that has overtaken so many of America's male workers, many men are realizing that the answer lies not only in reducing work hours and having more jobs (and more meaningful jobs) but also in defeating a mystique that has for so long made them synonymous with work. As we have seen, joblessness creates extreme gender-role conflict among men, leading to violence, increased physical and mental-health problems, and suicide. As noted by one research team, "unemployed men are particularly vulnerable to threats to their masculinity because work is so integral to a man's identity."[68] Those working in the men's movement must create alternative modes of identity for men so that they are not so vulnerable to the physical and psychological damage caused by the dislocation of work. They must be helped to have a meaning, and a masculinity, that is not inexorably tied to a life in the harness.

11

OUR BODIES, OURSELVES

Men's role—performing away from the home—is enough to lead either sex to drugs, suicide, and accidents. —Warren Farrell[1]

Society's expectations regarding the stereotypical male sex role exact costs on men's ability to seek and obtain health education, counseling and preventive and curative health care. —David Forrester, R.N.[2]

For all of us the age of twenty-five should be a time of hope and promise. Most men and women in our society have completed their education and are on the threshold of their adult lives. But for many men this time is often filled with unprecedented anxiety. Even college-educated men, or those receiving postgraduate degrees, can avoid the reality no longer. It is time for them to become breadwinners, to prove themselves in the marketplace. It is time to "separate the men from the boys," or at least the successes from the failures. The stress this creates in young men has been widely reported by psychology professionals around the country and is evident in several disturbing statistics. Consider, for example, the odds of a person living out their twenty-fifth year:

Females (white)	1,754 to 1
Females (black)	943 to 1
Males (white)	561 to 1
Males (black)	311 to 1

The odds for white women surviving are over three times that of white men. There is a similar discrepancy between black women and black men. The odds for white men are even significantly below those for black women.[3]

Also alarming is the dramatic increase in suicide rates for men aged twenty-five to thirty-four over the last two decades, as compared with the sharp decline in the suicide rate for women in the same critical age group:[4]

SUICIDE RATES PER 100,000 POPULATION, AGES 25-34

Year	Male	Female
1970	19.8	8.6
1988	25.0	5.7

The demand that they be breadwinners and the concurrent stresses of their work lives cause many men to be casualties at the very start of their careers. This trend continues throughout men's work lives. They die years before women and suffer far greater incidence of alcoholism, drug addiction, suicide, and many other diseases and disorders. In fact they are more susceptible than women to every one of the fifteen leading causes of death in the United States, including heart disease, cancer, lung disease, cerebrovascular disease, accident, and homicide. The industrial enclosure of men has been a health disaster for them.

The grim statistics on men's health also indicate the extent to which the masculine mystique has put men in a health bind. As millions of men's bodies are decimated by disease, addiction, and stress, the masculine mystique inculcates values that ensure that men will do little about their endangered health. At work and even at play men are taught to ignore illness and injury. Their machine-man view of themselves and their bodies—seeing their bodies as productive mechanisms programmed for constant performance and endless labor—keeps them from seeking medical help when they do become ill. Overall, men see doctors at only half the rate that women do. For most men locked into the competitive realities of the marketplace, illness, fatigue, emotional disturbance, and addiction are viewed with horror, shame, and fear. They signify that the machine has "broken down." And in a society that values men for their success, disease also signifies the most dreaded fate: obsolescence. When our machines break, we discard them; the mechanized male fears the same end. Therefore in the face of prospective loss of job and masculine identity, most men practice denial at the first sign of physical or mental-health problems.

The masculine mystique also teaches men to avoid sensible disease prevention and health promotion. Real men eat red meat, drink rather than seek help for emotional problems, avoid sensible nutrition, and work themselves to exhaustion. Note the disparity in preventive health behavior indicated by the following gender comparison:[5]

	MEN	WOMEN
Time spent using remote control	53%	34%
Arrested for drug violations	720,000	32,000
Calorie conscious	16%	36%
Smokers	30%	24%
Do not drink	24%	36%
Sometimes drink too much	38%	19%
Inpatients discharged for alcohol-related syndrome	631,000	211,000

Men also refuse to become educated about their bodies and illness. A 1992 national survey conducted for the American Medical Association by the Gallup organization revealed a continuing disparity between men and women in seeking medical help. Of the 759 men and 755 women surveyed, 29 percent of the men said they had not visited a physician in a year or more, compared with only 15 percent of women.[6]

Other recent studies underscore the fact that men are far less likely to notice or look for disease symptoms than women. A 1992 Boston University team found that women discover their own melanomas at a much higher rate than men. Melanoma is becoming a major killer of Americans. From 1950 to 1988 there has been an increase of more than 300 percent in incidence of the disease coupled with a jump in mortality of 150 percent. The greatest number of fatalities occur in men. According to the study, close to 70 percent of women discovered their own cancer, while only 40 percent of men did so. This difference helps explain why men are more likely to die from the disease, which is highly curable if caught early. The study had another significant finding: 23 percent of men, but just 2 percent of women, said their spouse found the cancers. Dr. Howard Koh, who led the study, says it confirms what dermatologists frequently see: "When a man comes in to have a suspected cancer looked at, very often he'll say, 'I'm only here because my wife made me come.' It's never the other way around."[7]

Recent surveys also show that men over fifty remain uneducated and unaware of the warning signs of common fatal diseases for older men. In one poll half of the respondents had no idea of what the symptoms were for prostate disease.[8] Even when men finally do seek medical care, they are far less forthright about their symptoms than women. Another series of surveys taken by the AMA/Gallup project in 1992 involved five hundred men over fifty, and three hundred physicians. One doctor in three believed that a majority of men avoided discussing prostate cancer symptoms during visits. Two out of three detected the same reluctance to discuss sexual dysfunction. Of the patients, 20 percent said they were embarrassed or ashamed to discuss symptoms of cancer. Even more men (25 percent) admitted shame and embarrassment about sexual problems. Many openly admitted that discussion of cancer or sexual dysfunction threatened their masculinity.[9]

These findings on shame among men about illness and sexual dysfunction are a testament to the continuing force of the masculine mystique. In the case of prostate cancer the results have been particularly tragic. There has been a 50 percent increase in the diagnosis of prostate cancer in the past twelve years, but a 40 percent increase in death rate, primarily because six out of every ten men diagnosed with the cancer have let the cancer go too far before consulting a physician, and have an advanced stage of the disease at the time of diagnosis. A prostate tumor can double in size in two to four years. Each year 200,000 new cases of prostate cancer are diagnosed, and more than 38,000 men die from the disease. Researchers predict that by the year 2000 annual increase in death from prostate cancer will be 37 percent and new cases will soar by 90 percent.[10]

Men's general shame about admitting illness is compounded when the issue involves sexual problems. For many men the embarrassment and fear in seeking help for sexual dysfunction is overwhelming. As has been noted, the masculine mystique demands that men be able to "perform" their sexual role in a machinelike fashion. So-called impotence stigmatizes a man as a failure—that is, demonstrates his inability to fulfill the dictates of the machine-, competitive-, and power-man mythologies. For many men it is their "worst nightmare," tearing apart relationships and marriages and seriously undermining their masculine identity.[11] Currently tens of millions of American men are labeled impotent—due to factors ranging from emotional stress, dysfunctional relationships, and marital discord to various diseases including diabetes, high blood pressure, and a variety of circulatory disorders. Each year there are approximately half a million outpatient visits and thirty thousand hospitalizations for "impotence" at a cost of around $150 million.[12]

Men's shame in the face of disease and sexual dysfunction

makes them poor consumers of medical care. The embarrassment of men who face health problems and their mechanistic views of their bodies results in a "quick fix" mentality where the male patient seeking medical care wants to "get it over with" as quickly as possible. Men rarely seek second opinions or actively question their doctors about treatment. "Women are much better consumers of health care," says Dr. Thomas Mertz, a prominent Michigan urologist. "They are much more inquisitive. They want to know about alternatives. In fact when I see male patients, the wife or daughter usually is there with a list of questions." Mertz prefers to have a man bring his spouse or other female relative to an examination. Otherwise "the guy goes home and his wife asks questions and he says, 'I don't know. He didn't tell me.' What he's saying is he doesn't want to think about it. Then I get three phone calls from the wife, son, and daughter to figure out what's happening to Dad."[13]

Men are also ashamed to admit, and are consistently misdiagnosed for, emotional and mental problems. Ignorance, denial, and insensitive health professionals are common. A timely example is the current misdiagnosing of men with depression. Depression has long been considered primarily a woman's emotional disorder. But a recent study reveals that the masculine mystique has played a hand in the alarming failure of the medical profession to diagnose the problem in men. A 1991 study published in the journal *Psychological Assessment* found that certain clinicians using standardized tests failed to recognize symptoms of depression in two-thirds of men.[14] According to the report doctors are less likely even to ask men about whether they are suffering depressive symptoms. Men also exacerbate the problem by not being forthright with doctors about their symptoms, often too ashamed or embarrassed to tell the truth about how they feel. Health writer Jane E. Brody summarizes:

> Historically it has been considered "unmanly" to admit to suffering from emotional problems. Rather than seek medical help for depression or even acknowledge that they may have such a problem, many men have traditionally handled their feelings by drink-

ing too much alcohol, taking mood altering drugs, being cranky or falsely cheerful, abusing their wives or children, becoming workaholics or exercise addicts or, with little or with no warning committing suicide. . . . On top of this, many doctors have been reluctant to delve into emotions with their male patients or even ask "embarrassing" questions that might reveal alcohol or drug abuse.[15]

As indicated by Brody, men's denial of emotional problems causes numerous additional health problems. Far more than women, men suppress their emotional symptoms and instead express their depression or anxiety through their bodies, leading to ulcers, tensions, muscle ache, fatigue, high blood pressure, and cancer—problems for which they are equally unlikely to seek medical help.

A CURE FOR BOYHOOD

The health crisis for males is not restricted to adults. There is a frightening increase in a variety of physical and mental disorders among boys. Few in our society are aware that seven out of eight children who are institutionalized in mental hospitals or similar institutions are boys. Whether the problem is autism, stuttering, or dyslexia, boys suffer in far greater numbers than girls. But perhaps the most alarming health problem for boys involves a significant, recent societal change in what we expect our "little men" to be.

We all remember the adage "Boys will be boys." It is part of American folklore: boys fighting or otherwise raising a ruckus while mother or teacher sigh in a Norman Rockwell–like tableau. Well, not anymore. According to numerous physicians and psychologists, much of the behavior formerly categorized as typical for boys could be a serious personality disorder requiring daily treatment with a powerful and potentially hazardous mind-altering drug.

Does a boy have trouble remaining seated when asked to do so? fidget or squirm when he is seated? have difficulty waiting his turn?

have difficulty playing quietly? have trouble following instructions or finishing tasks? have a problem with excessive talking? tend to interrupt or intrude on other children's games? have trouble listening? always lose things? often do physically dangerous things without thinking about the possible consequences? get distracted easily?[16] If he has any or all of these symptoms, he may well be diagnosed as suffering from conduct disorder or attention-deficit hyperactivity disorder (ADHD), as hundreds of thousands of boys are each year.

"There is now an attempt to pathologize what was once considered the normal range of behavior of boys," notes Melvin Konner of the departments of anthropology and psychiatry at Emory University in Atlanta. "Today, Tom Sawyer and Huckleberry Finn surely would have been diagnosed with both conduct disorder and ADHD."[17]

Hyperactivity, described early on as "an abnormal defect of moral control," has been sporadically diagnosed in small numbers of boys since the turn of the century.[18] For decades articles on the subject appeared only occasionally in scientific journals. Starting in the 1970s, however, "hyperactivity" became a near obsession in the psychiatric community. The last three years of the 1950s saw thirty-one articles on hyperactivity; the last three years of the 1970s saw seven thousand.[19] By 1980 hyperactivity was the single most common condition for which youngsters were referred to psychology clinics. Researchers were soon assuring teachers that each classroom had its percentage of hyperactive children needing to be drugged. And the experts told teachers where to look—80 to 90 percent of them would be boys.

The actual prevalence of attention-deficit hyperactivity disorder (ADHD) is still in dispute. Some studies estimate the rate of hyperactivity at 10 to 20 percent of children. A California survey puts it at a much lower rate, 1.19 percent. Still other nationally recognized experts use numbers ranging from 4 to 6 percent.[20] The large disparity in assessments of ADHD prevalence is credited to the fact that the current guidelines for diagnosis are so general as to be nearly useless. Some doctors even abandon the idea of a diagnosis altogether and go with their "gut reaction" when attempting to identify children with ADHD.

The arbitrary diagnosis of ADHD, and the significant differences in various assessments of its occurrence, has led some to question the rates at which it is diagnosed. Larry B. Silver, clinical professor of psychiatry at Georgetown University, comments,

Some children are given drugs they shouldn't be taking. . . . When a parent says the child can't sit still or pay attention, the physician needs to find out what's going on in the child's life. Maybe the parents had a big fight in August and Dad packed his bags and moved out. The child went to school in September and everyone is seeing him as anxious and distractible. . . . Giving an anxious child stimulants may lead to more anxiety. And a depressed child may show false positive response because stimulants can be antidepressants. ADHD is probably one of the least common causes of hyperactivity, distractibility and impulsivity.[21]

Family counselor Richard Woods agrees: "I've seen hundreds of cases when a child was diagnosed with ADHD when the real problem was caused by the child's divorced parents pressuring the child, causing a severe 'loyalty' conflict in the youngster."[22]

Some observers even question the existence of the disorder. Author and educator Alfie Kohn comments,

The wildly divergent estimates of prevalence [of ADHD] are disturbing enough in themselves, given that each percentage point stands for hundreds of thousands of children. But they also underscore the fact that different criteria for diagnosis produce different conclusions about whether a particular child will carry the ADHD label and, as a consequence, be required to swallow a drug every day. Most unsettling is a flicker of doubt about the integrity of the diagnosis itself. Can we in fact be confident that any child has a disorder called hyperactivity, or ADHD?[23]

However arbitrary the diagnosis of ADHD, the treatment is virtually certain: daily doses of Ritalin. Ritalin (the trade name for methylphenidate hydrochloride) is an amphetamine-type drug. It is a very powerful stimulant. The federal Drug Enforcement Administration (DEA) has classified Ritalin as a Schedule II controlled substance, the most potent category of drugs that can be prescribed. Other drugs in that class include morphine and barbiturates. For reasons as yet not understood, Ritalin, which is a potent stimulant for adults, has the effect of calming some children. It was approved for use in children in 1961.

There are major problems with Ritalin. For one it doesn't work for up to 40 percent of children diagnosed with ADHD. This is an extremely high percentage of failure for any drug. One researcher notes that "some youngsters even become worse on medication!"[24] Moreover many of those children who do respond to the drug also improve on a placebo. Pediatrician Esther Sleator followed a group of medicated children for two years and then began replacing the drug with sugar pills. Of twenty-eight patients, eleven continued to behave as if they were getting the real thing. Overall about 40 percent of all diagnosed ADHD children "improve" when given a placebo.[25]

Even those for whom the drug works face problems. Some children's behavior seems to "improve" only at relatively high doses of Ritalin. Such heavy doses can seriously reduce cognitive skills. This forces physicians and teachers to choose between students who are docile, drugged "zombies" and those using their thinking skills but showing ADHD symptoms. Giving children large doses of the drug raises other serious concerns. One researcher reports that "the [dosage] where teachers perceive the most improved classroom behavior is associated with side effects."[26] And Ritalin's short-term side effects can be severe. Insomnia, elevated blood pressure, facial tics, weight loss, stunted growth, suicidal behavior, and even Tourette's syndrome have all been associated with Ritalin use. The long-term physical and psychological impacts on children taking the drug are feared but not yet known. Some suspect that there could be a dangerous potential for long-term drug dependency. "Specialists see a number of young people who have taken stimulants every day of their lives from, say, ages 10 to 16, at which point both the children and their families are thoroughly dependent on a drug to maintain daily life," states Dr. Mark Stewart, a child psychiatrist at the University of Iowa.[27]

Ritalin's doubters include Howard Phillips, a retired representative of CIBA-GEIGY Corporation, which produces Ritalin. (MD Pharmaceuticals, Inc., produces a generic version of the drug.) "Frankly, I'm not that sold on Ritalin," states Phillips, who worked for CIBA-GEIGY for thirty years. "It's often used with a child who has an attention-deficit disorder as a marginal substitute for understanding parents or schools. Most of the problems can be overcome with a physically exhausting sports program, a check on diet—which can be a factor—and a good school situation. A couple of my sons were hyperactive, one of them was diagnosed as having ADHD, and we worked it through without Ritalin."[28]

Whatever its drawbacks and whoever its doubters, Ritalin use has increased dramatically in recent years. Pharmaceutical companies in the United States have bumped up production by 250 percent since 1991. Moreover, despite ongoing controversy, there is greater acceptance of Ritalin today, especially among educators and health professionals, than in the early 1980s. One study in Baltimore County, Maryland, found that the use of the drug on children had been doubling every four to seven years since 1971. By 1987, 5.6 percent of all public elementary school students in the area were receiving the drug. The male-female ratio for those being medicated varied from 8:1 to 5:1.[29]

There has been little public protest of the explosion in Ritalin prescription and use in the United States. There has also been scant acknowledgment or criticism of current education practices that deem it necessary to have so many boys drugged for years at a time. Moreover few of the thousands of articles on Ritalin contain any discussion of the reasons for boys being the vast majority of those receiving the potentially hazardous drug treatment.

Clearly the Ritalin crisis is a flashpoint in the relationship between our parenting, educational and child care systems and boys. The routinization of education, the increased use of child care and after-school programs, the lack of playtime for many boys in single-parent or two-working-parent households, and the lack of male presence in childhood and in early education are causing a chain reaction that is resulting in massive emotional trauma in America's young men. Over the last generation this has finally devolved into the drugging of millions of boys with potentially toxic chemicals.

One reason for the intolerance of formerly acceptable boyhood behavior, and the massive use of Ritalin, by our education system is that men and women, educators and parents, share the view that the proper role for men is as cogs in the economic wheels of our society. This prompts our society to acquiesce in the destruction of that part of boys that resists or comes in conflict with this fate. Many of the characteristics demanded of a child to avoid an ADHD diagnosis—sit still, don't fidget, don't talk, wait your turn, don't get distracted, don't lose things, complete activities—sound like the description of a docile office worker, not a boy. Science reporter Natalie Angier notes that the requirements of the postindustrial, computer-oriented job market have contributed to the exponential increase in Ritalin use; parents fear that the boy who is restless, adventurous, or a daydreamer will, in the future, lose out to the boy "who can sit still, concentrate and do his job 10, 12, 14 hours a day."[30]

Overall it is remarkable that Ritalin use on boys remains such a hidden part of the current health crisis in America. One can only imagine the protest that would be occurring if 80 to 95 percent of those being given this drug were girls for behavior viewed as typically female. And one can only wonder at men who will not raise their voices to protest what is being done to their sons.

THE ROID RAGE

As hundreds of thousands of children, mainly boys, are drugged for a behavior disorder virtually undiagnosed three decades ago, a staggering number of older boys are getting hooked on hazardous drugs, primarily to conform their bodies to the masculine-mystique ideal. Steroid use among America's young men is skyrocketing.

A report issued by the congressional General Accounting Office in 1989 reviewed fifteen studies on the use of anabolic steroids among students and athletes. The GAO report found that steroids had been or were being used by as many as 6.6 percent of the twelfth-grade males in the United States. Taken together recent studies indicate that approximately 500,000 male high school students use or have used steroids.[31] Steroid abuse by male high school seniors is nearly as widespread as the use of "crack" cocaine. Worse still, more than one-third of the users began using steroids at the age of fifteen or younger; two-thirds had started by the age of sixteen. And the phenomenon is not limited to any geographic area. Studies from several states all reported that up to 11 percent of high school males admit to having used steroids.[32]

More than 90 percent of steroid users who began at age fifteen or younger are repeat steroid users, and a high percentage (40 percent) of young men taking steroids are what is known as hard-core users. Hard-core and repeat users often practice steroid "stacking," or the simultaneous use of different steroids. In fact 44 percent of high-school-student users take more than one steroid at a time, and almost half have used both oral and injectable steroids.[33]

This epidemic of steroid use is caused in large part by hundreds of thousands of young men seeking the "perfect" male body stereotype as currently advertised throughout society. A 1990 Health and Human Services report indicated that 86 percent of steroid users were motivated by the attempt to "enhance" their looks. They take hormones to achieve the muscled archetype of the male body as presented in innumerable commercials, TV shows, and movies. The mechanistic, hairless, "pumped-up" body is viewed by most boys and girls alike as *the* masculine ideal. A high percentage of these boys use weight lifting along with steroids in their obsession to achieve the "right" look. A congressional report on steroid use notes that "in our society, which is filled with images of [body] flawlessness and excellence, steroids hold the promise of perfection. The promise is shattered, however, when individuals are faced with the brutal reality of steroid abuse." The self-destructive drive of male teenagers to eschew the ninety-pound weakling look for the "machine man" pumped-up ideal has led some to compare steroid use for young men to anorexia among young women.[34]

Another major factor in steroid use is the drive to increase body size and strength in order to create the "winning body." According to most reports, athletes are among the most common users of anabolic steroids among high school and college students. As noted in a prior chapter, 84 percent of anabolic-steroid users participate in high school sports, and between 15 and 20 percent of college athletes report using steroids.[35] Tommy Chaiken, a former football player at the University of South Carolina, describes a typical college "shooting party":

> Seven or eight of us heavy users got together in a dorm room and started shooting each other up. Guys would show up with their bottles, and there'd be a lot of chatter: I shoot you, you shoot me. . . . We tried to be careful how we injected each other . . . but sometimes you'd hit the sciatic nerve or something, and the guy's legs would buckle. I mean none of us were doctors or anything. But we were needle happy. We would have injected ourselves with anything if we thought it would make us big.[36]

Steroids are dangerous. Studies suggest that steroids may increase the risk of heart disease; produce liver toxicities; affect sex characteristics and reproductive capacity; and ironically, in children and youth, result in stunted growth.[37] Steroid use can also create casualties in other ways. Use of the drug can cause severe psychological disorders. Injecting synthetic testosterone in men and boys can create what are termed roid rages. These rages lead to many homicides each year and also contribute to the growing epidemic of teenage male suicide. A congressional report documented the following "typical" steroid incident:

> At age 13, Mike Keys began weight lifting to build his slender frame into the muscled male body ideal. By age 17, Mike Keys

stood 5'9", weighed 193 pounds and injected himself daily with testosterone obtained from a local gym. Never satisfied with the results, Mike continued to take steroids, despite pleas from his family to stop. His grades began to slip, he threw temper tantrums, and his mood swings worsened. According to his parents, on the morning of December 16, 1988, Mike was fine, even cheerful. The next evening Blaine Keys discovered his son's body lying next to his weight-lifting equipment—dead from a suicide.[38]

As society struggles with the steroid-use epidemic, the use of another body-building drug has also reached crisis proportions among young men: synthetic human growth hormone. Prior to the advent of genetic engineering, human growth hormone was used to help pituitary dwarfs gain height. The hormone was extracted from human pituitary glands taken from cadavers. This method was abandoned when batches of natural growth hormone became contaminated with a fatal virus causing Creutzfeldt-Jacob disease. By the mid-1980s biotechnology companies began developing genetically engineered human growth hormone, and soon were manufacturing the hormone in industrial quantities. With its great availability, genetically engineered HGH is joining anabolic steroids as the body-building drug of choice for many teenagers and athletes. As with steroids HGH use by teenagers or adults is illegal. But HGH has an advantage for muscle builders and athletes: Unlike steroids, its use cannot be detected by drug tests.

Black-market–HGH use among male teenagers attempting to "pump up" is soaring. In a March 1992 poll 5 percent of suburban tenth-grade boys surveyed stated that they used genetically engineered human growth hormone.[39] But HGH abuse by muscle builders and athletes is not the most egregious misuse of the hormone. The genetically engineered hormone is being used on thousands of U.S. children every day. These youngsters are not using this drug at their own choosing. They are not bodybuilders going for the perfect body or athletes seeking to improve performance. The parents of these children are not obtaining the genetically engineered drug on the black market. In fact it is often being prescribed by negligent and misinformed family doctors (the use of HGH on many of these children is just as illegal as its use by athletes or youthful musclemen). These children are being subjected to the extraordinary physical and psychological risks of daily genetically engineered hormone injections for only one reason—their parents feel that their bodies are "wrong," that they are too small to be successful. Nine out of ten children being given genetically engineered growth hormone to increase their size are boys. It is estimated that close to $700 million of this hormone is sold annually.

TOTAL MALE CARE

Remarkably, given the clear evidence of a spiraling health crisis for men and boys, there have been few efforts to establish centers for men's health. By contrast there are over two thousand women's health centers across the country. However, several years ago one doctor, urologist Kenneth A. Goldberg, saw the health bind that was decimating so many men and decided to do something about it. In 1989 Dr. Goldberg opened the Male Health Center in Dallas, Texas. It was the first center in the country specializing in treating male health problems. The stated purpose of the center is simple: to help men live healthy and active lives. The center's strategies for improving men's health include early diagnosis and treatment of health problems, support during and after care, and education for men about their bodies so that future health problems can be avoided.[40]

The center is a labor of love for Goldberg, a dream that took him over a decade to realize. Goldberg's early experiences as a urologist were more than enough to convince him that men were in need of a special kind of health care. He recalls one patient who came in for a second opinion on the effectiveness of the testosterone injections another physician used to treat his impotence. During the visit the patient mentioned as an aside that he had trouble urinating. "As soon as

I examined his prostate I knew he had cancer. It had already spread . . . it had to have been there for years."[41] After several similar experiences Goldberg staked his future on the premise that men's aversion to taking care of themselves could be overcome with the right approach. "The problem is a combination of men not coming in and physicians not being accustomed to address the needs of the entire man and all the conditions and problems men have," says Goldberg.[42]

Currently the center's staff consists of three urologists, two family physicians, a psychologist, a physician's assistant, and two medical assistants plus about a dozen volunteer "patient educators." Most of the patient educators are prostate-cancer survivors whose main job is to help put new patients at ease by providing a quick overview of prostate disease and relating their experience fighting it.[43] The education approach is key in encouraging men to come to the center. David Sunderlin, the center's patient-education coordinator, says many men call the center anonymously several times "just to talk to somebody" before they finally identify themselves and make appointments. It's his job to be encouraging and supportive in handling the original calls from men. "I've had patients who were treated for impotence or prostate cancer come to me six months later and say 'You're David, aren't you? We talked a couple of times on the phone last year. I just wanted to say thanks.' " Sunderlin appreciates the importance of gaining men's trust in order to break the masculine mystique's shaming of men in need of care. "They think of me as a friend."[44]

The center has also come up with another strategy with which to combat men's reluctance to care for their health. Starting in 1991 it began an outreach program in Dallas where employers contract for job-site cancer screening for prostate, skin, and testicular cancer. Thousands of workers are screened each year. Dr. Joey Hamilton, who works part-time at the center, says the job-site screenings remove yet another excuse men often use to avoid seeing a physician: "It's a matter of convenience. A lot of men say they cannot afford to take a half day off work to see a doctor for an exam. When we show up at their job, it's only 30 minutes or so out of their day."[45] Hamilton estimates that the screenings reveal the need for follow-up in about one-third of patients.

Goldberg's dream, and his persistence and courage in realizing it, has been a boon to thousands of men. As of 1992 over twenty-five thousand men contacted or came to the center. While the majority of these patients came from Texas, many have traveled from as far as Florida and Alaska to be treated.

Recently other attempts have been made to address the health crisis for men. Dr. Goldberg is on the advisory board of the Men's Health Network, a new organization formed in 1992 to promote men's health as a vital national issue. "We've seen 20 to 30 years of networking and consciousness raising from the women's health movement, and the results have been impressive. It presents a model for us to emulate," states Ron Henry, cofounder of the Network.[46]

The Network, run from a small office in Washington, D.C., has several straightforward goals that include: saving men's lives by reducing the premature mortality of men and boys; increasing the physical and mental health of men and boys so that they can live fuller and happier lives; and significantly reducing the cycles of violence and addiction that afflict so many men. The Network is seeking to employ several strategies to achieve its ambitious goals. These include sponsoring national education campaigns to promote public and media awareness of men's health issues and to disseminate vital information on how to prevent disease, violence, and addiction; compiling a data-collection system that will allow the Network to act as a national clearinghouse for information about men's health issues; providing and maintaining an ongoing network of health care providers and services that deal with men's health issues; and actively working with policymakers and agencies to initiate better government programs on men's health issues and to ensure adequate funding for research and education on men's health needs.

The Network is unique in seeking to address a vast scope of men's health issues—from male-specific diseases, teenage suicide, and the plight of veterans, to the psychological impacts of divorce and the special health needs of older men. As with Goldberg's Male Health Center, those involved in network building are aware of how their work challenges the masculine mystique. Network spokesperson Jim Sniechowski notes, "The message we're trying to get out is that it is not unmanly to take care of your body. Getting health care allows men to fulfill themselves and breaks the view that they are mere productive machines. Restoring our physical and mental health is the most manly thing a man can do."[47]

GETTING WELL

Every man can do something about the male health crisis. The most obvious step is for men to seek medical help openly and quickly when necessary. Men are not invulnerable machines, and their health and well-being are more significant emblems of masculinity than their enslavement to work. As indicated by Dr. Goldberg's unique work, male health professionals can also play a significant role in addressing the health bind. Medical professionals with courage and capital can seek to emulate the actions of Goldberg in establishing health centers for men.

Activist organizations and networks can help provide education and outreach to men around the country. They can be catalysts that join men together to fight threats to male health including suicide, drug and alcohol abuse, AIDS, prostate and testicular cancer, and stress-related diseases. Corporations can play a vital role in men's health by sponsoring and instituting workplace screening for men for a variety of cancers as well as hypertension.

The federal government must also be encouraged to play a more aggressive role in protecting men's health. For one the National Institutes of Health (NIH) spends twice the funds on women's health that it does on men's health. The agency has just initiated a new Office of Research on Women's Health; a similar office for men's health is urgently required. Such an office could begin research on crucial men's health issues that no health agency has adequately studied. These issues include the following:

- Men's high rate of suicide
- The overdiagnosing of attention-deficit disorder and the over-prescription of Ritalin
- Steroid and human growth-hormone abuse
- Dyslexia
- The impacts of school sports on the health of boys and young men
- Male depression
- Male sexual dysfunction, including "impotence"
- Prostate cancer
- Testicular cancer
- Male violence
- Post-traumatic stress syndrome among veterans
- Estrogen chemical pollution and its impact on men's reproduction
- Male-specific genetic diseases

Ultimately, addressing the men's health crisis will require a fundamental restructuring of our personal and public understanding of health. For decades American medicine has been dominated by the same efficiency and power ideology that are the underpinnings of the masculine mystique. We favor "gee whiz" quick fixes, and the media plays up intrusive medical advances such as heart transplants far more than it does breakthroughs in our understanding of nutrition and stress, which are ultimately far more effective in halting disease. In resolving their health crisis men must recognize that medicine is as culturally determined as any other pursuit. There is a reason why the last few centuries of Western medicine led to the attempt to transplant a baboon heart into a baby in Loma Linda, California, whereas three thousand years of Chinese medicine resulted in the holistic methods of acupuncture. Just as the ideologies of recent centuries destroyed the holistic masculine in the West, they also undermined a holistic approach to medicine.

For generations, then, our system of health care has been founded on developing cures for disease and then debating who will pay the skyrocketing price. As health costs soar, it is time to promote a wellness-based health system, a system focusing on preserving health instead of treating disease. A wellness-based health system would concentrate on restructuring our society and environment so that they are more conducive to health. It would help retrain our habits and choices to achieve and preserve health.

Without question, men are far less likely than women to take sensible steps toward disease prevention and health promotion. Too many men are not exercising their bodies, and are getting increasingly sick from poor diet and physical neglect. Unfortunately our fast-food industry, cigarette companies, alcohol distributors, TV networks, and advertisers continue to aid and abet this unhealthy lifestyle. For their part the pharmaceutical and medical-technology industries and our health providers and doctors, to a large extent, turn a deaf ear to the call for a reorientation in our conception of health. There are untold profits to be made from sickness and far fewer financial rewards to be gained from wellness.

Studies now show that 70 percent of all illness is preventable.[48] A primary culprit is saturated fats, which have been linked to heart disease, cancer, stroke, and diabetes. While a thick steak may be advertised as just the food to fuel the male machine, there is nothing particularly manly about a heart attack or obesity. While most of us would smile at the male adage "I'd rather have a bottle in front of me than a frontal lobotomy," the truly masculine recourse to emotional problems is therapy, not alcohol, which is a leading killer of men. Though men have cut down on smoking and in large part rejected the view of smoking as masculine or sexy, smoking is still a major contributor to male fatalities. Studies show that more men smoke than women and that smoking takes an average of eighteen years off the average male life expectancy.[49]

Health care reform will be a central issue in America over the next few years. Masculinist activists should take advantage of the moment, seize the initiative, and help redirect the health vision of the nation away from one of sickness to one of wellness. If they fail to do so, the health of the American public, and as we have seen, especially that of men, will continue to deteriorate from an ever-worsening lifestyle while medical costs will continue to rise.

Fortunately there are models for the preventive-health system that would do so much to help men. In the past decade several highly successful preventive-health pilot programs have been established around the country. For example, the city of Birmingham, Alabama, with the help of a $1.5 million grant from the National Institutes of Health (NIH), carried out one of the most innovative and effective wellness programs ever attempted at the workplace. The results were both dramatic and revealing.[50]

Government workers were provided a range of intervention programs including seminars and workshops on weight loss, nutritional education, cholesterol/triglyceride reduction, blood pressure control, stress management, smoking cessation, and physical fitness. City employees attended all sessions on city time during regular work hours. In addition employers were encouraged to take part in more comprehensive after-work wellness programs at city expense.

To ensure maximum participation and to encourage a real commitment on behalf of the employees, a number of incentives were built into the wellness program. Participants received "good health dollars" for attending intervention programs and for realizing goals. The "good health dollars" were gift certificates to a wholesale merchandise store. Achievement was also rewarded with other small gifts, including gym bags and T-shirts. After the first year the winner of the wellness lottery received two round-trip tickets to the Caribbean.[51]

The results of the program were impressive. Many of the participants lost weight, changed eating habits, stopped smoking and drinking, and began a rigorous exercise program for the first time in their adult lives. With the improved health came a lowering of health costs. The health gains made by participants saved the city more than $11 million in medical costs by the end of the fifth year of the wellness program. The city estimated that it saved nearly ten dollars in health costs for every dollar invested by the city and the NIH in the wellness program.[52]

Similar wellness programs could be initiated throughout the country. Wellness programs could also be mandated for every grade school, junior high, high school, and college in the country receiving federal, state, and local financial assistance. In that way good health habits could be entrained early.

For the millions of unemployed Americans and for those who are homeless, basic wellness programs should be established in neighborhoods and communities throughout the country to dispense information and train neighborhood people to provide vital information on wellness to local residents.

The federal government should also consider extending additional financial assistance to upgrade municipal parks and recreational and sporting facilities in the inner cities. This could be a boon to many inner-city boys and could be used as a tool to provide expanded physical fitness programs for those millions of Americans who will not be reached by employer-sponsored programs.

Finally, the preventive approach to men's health must deal with the most direct result of the masculine mystique: stress. Stress has destroyed untold millions of men through heart disease and numerous other illnesses, and stress is a function of the impossible demands the mystique makes on the bodies and minds of men. The International Labor Organization, a United Nations agency, estimates that job stress costs U.S. employers more than $200 billion a year in lower productivity, absenteeism, rising insurance costs, and other medical costs.[53] While men cannot immediately escape the economic and social structures that have overemphasized profit, power, and competition, they can try to free their minds from the entrancements of such a system. They can develop interests in family, friends, community, and nature that balance the work obsession.

The men's health crisis provides men with a clear mission. They need to be leaders in initiating and supporting holistic health and psychotherapeutic approaches that directly link health threats to men to the coercive nature of the masculine mystique and the current economic system. Changes in diet; reduction of smoking, drug, and alcohol use; less stressful work environments; and greater nurturing and caring for men by other men are all essential, interconnected aspects of any male health initiative.

12

A MAN'S NATURE

The world needs a man's heart.   —Joseph Jastrab[1]

*If men cannot imagine a masculine connection to nature, if it is
conceived as being other than them, then their feelings of separation
may breed alienation from life.*   —Aaron R. Kipnis[2]

Wally Aiken lives in East Palestine, Ohio. He is employed as a grinder in a foundry. For years Aiken worked the second shift, and he did so on purpose. He needed his mornings free for his unique avocation. As he expressed it, "The past several years I have been trying to reclaim some strip-mined land."[3]

The destroyed land that Aiken had targeted for reclaiming is about a half mile from his home. It consists of forty-two acres, forty of which he had picked up at an auction sale for $750. The land had been stripped for coal on several occasions over four decades. When Wally first started working on the land in the mid-1970s, it was a complete casualty of strip-mining. Its ravaged geography consisted of six- to twelve-foot ridges of soil and rock populated by a motley variety of opportunistic vines, briars, shrubs, and trees. Seemingly undaunted by the task of turning this land into a farm, Wally, who had no previous agricultural experience, invested in an old Allis-

Chalmers bulldozer and began the arduous task of clearing the land. Predictably the work was slow. Each acre required 170 hours of work to backfill and grade. Once the bulldozer work was finished on a given plot, Aiken did what he calls groundwork, which involved clearing away larger stones, tree branches, and roots. After the difficult clearing chores were complete, the ground was ready for seeding. Aiken sowed the land with rye and a mixture of grasses and legumes: timothy, orchard grass, tall fescue, red clover, alfalfa, bird's-foot trefoil. Once the seed was in the soil, Wally covered it with a mulch of manure or old hay.[4]

Each step took time, and required both labor and luck to work. Wally describes a typical sequence of problems on one section of his land:

> Since I was filling against a hillside, the finished grade was a slope. I knew I had to get some cover established as quickly as possible. I skipped picking up the stones, etc., and disked it lightly, then planted my grass-legume mixture. I then went over the whole thing with a cultipacker. I next spread out several hundred bales of spoiled and low-quality hay I bought. Well, it didn't rain, and it didn't rain, but the seedlings sprouted anyway just from the moisture in the ground. Weeks went by and still no rain. Then came hurricane Frederick. It rained and rained. I was afraid to look at my future pasture, but finally did. I was surprised to see that it had fared pretty well, considering the volume of rain we had had. It had washed in places to be sure, but the damage was small. The washes were quickly filled with more hay. I think the hay mulch was the real lifesaver in this instance. The grass and legumes made several inches of growth before winter came.[5]

Slowly but surely Wally healed the ruined strip-mined land. After several years he had cleared enough land to create a small farm. Land that had been virtually destroyed now held a dense, thriving stand of pasture plants. The soil had become rich and fertile.

Farmer and essayist Wendell Berry, who first reported on Aiken's land-recovery efforts, summarizes his unique accomplishment:

Wally Aiken is doing what he set out to do; he is making a farm out of the spoil left years ago by people who turned good land into money and smoke, in contempt of everything that might come after them. That they have had human successors at all here, where their destructiveness is bewildering and depressing, and in a nation where the care of such land is a mixture of bad habit and shoddy policy, is itself a kind of wonder.[6]

Aiken's goal in working the near-ruined land was to make it a working farm, but as the work progressed, he found that the process proved as healing for him as for the land. "It is nice to have something to devote oneself to, to care about and be part of," Aiken remarked.[7]

MEN AND THE EARTH

Of all the tasks of the masculine revolution none is more important than that of revitalizing men's husbanding and stewarding of the earth. It is important to remember that a sustainable environment is not just one issue among many for men. Rather it is the context for all social and personal issues. For without a biosphere that can support life there are no other issues.

The call to protect the earth is urgent. Today humanity faces the first truly global environmental crisis in recorded history. In the past few years the public has been jolted by revelations about ecological threats to our biosphere that it had not even suspected existed—ozone depletion, acid rain, species extinction, global warming. The current crisis is unprecedented. While our ancestors experienced numerous man-made threats to ecological stability, the effects of these ecological problems were localized. Now humanity, through its industrial way of life, has affected, perhaps inalterably, the very biochemistry of the planet. Lacking precedents for dealing with this crisis, some deny it exists, others work frantically for solutions, and the majority, overwhelmed by the daily difficulties of life, do not act.

One of the most unfortunate effects of the masculine mystique is that it has fostered a view among many men that environmentalism is "unmanly" and, even worse, that wanton exploitation of land and resources is a masculine ideal. We have seen how the masculine has come to be closely identified with technology and production, while the organic and generative are associated with women. Many now fall into misandry by claiming that men are genetically and hormonally predisposed toward destruction of the natural world.

The irony of this view of men and nature is that masculinity and the earth have been cocasualties of the same historical process. The ideological and social forces which removed men from their land, enclosed them into the factory system, and then annihilated traditional concepts of masculinity are the same forces that have fostered the destruction of so much of the earth.

As was described earlier in this book, the doctrines of mechanism and the market attacked both the earth and men. The Enlightenment philosophers began by conceptually reducing all living things to a collection of quantifiable objects. They and their successors put forth the view that the entire biotic community, including humans, were little more than biological machines. Under this mechanistic rubric men were seen, and were made to see themselves, as so many human "tools" that could be used in industrial production and then discarded. By the same token, the natural world was seen as so many exploitable objects, also to be consumed in the endless technological pursuit of profit and wealth.

Similarly the market dogma of self-interest led to the fiction that human labor was a commodity like any other that could and should be sold under the laws of supply and demand. This caused a revolution in the lives of men as they were forced to sell themselves as workers in order to avoid destitution. The same commodification process was responsible for the lifting of long-standing legal restrictions on the sale of land and the subsequent unrestricted purchase and use of land for production and profit.

The power ideologies of the last centuries have not only subjected the vast majority of men to subservience and obedience but have also subjected nature to a heretofore unimaginable exploitation. Ultimately just as power, manipulation, self-interest, and the ethics of efficiency and progress became staples of the masculine mystique, they also provided a new and disastrous blueprint for man's relationship to his environment.

Moreover the history of the destruction of gender in our society actually mirrors the destruction of biological diversity in the natural world. In agriculture we have bred monocultured hybrid "super-yield" plants and animals that have little semblance to any natural species. The biological diversity of these plants and animals is consistently sacrificed in the process of making them ever more efficient and profitable. Additionally each year economic development causes thousands of species to lose their habitats, many becoming extinct.

Over generations the characteristics and archetypes of each gender have been similarly reduced, contracted, and disfigured to fit the requirements of the industrial system. As men became the primary cogs in the economic and productive system, their gender was sacrificed on the altar of production, and in place of their native characteristics the system substituted the masculine-mystique ideals—machinelike efficiency, hypercompetition, self-interest, autonomy, and the idolization of technological power. Women were marginalized and banalized as "homemakers" and orchestrators of domestic consumption in a system that had destroyed community, extended families, and any real sense of a rooted home. Now, as the postindustrial workplace can use both genders more equally, there is a new call for both genders to be made extinct and to put in their place a new androgynous humanoid, fully indoctrinated with the market and technological mystiques, with consumption as its sole goal. The diversity of gender continues to be sacrificed for the same reason and in the same manner as the diversity of the rest of creation.

INTIMATE POLLUTION

The destruction of the earth affects men physically as well as psychologically and spiritually. As with women and children, men's bodies become the repositories of many of the chemicals used on our food and the pollutants that factories spew into the air. This affects men on the most intimate of levels. Even as we destroy the regenerative carrying capacities of the land, oceans, and air, we may be doing the same thing to the generative potential of the male body.

For several years Louis Guillette has been conducting research on alligators in Florida. Over time he began to see significant reproductive problems in the alligators. Over the years, the alligators' penises became smaller and smaller, ending up a quarter of their normal size. The alligators' testosterone levels also diminished significantly. Many became sterile. Guillette subsequently met a researcher who had seen similar effects on lab mice exposed to a chemical in the DDE family, chemicals formed when DDT decomposes. Guillette then recalled that thousands of gallons of DDT had been spilled into the Florida lake in which the alligators he had been studying lived. "I think we have a problem here," Guillette recently told a congressional panel. Humans are frequently exposed to numerous chemicals like DDE that can seriously disrupt sexual development, he explained, and therefore "every man in this room is half the man his grandfather was."[8]

While Guillette may be guilty of hyperbole, still, since 1938 sperm counts of men in the United States and twenty other countries have dropped by an average of 50 percent. At the same time testicular cancer has tripled. Many researchers suspect the culprit is men's early exposure, perhaps in breast milk, to certain chemicals that have built up in the mother's body. Hundreds of chemicals used since World War II—PCBs used in manufacturing, certain pesticides, plastics, chlorine compounds used in bleaching paper—are now suspected of having a negative impact on male sperm count and genital development.[9]

Restoring masculinity, both figuratively and apparently physically, means breaking the masculine mystique and seeking an atonement (at-one-ment) with the natural world. Men must reestablish their identity with the earth, a relationship that was shattered during the trauma of enclosure and industrialization. This means actively healing the earth from the excesses of exploitation, and by doing so healing the wounds that have been inflicted on men by their forced alienation from nature. It means transforming the idea of economy from one of consumption and gross national product to one of sustainability and conservation. Ultimately it requires the re-marrying of economy with ecology. Understood in this fashion, the politics of masculinity are inseparable from the politics of ecology. And as shown in the work of Wally Aiken, this personal and political transformation can begin with each individual man.

To recommit themselves to the natural world, men must, in whatever ways they can, maintain a daily relationship with the earth. Wendell Berry has pointed out that the ecological crisis is also a crisis of agriculture. If men are to recapture a true sense of stewardship and husbandry and affirm the "seed-bearing," creative capacity of the male, they must, to the extent possible, become involved in sustainable agriculture and organic farming and gardening. Men should also initiate and support legislation that sustains our farming communities.

Perhaps the most direct way to recapture stewardship is to tend a garden. For those fortunate to have some land, a personal garden is possible. For others, taking part in community gardens or parks can be equally rewarding. As Aiken discovered, working with the soil reconnects us to the cycles of nature and teaches many lessons about diversity, stability, life, and death. Involving young men in gardening is equally important. Aside from learning to love dirt and plants and the pride of growing their own food, gardening can be an important antidote to "TV time."

Planting trees is also an expression of husbandry. Tree planting is an important way of improving urban environments. Moreover planting trees is a spiritual as well as a physical act. Creating new life in a new place—life that can with a little luck last centuries—is a powerful antidote to the quick-consumption pathology of the masculine mystique. Additionally the tree affirms the generative masculine. In many ancient cultures the tree is a powerful symbol of the masculine. In the art of the ancients the phallus itself was often portrayed as "the tree of life." Many local environmental groups have tree-planting projects with which volunteers can become involved.

Men should also become what Robert Bly has called "inner warriors" for the earth, involving themselves in nonviolent demonstrations and other activities to preserve the natural world. Each man can also join the fight to pass laws that protect our land, air, and water. Major legislation on these issues as well as important energy issues such as improving the fuel efficiency of America's number-one polluter and men's primary fantasy machine—the automobile—are at any given time making their way through Congress and local legislatures. Too often there has been a masculine-mystique–inspired gender gap when it comes to support of environmental legislation, with men supporting such legislation less than women.

Additionally an important aspect of husbandry is defense of family. As we have seen, pesticides and other toxic pollutants that poison our food, homes, water, and air represent a real danger to men and women, but they are especially dangerous for children, whose bodies are still growing. Men need to be adamant in their call for limitations on the use of such chemicals.

GOING WILD

Masculinity needs to restore not only the virtues of stewardship and husbandry but also those of wildness. The enclosure of men was also accompanied by the destruction and industrial enclosure of more and more wilderness. Men lost the wildness in themselves as they exterminated it from their natural surroundings. Men need to reverse this impoverishment of the earth and of the masculine spirit. As has been described in Chapter Eight, thousands of men are returning to the wilderness in men's gatherings to regain the elemental and chthonic strength that modernity and the marketplace have sapped out of them. Men are taking up drumming and dancing and even North American Indian rituals in an attempt to recapture in themselves the rhythms of wildness.

These men have understood the central lesson of wildness, namely that its recovery can only be accomplished through the actual experiencing of wilderness. As Sam Keen writes,

Wildness, first and foremost, comes from identification with the literal wildness—rugged mountains, virgin forests, barren tundra, the habitat of untamed grizzlies, undomesticated wolves, fierce mountain lions. Wildness is no metaphor whose meaning we may learn when we are comfortably housed within a city or enclosed within boundaries of the civilized psyche. We need large expanses of untouched wilderness to remind ourselves of the abiding fundamental truths of the human condition: We are only a single species within a commonwealth of sentient beings.[10]

As such, men must heed the example of America's patron saint of wilderness, John Muir. Muir, born in 1838 in Scotland, came to America as a boy and later became the country's premier poet of, and spokesman for, wilderness. He had standard advice for the American men of his time, who were the first generation to become industrialized: "Keep close to Nature's heart, yourself: and break clear away, once in a while, and climb a mountain or spend a week in the woods. Wash your spirit clean."[11]

Each man needs to enter the wilderness. Some will do so in groups. Others, like John Muir, will prefer to explore the wild alone. Some are content to hike and camp. Others will light night fires and dance, drum, and sing. Still other men will be drawn to the traditional outdoor crafts such as fishing (to be carefully distinguished from much of current "outdoor sports," which too often means the seeking of "trophies"—large fish and mammals—with high-tech machines).

As men return to the wilderness, they reinhabit psychic and physical places from which they were exiled generations ago. Yet only the most myopic of men would return to the wilderness in search of spiritual resuscitation without also seeing that the wilderness itself was threatened and needed protection. In the last years of his life John Muir called for "wilderness-minded" men to save the wilderness from destruction. In 1892 he founded the Sierra Club to defend California's wilds. He himself had been forced from a life of celebration of wilderness to one of political activism by, among other industrial invasions, the proposal to dam Hetch Hetchy, a stupendous valley just north of Yosemite. Muir had spent years living in the California wilderness and was shocked by the proposal to dam the magnificent site. "Dam Hetch Hetchy," Muir stormed when he first heard of the proposal, "as well dam for water-tanks the people's cathedrals and churches, for no holier temple has been consecrated by the heart of man." For ten years Muir fought to save the valley against those who "seem to have a perfect contempt for Nature, and, instead of lifting their eyes to the God of the mountains, lift them to the Almighty dollar."[12] He, and the mass national campaign that he led, convinced the Roosevelt and Taft administrations to refrain from building the dam. However, in 1913, Woodrow Wilson finally approved the dam, and the battle over Hetch Hetchy was lost. One year later Muir died. Despite the failure to save his beloved valley, Muir's vigilance and public crusade were key to the creation of several national parks and the fostering of the wilderness ethic in America.

Each man has an obligation to work with others to defend the wild in himself and at the same time defend the continuing survival of wilderness on our planet. Many local and national environmental organizations have initiatives to help protect the wilds. However, the first step in the preservation of wilderness is its recovery in the hearts and minds of men.

The last chapters have surveyed the vast battleground on which men are struggling to overcome the masculine mystique and to establish a right relationship to family, work, health, and the natural world. This basic agenda is fundamental to the men's movement and to any alleviation of the hidden crisis.

However, men also need to include in their efforts a deeper commitment to those who, under the aegis of the masculine mystique, have lost the most. As described in the next section, the plight of these men must become a central focus of the masculinist movement.

PART IV

THE LOST MEN

13

THE DEAD IN THE LIVING

In killing the grunts of North Vietnam, the grunts of America had killed a part of themselves.
—Charles Anderson[1]

Steve Graham was a seventeen-year-old high school dropout. In the late 1960s he joined the army with the promise that he would be trained as an airplane mechanic. Instead of working with planes, Steve was sent to Vietnam and into combat:

We were on a platoon-size sweep, trying to run anything up in the mountain down into this big valley. We did this for three days, with Nef walking point for our team. Nef was the grungiest grunt you could be. He had leather straps hanging off his wrist; he carried a big machete; he had lots of stories.

One morning me and Nef and my friend Doc were up on the ridge smoking a joint and the word came up from the lieutenant: "I want you guys down across that creek at the bottom in thirty minutes." So we went down a high speed trail. We could see that people had been moving down this trail recently. We came into this little area where things had been crushed down, where quite a few people had been sitting. There were NVA [North Vietnamese Army] rations all around. Me and Nef and Doc moved out again. I said, "Nef, be careful." He got up and started walking through this elephant grass.

There was no marking for this booby trap, 'cause I was looking. They had just left and set the booby trap on the way out and didn't mark it. The trail almost disappeared through the elephant grass and Nef tripped the wire. I heard the spoon come off the grenade, a very distinctive sound. I turned around to dive off in the opposite direction, but Nef was totally unaware that he had hit a trip wire. He called back, "Did you see what I dropped?" Because of his calmness I thought, "Well, he must have dropped something off his pack and that's what I heard." So I turned back toward him and said, "Man you scared the shit out of me." Then this grenade went off as I was taking a step toward him. . . . He got blown one way and I got blown the other way. I never lost consciousness. I remember going through the air and landing on my right elbow yelling, "Shit!" I looked down at my legs and they were totally laid open. I tried to yell for Doc and I couldn't yell. It was like I was underwater. I couldn't hear nothing. I started relaxing and looking around. I could see branches falling off of trees so I knew we were being shot at, but I couldn't hear any of it.

It seemed like a lifetime for the helicopters to get there. . . . They sat me on this thing and pulled me up to the helicopter. I remember looking down at everybody lined up to the helicopter. They all waved to me and I waved to them. It was the strangest feeling: I knew I was going home, but I didn't know if I was going home alive or dead.

Up in the helicopter, that's when the pain started hitting. They brought Nef on behind me. He was dead when they put him on. They stuck a tube down his throat real quick and started breathing for him. I looked out over Vietnam and all I could see was graves. That's all I remember until we landed 'cause I passed out. Later this one guy told me: "You were lucky, 'cause you died." . . . He said I had stopped breathing for sixty-three seconds.

They got us to the hospital and in this big ward . . . all around me was death, people dying. . . . This nurse was holding my hand while the doctors were working on my leg to try and stop the bleeding. . . . I hadn't been given any morphine or any pain medication at all. Things are really starting to hurt, and I'm starting to have a hard time breathing 'cause the blood is getting into my lungs.

Finally, they pushed a metal tube down my throat and sucked the blood out so I could breathe again. . . . Nef was still with me in the hospital. He had died a couple of times but they managed to get him breathing again. Now he was blind and I think part of his brain was missing. He had lost a chunk of his head in the explosion. We lay there together. Out of the corner of my eye I could see Nef's legs, little movements. He would lay there all day long complaining about these purple spots he saw in his blindness. . . .

After a week they flew us to Japan. Nef finally died for good. They operated on me there, my legs and my throat. . . . Six times they operated on me. I had to eat through a tube up my nose for about four months. A piece of shrapnel had shattered my voice box, severed a vocal cord, and lodged in my esophagus.

So that's why I still can't talk. This one vocal cord is cut, and the other one supposedly is paralyzed. There's a big air space there, so all I can do is whisper. It was hard to get adjusted to the loss of my voice. I used to sing. I had always thought that would be my career: in music, either singing or playing the guitar.

And the everyday things, I was embarrassed by it. I'd have other people make my telephone calls, because whenever I'd try and call someone they'd think it was an obscene phone call or they'd just hang up. Or even when I'd go up to order a hamburger where music is played overhead in a speaker, I couldn't do it. I'd always need someone to order for me in a restaurant. . . . All the time I was with my first wife, she did a lot of my communicating with the world. . . .

When I talk to other people about my views it usually ends up getting into death. That generally turns people off. I attribute a lot of it to Vietnam, because death was such an everyday thing. Someone is there that you like, and the next day they're not there anymore. Sometimes you can't even find pieces of them. You realize how meaningless your life is. There's nothing for you to do. . . .

People talk a lot about "delayed stress syndrome" from Vietnam. For myself, I have a hard time with depression and that death thing. . . . Sometimes I think: "Why can't I really get into something? Anything: believe in God, do something I like, get a job helping other people, whatever." But I can't make it important enough for me to do it. Everybody knows that death is scary, but then they just don't think about it anymore. They forget about it and go back to doing what they were doing. Somehow I can't forget about it that easily.[2]

Steve's story and personal tragedy graphically symbolize the plight of millions of veterans from Vietnam, Korea, and World War II, men whose voices cannot seem to reach the bureaucracies of government or the hearts and minds of American society.

The mechanized wars of this century have accounted for over one hundred million young men dead or seriously wounded. As was the case with Steve, death, injury, or disfigurement in modern warfare are mostly anonymous incidents where shrapnel, grenades, bullets, mines, or bombs, often delivered from long range, chew up the bodies of combatants. As the machines of war were developed, the hundreds of millions of men who fought modern wars were confronted with a battlefield, and a human reality, that were unprecedented. Historian Martin Van Creveld describes this new twentieth-century phenomenon:

> Ultimately the net effect of the progress in weapons technology was to increase enormously the volume of fire that could be delivered, the range at which it could be delivered, and the range and accuracy with which this could be done. The combination of all three factors meant that, square meter by square meter, the battlefield became a deadlier place than ever before. Metal in the form of bullets from quickfiring rifles and machine guns, as well as fragments from artillery shells, came hurtling through the air in quantities that would previously have appeared absolutely incredible.[3]

Over the last century as warfare became a mechanized "storm of steel," the tactics and garb of war had to adjust. Gone were the cavalry charges and hand-to-hand combat of the past, as were the classic formations of soldiers standing shoulder-to-shoulder walking erect into battle. Soldiers were now ever more widely dispersed and permanently crouching to avoid the hail of fire. As a result the modern battlefields have what one commentator called an "eerie, empty look." Traditional uniforms, bemedaled, gaudy, and multicolored, gave way to camouflaged coverings in field gray, olive green, or earth brown, which were likely to be stained by "greasy-grease." Ceremonial plumed or spiked hats gave way to steel ones derived from those long worn by miners and thus symbolic of the transformation of war from an essentially aristocratic pastime to deadly industrial-type work.

By World War I combat was no longer about men against men but rather men against machines. At Ypres in 1915, 100,000 young men were gunned down in a single day without seeing the machine gunners who caused their deaths. While the wars of yore usually involved symbolic victory of small groups of men in ritualized battles, World War I and the wars that followed it were about mass extermination of armies. As noted by historian Richard Rubenstein in his discussion of the battle of Verdun, in which a million men died over a period of nine months, "In modern warfare, there is no knightly comradeship. The objective is often to deprive the enemy of his basic instrument of violence, his Army. In essence the . . . strategy was biological. The objective at Verdun was to exterminate as many of the enemy as possible. . . . *Both the British and the German generals made the same decision: their country's young men were expendable.*" (Emphasis in original.)[4]

The World War I fire zones introduced a generation of young men to experiences unimaginable except as a fanciful imitation of those attributed to hell. The young men walking into this inferno were totally unprepared for it. Their minds were full of images of war in prior times. Led by patriotism and jingoistic demonization of the enemy, the young soldiers imagined glorious fighting where death if it came would be honorable.

Instead of an initiation into manhood, most found industrial-type slaughter—deafening firepower rocking mind and body; a rain of bullets and shrapnel filling the air; the bodies of tens of thousands of dead young men strewn helter-skelter over miles of barbed wire; the nauseating stench of decaying bodies, burning flesh, and acrid mud; the earth itself pockmarked and blasted out of recognition by artillery fire. Every day they saw thousands of grotesque deaths and dismemberments that nothing could have prepared these young combatants for. One British private in World War I remembers his friend hit in the head by a burst of machine-gun fire: "His blood and brains, pieces of skull and lumps of hair, spattered all over the front of my greatcoat and gas mask. I stood there trying to get the bits off."[5] To complete the analogy to the classic picture of the inferno, toxic and asphyxiating gases released from cylinders or bursting from artillery shells quickly filled trenches and foxholes choking and killing wherever they fell, causing whole battalions to run in panic.

By World War II major technological developments had made the killing fields even more nightmarish. Air power meant that death could now be delivered at will from the sky. Tank technology greatly accelerated the fury of land warfare. The additions of submachine guns, flamethrowers, and light artillery to the arsenal of the infantry soldier added further to the already overwhelming repertoire of death.

No century in human history can match the current one in sheer numbers of human beings slaughtered in war. And along with the increasing volume of civilian casualties, the mechanized wars of modernity created nothing short of a holocaust of young men. We tend to forget how young these men were when they were offered up as the fodder for the war machines. The expressions *doughboys, our fighting boys*, and *the boys at the front* were not hyperbole. The average age of the World War I casualty was 17.8 years of age. The age of the average soldier fighting in Vietnam was 19.2 years of age. Most of our modern warriors were indeed little more than boys; most of them were scared boys. A British artillery officer in World War I wrote a letter to a nurse confessing that "what we need most when our strength is spent—women who are so shameless in their pity that they will mother us. We daren't ask it ourselves. If you don't guess we will never tell you."[6]

The attitude of the public about war has still not caught up with the modern technological reality. We still associate war with chivalric courage and valor, yet it is mostly about long-distance murder. We insist on treating the actions of our soldiers as heroic even when they involve the mass genocide of the battlefield, the bombing of cities, or the computerized destruction of modern air warfare. In the new age of total war the civilians of countries invaded or destroyed know differently. The Europeans who survived mass firebombings of their cities and battles in their streets need no lessons on modern warfare. The citizens of Korea, Vietnam, Cambodia, and Iraq understand. But America, whose cities have never been bombed and whose country has not been invaded in the age of modern warfare, has been developmentally arrested in its view of war.

Veterans who survived the battlefield face the brunt of this social pathology. They have seen firsthand the dreadful reality behind the mythology of modern war. They have learned that they are not precision fighting "machines" but rather men, often panicked and frightened, put into battle situations that are remarkable mainly because of their confusion and anonymous slaughter. They have learned that in modern warfare the noble warrior is at best merely an obedient soldier and at worst a straightforward murderer, often of civilians. One American officer in Vietnam summed up what happens to the minds of the basically decent American conscripts once they are confronted with battle:

> You put those kids in the jungle for a while, get them real scared, deprive them of sleep, and let a few incidents change some of their fears to hate. Give them a sergeant who has seen too many of his men killed by booby traps and by lack of distrust, and who feels that Vietnamese are dumb, dirty and weak, because they are not like him. Add a little mob pressure, and those nice kids . . . would rape like champions. Kill, rape and steal is the name of the game.[7]

Paradoxically many veterans also learn that the dehumanization of the enemy being accomplished by the press and government at home, and by their officers in training, is false. They learn that "the enemy is us." One American infantryman remembers when this occurred to him in Vietnam: "One day during a fire fight, for the first time in my life, I heard the cries of the Vietnamese wounded, and I understood them. When somebody gets wounded, they call out for their mothers, their wives, their girlfriends. There I was listening to the VC cry for the same things. That's when the futility of the war dawned on me."[8]

After victorious wars some veterans received parades upon returning home. Others, including many of the veterans of Korea and Vietnam, did not. For a short time some of the veterans become the heroes that the government and the public want, but then they are forgotten. Few civilians want to hear that their view of war is a myth, that the slaughtered enemy were people just like them, that our courageous fighting men were more often simply the operators of machines of long-range destruction and at times the murderers of civilians. Isolated, the veteran carries the burden of the war's vileness on his own shoulders, unable to find anyone to share or understand his experiences. This aloneness leads him to relive his war experiences daily; often he sees only one way out of his isolation and pain: some form of self-destruction.

As part of American society's avoidance of the real facts of war, there is little public pressure to truly care for its wounded men—those like Steve whose bodies have become emblems of the reality of modern warfare. Ron Kovic, author of *Born on the Fourth of July*, remembers being in a U.S. hospital paralyzed by a bullet wound in Vietnam. He saw little compassion or gratitude. "Urine bags are constantly overflowing on to the floor while the aides play poker on the toilet bowl in the enema room. . . . The sheets are never changed and many of the men stink from not being properly bathed."[9]

Author and Vietnam veteran Michael Uhl writes eloquently of what would be required if American society were truly to understand the pain of many veterans:

Unfortunately, while there presently is some renewed interest in Vietnam veterans, most of the organizations and individuals involved are trying to deal with the war related pain of vets without understanding its true source. They'd rather try to change the way veterans feel about their war experiences . . . than deal with the society capable of creating such brutalizing and dishonorable war machinery. . . . If average Americans could grasp for one instant the meaning of body count and apply it to an American child; if they could see a little Yankee girl aflame with napalm running naked down some suburban asphalt street, or imagine their own community transformed into a free fire zone beyond the protection of any convention of war, they might gain an insight into the darker side of American power. . . . And might not Americans then embrace the Vietnam veteran and share and understand his pain and disaffection? . . . What a burden would be lifted![10]

Regrettably in the over two decades since Vietnam this public exercise has not been undertaken. The romance of war, and the glorification of the modern soldier as a kind of courageous robopath, have continued unabated. The truth about modern warfare remains repressed by society, and therefore stays the burden of the veteran. Some can forget. Others, like Steve, can't.

MINDS IN BATTLE

The victims of modern war are not only those who were killed or maimed. There are millions of veterans in the United States and around the world who are permanently psychologically scarred by what they saw, what happened to them, and by acts they committed. In World War I those who showed extreme psychological distress after battle were called cowards; some were even shot. Later their condition was diagnosed as "shell shock." By 1939 over 130,000 World War I British vets were on disability based on psychological trauma experienced in the war. In World War II and Korea it was called battle fatigue. Often as many as 20 percent of U.S. troops were evacuated from battle sites in these wars as "psychological casualties." After Vietnam—too long after, it took almost a decade—a new term was coined for it: post-traumatic stress disorder.

Throughout the 1970s psychologists were noting that veterans were reporting numerous symptoms, including sleeplessness, severe headaches, recurrent nightmares, flashbacks, and sudden and unprovoked outbursts of violence. Many veterans seemed unable to connect with normal life, some plunging into drugs and alcohol abuse. Others, like Steve, simply withdrew from society, living in what one psychologist called "psychic Vietnam." Despite the increasing number of reports on trauma symptoms of Vietnam vets, experts remained divided on whether the veterans' symptoms were related to their war experience. As a result for years after the war there was no consistent diagnosis or treatment of stress disorders associated with service in Vietnam. Art Blank, a psychiatrist who heads the Veterans Administration's (VA) readjustment counseling service and a Vietnam vet himself, commented on the lengthy struggle to get the government and the mental health profession to recognize the problem. "It took a significant political and professional effort just to bring about a basic recognition of the condition. You could almost say there had to be another war fought."[11]

Eventually this war was won. In 1979 Congress authorized the VA to open a string of outreach and counseling centers for veterans. Over the next decade more than half a million vets were treated at the centers, as were 150,000 family members. Subsequently the psychiatric profession joined the government in acknowledging what they should have known for a long time—that if an individual, even a supposedly invulnerable trained "killing machine," undergoes sufficient trauma, sees enough horror, he can suffer disabling psychological damage. In 1980 post-traumatic stress disorder (PTSD) was included in the diagnostic manual of the American Psychiatric Association.

The toll in men's lives caused by the delay in treating veterans' mental problems had been high. By the time the government had acted to deal with their mental health problems, over 400,000 Vietnam veterans were in prison, on probation, or awaiting parole. Even more tragic, over 100,000 Vietnam veterans have committed suicide after returning home from the war, almost twice as many as died in combat.[12]

It is of course shocking that it took government and the mental health profession so many years to recognize that war sinks a painful shard into the souls and psyches of so many men. The delay is added testimony to the deep societal denial of the real nature of modern warfare and what it does to men. However, the refusal to recognize PTSD also demonstrates how prejudiced our society remains in its views of men.

Men, especially the machine men of the military, are not supposed to be helpless, depressed, or unable to handle life. The masculine mystique causes the ostracism of men who ask for help, who experience fright, horror, and, worst of all, who have become dependent on people or the government. After all, real men pull themselves up by their bootstraps and don't go "crybabying" about jitters or bad dreams. Even some vets have scorned those shown by the media who were suffering, including those seen weeping at the Wall or other Vietnam memorials. "Excuse me while I barf," wrote one Viet vet in a *Wall Street Journal* op-ed piece. "The vast majority of men who fought in the war . . . simply do not fit those images. Many of us are embarrassed by them."[13]

Whatever the scorn, or expectations, of society, many veterans could not simply reenter society and return to normal life. Their minds had become the final battlefield of the war. They had experienced too much death to fully live again. In 1988 a Veterans Administration–funded study reported to Congress that 15 percent, or about 470,000, of the approximately 3.14 million men who served in Vietnam were being treated for PTSD in that year alone. Soon it wasn't just Viet vets. As PTSD became better recognized, veterans from World War II and Korea began to seek treatment of their trauma symptoms. Many of these men had suffered for decades without seeking help, afraid to admit their problems to a society that didn't want to hear. Now over one-third of all PTSD patients are from wars prior to Vietnam.[14]

Our society has been so unable and unwilling to hear the reality of the veteran's pain that, on occasion, it has killed the bearer of the message. Wayne Felde landed in Vietnam on his nineteenth birthday, in March 1968. A week after he arrived in Vietnam, Felde was flown by helicopter to Landing Zone Polly Ann near Kontum. He could not join his unit immediately because they were away fighting the Vietcong. When the helicopters returned with the casualties, he unloaded dead bodies until nightfall. The next day he joined a firefight that lasted two hours. Afterward he and another soldier went to recover the body of a member of their squad, who had been captured and subsequently killed. When they found him, they saw that his body had been napalmed after death. When Felde attempted to lift the corpse, the legs came off. Later Felde recalled "picking up pieces of our guys to send home. . . . I cried for guys I didn't even know. I thought of their moms and my mom and someone offered me a reefer. I never smoked it before, [but] . . . I smoked it then and from then on."[15]

During his year in Vietnam Felde saw and experienced the horrors of the war. He held the quivering intestines of a friend dying of a mortar-round wound. He watched a lieutenant perform a "gook abortion"—slicing open the abdomen of a pregnant Vietnamese woman with a machete. After his return to the States Felde had recurring nightmares and flashbacks of his Vietnam experience. The sight of rice on a plate could trigger vivid memories of Vietnam that resembled psychotic hallucinations.[16]

Felde did not have to go to Vietnam. Raised in Maryland, he was the sole surviving son of a World War II veteran; he could have obtained an exemption. But he decided to serve his country and successfully arranged to get himself drafted. Felde went to Vietnam as a patriot. But, as he later told a jury in Louisiana, he returned "not a criminal but a troubled and wrecked man."[17] His last few months of service in the States were filled with heavy drinking and a near-fatal car accident. He spent the next two years in and out of college and holding fifteen different jobs, each of which he quit. He married his high school sweetheart, but the marriage lasted only six months. In 1972, while on a drinking spree, Felde got into a fight with a coworker, who was an ex-convict. As they struggled for a gun, the man was killed. When the police arrived, Wayne went berserk, yelling, "Vietnam, Vietnam, come and get me!" He spent three years in jail and then escaped. After two years in hiding or on the road, he surfaced in Shreveport, Louisiana, to be with his mother, who was dying of cancer.

A week after his mother's death Felde was again arrested. While in custody he took out a .357 Magnum which had been overlooked by the arresting officer, and in what he says was an attempt to kill himself, the gun went off. In the fracas Felde was badly injured, losing a kidney, part of his liver, and permanently crippling his right leg. A bullet fired by Felde split on one of the police car's seat springs and killed an officer after severing a vein in his groin.

At a subsequent trial Felde was convicted of first-degree murder and sentenced to die in the electric chair. Philip Caputo, noted author and fellow Vietnam veteran, questioned the verdict. "Felde was not at the scene of either crime. He was where he has been for nearly 14 years, at a place called Fire Base Polly Ann."[18]

After Felde's conviction the web of symptoms involved in PTSD became better known, and the disorder was successfully used as a defense in murder trials. However, the Louisiana Board of Pardons turned down Felde's plea for clemency based on his suffering PTSD. According to those who knew him, Felde abhorred the idea of asking for clemency, feeling, correctly as it turned out, that government bureaucrats would not understand. A week before he was executed, Felde told his lawyer, "They can kill the messenger but they can't kill the message of what the Vietnam War did to people like me." On March 14, 1988, ten days before his thirty-ninth birthday, he was killed by "enemy fire," consisting of the 2,300 volts of Louisiana's electric chair. After the execution one commentator suggested that there should be a special section of the Vietnam veterans memorial—an area that is devoted to listing men like Wayne Felde and so many others—men who died in Vietnam but lived to tell about it.

AGENTS OF DEATH

Many veterans return from war carrying not only the psychological burden of the war but also a toxic and potentially fatal part of the battlefield in their biological systems. The gas victims in World War I returned home to slow deaths by asphyxiation. World War II veterans who fought in the Pacific theater came home with exotic illnesses, and a few were victims of Japanese biological warfare. Many Korean veterans returned from the war to become "observers" at various atomic-test sites, where they were exposed to cancer-causing radiation. Persian Gulf veterans are already reporting a range of illnesses believed to be caused either by air pollution from the oil fires in Kuwait, low-level exposure to chemical weapons, or unapproved genetically engineered vaccinations that they received.

Vietnam veterans were no exception. Tens of thousands of soldiers were exposed to toxic chemicals when 18 million gallons of the herbicide Agent Orange were sprayed from the sky, wiping out much of what was green and growing in Vietnam. The herbicide sprayed on and around these men was not the garden variety used at home in the United States. It was purposely manufactured to be more potent and more toxic because the manufacturing of the higher-powered chemical was cheaper and faster.

The Pentagon's defoliation program for Vietnam, begun in 1962, was called Operation Ranch Hand (originally it had the more apt title Operation Hades). By 1967 the program was spraying herbicides over 1.5 million acres of Vietnamese foliage and 221,000 acres of croplands. By the time the program ended in 1971, an estimated 6 million acres of Vietnam had been hit with herbicides. Fed by the Ranch Hand program, herbicide manufacturing became one of the growth industries spawned by the war. Annual sales increased from $12.5 million in 1966 to $79.8 million three years later. Eleven chemical companies, including Dow, Monsanto, Hooke, and Velsico, shared the booming business.[19]

Within a few years of the war's end thousands of vets were reporting severe medical problems ranging from non-Hodgkin's lymphoma—an extremely rare cancer—to soft-tissue sarcomas, and numerous other debilitating and fatal diseases. Many in the medical profession began linking these diseases to exposure to dioxin and other chemicals present in Agent Orange.

Numerous birth defects have also been associated with exposure to Agent Orange. Jim Wiggens, a Marine veteran from New York, described the devastating effect he believes Agent Orange had on his family. "Four of our seven children were born with birth defects, primarily malformed legs and feet. My wife has also suffered two miscarriages. She didn't serve in Vietnam, but she feels like she did."[20] Diseases caused by dioxin and the other chemicals in Agent Orange can have a latency period of decades. First- and second-generation victims of the disease continue to emerge with each passing year.

In the 1960s Air Force scientists who helped create Agent Orange knew about the toxicity of the herbicide they were spraying in such massive amounts.[21] Yet the federal government has only now begun to accept liability for the horrible impacts on veterans caused by Operation Ranch Hand. Up until recently the Department of Veteran Affairs had recognized only chloracne, a severe skin rash, as directly linked to Agent Orange exposure. For all the other serious diseases and birth defects associated with the herbicide, Congress, under extreme pressure from chemical companies, had said no. Veterans and their families who suffered disease or birth defects due to exposure to Agent Orange, or families of veterans who died of Agent Orange exposure, were not covered for treatment or compensation. Scientific studies that would have supported the veterans' claims on Agent Orange exposure were either sabotaged or misrepresented.

Recently the VA has added several other diseases, including a variety of cancers, to the list of illnesses that would now be covered by VA care and compensation. While welcome, the additions did not come in time for thousands who died of these diseases without any coverage. Additionally, since the average VA claim now takes up to five years to adjudicate, many more Agent Orange victims will die waiting for some help from the government they served.

In the late 1970s some Agent Orange victims sued the manufacturers of the defoliant. They litigated in the hope of receiving a justice from the courts better than that which they were getting from Congress. In 1984 the manufacturers of the herbicide settled the class-action lawsuit. The settlement called for $180 million to be distributed among the victims. By 1991 almost fifty thousand claims seeking compensation under the settlement had been filed. After years of delay and further litigation thousands of vets have received settlement payments of between $3,500 and $18,000.

Many vets are outraged at the settlement. They noted that a few thousand dollars are clearly insufficient to compensate individuals for fatal cancers or severe birth defects in their children. Most veterans involved feel that the case was settled prematurely, once again leaving sick veterans and their families out in the cold. Others feel that the settlement was arrived at to avoid telling the American people the truth about Agent Orange and the cynical manner in which it was used. One vet stated, "The Vietnam veteran would rather have this history recorded for all time than worry about claims awards."[22]

The belated acknowledgment of PTSD and the agonizing struggle of Agent Orange victims to get compensation is part of a larger pattern of treating vets as subcitizens. Gas victims of World War I, battle-fatigue victims of World War II, the army mustard-gas volunteers who were experimented on during World War II, the navy men who built ships in the forties and fifties with asbestos and ended up with severe lung disorders, the tens of thousands of soldiers exposed to radiation from being ordered to witness atomic tests—all spent decades trying to get treatment and compensation for the disease and death that they endured due to their service in the military.

The message taught by the struggle of these veterans is clear. When the shooting stops, when the man is no longer needed as a cog in the war machine, he is forgotten. Entranced in our worship of war, we like to romanticize and honor war heroes of decades past. Movies and White House ceremonies honor the modern warriors, generally for political gain. We have seen the ritual replayed in Margaret Thatcher's war in the Falklands and George Bush's in the Persian Gulf. We remain numb, however, to the reality of war and the reality of the lives of the multitude of men in hospitals, jails, drug centers, and withdrawn in homes around the country—men who, far from fighting for medals, are fighting for understanding, care, and often their lives.

America's veterans have borne much of this in relative silence. Men like Steve Graham are literally silenced. Others have withdrawn. Many are too discouraged or poor to keep fighting the unequal battle against government bureaucracies and corporate and public indifference. These men need help, yet few nonveteran men, or women, have spoken up for them.

One exception is Tod Ensign. Ensign has worked with veterans since 1969. He is a lawyer and longtime social-justice activist. Ensign's organization, Citizen Soldier, is described as a veterans/GI advocacy organization, and it lives up to its description. It is among the feistiest and most effective groups working on veterans' issues. The group, through its small office in New York City, has a large educational outreach on veterans' concerns, conducts health studies, and litigates (as it did on Agent Orange).

Ensign puts the veterans' plight into the context of the economic and social system in which they live. He notes that many veterans are only valued so long as they can "walk up a hill and stop a bullet." Once home, there is no safety net for these men, and they too often fall into joblessness, hopelessness, suicide, and violence. An early reader of Herb Goldberg's works on men, Ensign also understands how our society's reductionistic view of men contributes to the plight of veterans: "America's warriors have been treated like so many no deposit, no return bottles," Ensign states. "Once the contents are consumed the empties are thrown on the junk heap."[23]

The immediate solutions for many veterans fought for by Ensign and others are not complex: better treatment and compensation for PTSD, treatment and compensation for all Agent Orange victims, changes in the laws to make civil actions against Agent Orange makers easier, a new system that allows VA claims to be adjudicated quickly, and support for veterans' groups so that the new veterans created by American conflicts overseas are fully protected upon their return.

The implementation of these cures are, however, more complex. They often involve bucking powerful corporate and government entities. Moreover, the veterans issue will become more urgent as America's 27 million vets become older, requiring more care just as the government has frozen appropriations for the VA.

Addressing the problems of veterans also involves a radical shift in our social perception of modern warfare. Until the public is ready to hear about the reality of the wars we fight, the vets will go unheard and their physical and psychic sufferings will be borne alone.

Finally, we must also examine our attitudes about men—especially the masculine-mystique view that men validate themselves by becoming the invulnerable, efficient killing machines glorified by our robopathic military. Why do we as a nation feel that veterans who have been injured and psychologically scarred in service are not fully worthy of our gratitude, respect, understanding, and help? Why do we forget them so easily, especially when the war is not won? Why do we demand perfect heroes and then cast away real-life victims? Is a young soldier's broken body or mind any less worthy of compassion than a woman's or a child's?

14

THE INVISIBLE MEN

Got one mind for white folks to see,
'nother for what I know is me;
He don't know,
He don't know my mind, when he sees me laughing
Just laughing to keep me from crying —R. Ames[1]

My first victim was a woman—white, well dressed, probably in her early twenties. I came upon her late one evening on a deserted street in Hyde Park, a relatively affluent neighborhood in an otherwise mean, impoverished section of Chicago. As I swung into the avenue behind her, there seemed to be a discreet, uninflammatory distance between us. Not so. She cast back a worried glance. To her, the youngish black man—a broad six feet two inches with a beard and billowing hair, both hands shoved into the pockets of a bulky military jacket—seemed menacingly close. After a few more quick glimpses, she picked up her pace and was soon running in earnest. Within seconds she disappeared into a cross street.

That was more than a decade ago. I was twenty-two years old, a graduate student newly arrived at the University of Chicago. It was in the echo of the terrified woman's footfalls that I first began to know the unwieldy inheritance I'd come into—the ability to alter public space in ugly ways. It was clear that she thought herself the quarry of a mugger, a rapist, or worse. Suffering a bout of insomnia, however, I was stalking sleep, not defenseless wayfarers. . . .

In that first year, my first away from my hometown, I was to become thoroughly familiar with the language of fear. At dark, shadowy intersections, I could cross in front of a car stopped at a traffic light and elicit the thunk, thunk, thunk, thunk of the driver—black, white, male or female—hammering down the door locks. On less traveled streets after dark, I grew accustomed to but never comfortable with people crossing to the other side of the street rather than pass me. . . . I [still] often see women who fear the worst from me. . . . I understand of course that the danger they perceive is not a hallucination. Women are particularly vulnerable to street violence, and young black males are drastically overrepresented among the perpetrators of that violence. Yet the set truths are no solace against the kind of alienation that comes of ever being suspect, a fearsome entity with whom pedestrians avoid making eye contact. That first encounter, and those that followed, signified that vast gulf. . . .

Over the years I learned to smother the rage I felt at so often being taken for a criminal. Not to do so would surely have led to madness. I now take precautions to make myself less threatening. . . . And on late-evening constitutionals I employ what has proved to be an excellent tension-reducing measure: I whistle melodies from Beethoven and Vivaldi and the more popular classical composers. . . . Virtually everybody seems to sense that a mugger wouldn't be warbling bright, sunny selections from Vivaldi's *Four Seasons*. It is my equivalent of the cowbell that hikers wear when they know they are in bear country.[2]

The 1992 riots in Los Angeles once again revealed the wound at the heart of urban America. Messages of concern and healing were mixed with those reminding us that no society can exist without "law and order." Code words were used back and forth, but it was apparent to all that the majority of those who rioted were black. However, the palpable fear that the riot caused many in the white as well as the black community was not a fear of black people. It was primarily a fear of the violence of young black men.

Fear of black men has become a reflex in urban life. It is a routinized apprehension that occasionally becomes heightened to near paranoia when a long-dormant inner-city volcano suddenly erupts, and we see the anger and violence of yet another alienated, dispossessed generation of black youth. The apprehension about black men is often justified. Black males do commit a disproportionate number of violent crimes. Yet as described in the words quoted above of Brent Staples (a distinguished editor and journalist with *The New York Times*), the societal fear of these young men affects not only those who feel it but also those who are feared.

The added frustration and irony for African-American men is that though they are feared, it is really the black males who have cause for fright. They, among all other segments of the population, are the most frequent victims of violent crime. Overall, black men are victimized by violent crimes (defined as robbery, rape, and assault) 25 percent more than white males, 50 percent more than black females, and 200 percent more than white females. Forty-five percent of black males will become victims of violent crime three or more times in their lifetime. A black man has a 1-in-28 chance of being murdered; the average American has a 1-in-53 chance. For black men ages fifteen to thirty-four the leading cause of death is homicide.[3] The situation is worsening. According to a study by the Centers for Disease Control, the last years of the 1980s saw the murder rate for black youths between fifteen and nineteen nearly double. "In some areas of the country," said Robert Froehlke, principal author of the CDC study, "it is now more likely for a black male between his fifteenth and twenty-fourth birthdays to die from homicide than it was for a U.S. soldier to be killed on a tour of duty in Vietnam."[4]

It is not just violence. If there were a hierarchy of victimization in this country, black men would be at the top. Black men have the lowest life expectancy of any group in the United States. They rate highest in a number of areas, including high blood pressure and certain cancers.

At the same time, as a group they rank the lowest in health insurance coverage. Suicide rates for black males have also soared, and suicide is now the third-leading cause of death (after homicides and accidents) among black males in the eighteen to twenty-nine age group.[5]

Nor has the education system helped. For too many young black men academic failure is endemic, and alienation from the education system near total. Black males leave school due to discipline problems twice as often as black females. By the eighth grade (thirteen years of age) 45 percent of black males are at least one year behind. One 1990 study in Milwaukee revealed that black boys accounted for 50 percent of all suspensions in the city's school system even though they made up only 27 percent of the school population. The study also found that 80 percent of the city's black male high school students earned less than a "C" average. A Department of Education survey showed that in 1989, 17.5 percent of black males (aged eighteen and nineteen) had left high school without graduating. Four times as many black women as men attend our nation's universities. And since 1976 the percentage of male black high school graduates who have enrolled in college has steadily declined. Now there are more black males aged twenty to twenty-nine in jail than in college. Some have estimated the rate of functional illiteracy among black males to be an astounding 45 percent.[6]

The economic reality for black men is equally bleak. In 1990 the unemployment rate for black males was 11.8 percent, over two times higher than that for white males. Joblessness among black male teenagers is even more alarming, consistently hovering over 35 percent. During the 1980s 46 percent of black men between the ages of sixteen and sixty-two were not members of the labor force. In the recent recession blacks lost proportionately more jobs than any other population group. Black men in "blue collar" jobs were especially hard hit. One out of every three blue-collar workers laid off was black.[7] What was a recession for the rest of America was a depression for blacks. As the adage goes, "When the American economy gets a cold, the black community gets pneumonia."

The increasingly dire situation for black men has led one black sociologist to declare black males "an endangered species." Observers like Alvin Poussaint, associate professor of psychiatry at Harvard Medical School, share the foreboding. "Everywhere you look, black males are in trouble," says Poussaint. "And the more the black male falls behind and gets damaged, the less available he is to become a good father, brother, or grandparent. This is not just a personal disaster, it is a profound loss to the black community's stability and strength."[8]

Over the years many have attempted to account for the lack of African-American progress along the main avenues of achievement in our society, and especially the plight of the black male. In 1965 then–assistant labor secretary Daniel Patrick Moynihan issued a report entitled *The Negro Family: The Case for National Action.* The Moynihan Report articulated the highly influential "family instability thesis," namely that slavery caused a disruption in black families from which the African-American community has never recovered. As for the African-American male, the report noted that in slavery the "Negro male was particularly likely to be transferred from owner to owner, so it was nearly impossible for him to maintain lasting relationships with Negro females and any children he might father."[9] Consequently, according to the theory, a mother-centered family developed among blacks to a far greater extent than among whites. Under these circumstances the black male did not acquire strong family responsibilities, nor did he have the influence of a strong father role model.

While few would question the trauma of slavery on the African-American community, a review of the history of the black experience over the last century shows a far more complex socioeconomic basis for the current condition of black men than presented by Moynihan and the other family-instability theorists.

WHO NEEDS THE BLACKS?

In 1910, 73 percent of the nation's black population lived in rural America, 91 percent in the South. There the black population worked primarily as agricultural workers in sharecropping circumstances that had altered little since the days of Reconstruction. The white population of the South had an ambiguous relationship with the blacks; while there was much racial hatred, nevertheless the black was a vital cog in the South's economy. One observer at the turn of the century wrote, "One of the most significant things I saw in the South—and I saw it everywhere—was the way in which the white people are torn between their feelings of race prejudice and their downright economic needs. Hating and fearing the Negro as a race (though often loving individual Negroes), they yet want him to work for them; they can't get along without him."[10]

Most blacks remained in the South throughout the first decades of the century picking cotton and performing other vitally needed low-level agricultural work. Some did leave seeking better work in the North, especially after World War I. At that time new legal restrictions caused a halt in the flow of immigrants from Europe, who had been the main cheap labor force for factory owners. The absence of European immigrants provided new opportunities for black workers in the northern industrial work market.

Beginning in the 1930s and extending over the next several years, several factors joined together to change forever the lives of the millions of blacks remaining in the South. It began with the introduction and increasing use of the tractor, which allowed southern farmers to mechanize many tasks that heretofore had been done by blacks. The mechanical replacement of black farm labor culminated in the invention of the mechanical cotton picker in 1944. Five years later 94 percent of cotton in the South was still being picked by hand. But by the late 1950s only 22 percent was being picked by hand. By 1975 all cotton was being picked by machine.

As machines replaced farm labor, southern farm communities disintegrated. Between 1940 and 1960 southern farm labor declined from 4.2 million to 1.7 million.[11] While the mechanization of agriculture was the chief cause of this steep decline, the increasing use of herbicides (rather than hand removal of weeds), federally mandated minimum wages for farm workers, and government restrictions on cotton production also contributed.

As technology and government policy had made the southern blacks obsolete, they became the victims of a kind of technological enclosure that finally forced them from the land that had been their meager livelihood for decades. As with the victims of past enclosures, the southern blacks became economic refugees. More than five million blacks left the South looking for work in the North between 1940 and 1970. It was undoubtedly the largest migration in U.S. history. The economic refugees flooded to the major urban areas on the eastern seaboard, in the upper Midwest, and in California. Once in the cities, black workers sought desperately to gain jobs in the manufacturing sector.

One southern lawyer, observing the beginnings of the mass migration in 1947, sensed its ominous implications:

> Five million people will be removed from the land within the next few years. They must go somewhere. But where? They must do something. But what? They must be housed. But where is the housing? Most . . . are farm negroes totally unprepared for urban industrial life. How will they be absorbed? . . . What will the effect be upon race relations in the United States? Will the victims of farm mechanization become the victims of race conflict?
>
> There is an enormous tragedy in the making unless the United States acts, and acts promptly, upon a problem that affects millions of people and the whole structure of the nation.[12]

The United States government did not act. At first this inaction did not seem as catastrophic as imagined by many. Numbers of blacks did find work in the urban factories. During World War II there were jobs in the booming wartime production industries. Blacks were able to retain many of those jobs as the postwar era saw an explosion in manufacturing productivity. By the mid-1950s around a quarter of all workers at Chrysler and General Motors were black.

However, just as the southern black refugees began to gain an employment niche in the manufacturing sector, another technological revolution made them obsolete once again. Starting in the late 1950s automation came to many U.S. industries. Soon company after company was investing in the new automation technology. Machines began to replace men at a rapid rate. Close to two million blue-collar jobs were lost in the decade between 1952 and 1962, and the losses were concentrated in the industries that had become the job base for the migrating blacks. In 1960 there were less than one hundred black workers among the approximately twenty thousand skilled workers at Chrysler and GM.[13] By 1964 blacks were experiencing a 12.4 percent unemployment rate, while white unemployment was less than half that total. Since that time black unemployment has consistently been double that of whites.[14]

Adding to the woes of black workers was that they soon became isolated not only from work but also from the workplace. For a variety of reasons, including new zoning restrictions, cost-cutting measures, and the fear of labor unrest, industry began moving its new automated factories to the suburbs. White workers and their families followed. The newly unemployed blacks remained in the inner cities, now devoid of jobs and any real access to jobs. Once again the black man's labor was no longer needed, and he was discarded as so much economic debris. Black workers and their families were doomed to become a permanent underclass.

The disenfranchisement of the black community affected all its members. Yet the black man was the hardest hit. Despite the claims of Moynihan and others, for generations the black male had worked the soil to support his family. He was by tradition the head of the household and had fully taken that responsibility. However, in the short span of three decades he was displaced by machines both in the field and eventually in the factory. His primary social role as worker and breadwinner was destroyed.

When government finally did step in, it created a welfare safety net for many black women and children but not for men. As will be explained in the next chapter the welfare system works actively to disenfranchise many black men and further alienate them from their families. Almost twenty-five years ago sociologist Sidney Willhelm described the condition of the black male worker:

> With the onset of automation, the Negro moves out of his historical state of oppression into one of uselessness. Increasingly he is not so much economically exploited as he is irrelevant. . . . He is not needed. He is not so much oppressed as unwanted; not so much un-wanted as unnecessary; not so much abused as ignored. . . . The Negro's anguish does not rise only out of brutalities of past oppression; the anxiety stems, more than ever before, out of being discarded as a waste product of technological production.[15]

The experience of becoming a discard in the modern technological labor market was a disaster for the black male's economic survival and also for his masculinity. The masculine mystique's insistence that a man is defined by his economic productivity, his competitiveness, his ability to amass material goods, and his power over other men is no less a mandate for black men than it is for white. Black men buy into the mystique, yet they lack the jobs and resources to conform themselves to it.

To compensate, many young black men take on what researchers term compulsive masculinity. Author Richard Majors points out that without jobs and finances the young African-American man has to become compulsively masculine if he is to retain the aura of manhood under our current mystique definition. "Proving his masculinity is a daily chore for the black male," Majors states. "It can never be taken for granted." The black man then becomes something of a caricature of the masculine mystique. "In compulsive masculinity, typical masculine values become a rigid prescription for toughness, sexual promiscuity, manipulation . . . and a willingness to use violence to resolve interpersonal conflicts." This unfortunate incarnation of the masculine mystique leads to much of the dysfunctional behavior seen among black males. As Majors concludes, "These values, perpetuated through male-to-male transmission in a tightly knit street culture, lead towards smoking, drug and alcohol abuse, fighting, sexual conquest, dominance, and crime."[16] Many researchers believe that the compulsive-masculinity message reaches black males at an early age. They have found that black male children may be at risk from the time they start school.

Around the country many black men have come together to deliver a message different from that taught by the masculine mystique and compulsive masculinity. They are actively becoming part of the education of African-American boys. They understand the structural nature of many of the problems afflicting black men and the African-American community, but they still feel that they can make a difference in the lives of boys.

MENTORING

"We know that what we've been doing in elementary classrooms is not working for a large number of inner-city boys," says Spencer Holland, a psychologist specializing in problems of inner-city schools. "And we know exactly what's missing from them: positive role models. These boys usually have all women teachers and they begin very early to define learning as a very feminine thing to do. At the same time they're growing up in an inner city, where the machismo is terrible."[17]

Unlike many other observers of the struggle of young minority men in this country, Holland decided to do something about it. Working with Washington, D.C.'s, Concerned Black Men organization, he initiated Project 2000. In the late 1980s Holland and several other volunteers, including businessmen, students, lawyers, and government workers, began actively participating in the elementary school education of inner-city kids. One stated objective of the Project 2000 program is "To provide inner-city elementary school-aged African-American boys with opportunities for one-on-one interaction with adult male role models in the school environment."[18] The program has targeted one school, Stanton Elementary

School, in southeast Washington, D.C., as its focus. In 1988 the volunteers started working with first-grade students. They will continue interacting with the same students through the elementary grades and junior and senior high until the students graduate in the year 2000. The project is named after this class of 2000.

Stanton Elementary represents a significant challenge for the project's volunteers. The school, which services 530 students, is situated in a neighborhood riddled with drugs and crime and beset with a nearly omnipresent sense of hopelessness. More than 60 percent of the students live in public housing, and 80 percent live in single-parent homes headed by a mother or grandmother. "We understand the limits of what we're doing," Holland says. "We can't change their home life, but we can change their attitudes about education. That's what this is about. Just for them to see it's all right to be a man and to like to read is a major objective."[19]

The project's volunteers are asked to have at least one visit per week with their assigned class. One visit every other week is a minimum requirement. Many volunteers exceed the minimum, and there is no restriction on the maximum number of visits per week. The volunteers also pledge to spend at least half the day at Stanton whenever they come.[20] In the classroom the volunteers work as teachers' aides, circling the classroom as a teacher gives a lesson, helping those in need and casting the occasional stern glance at those students who are not paying attention or are disruptive.

The project sets up near daily after-school tutorial services and stages annual Career Days, and Father-Son banquets for which all boys at the elementary school invite their fathers or another significant man in their lives to an afternoon of fun, games, and food. The volunteers have given books and supplies to Stanton and have taken boys on numerous field trips.

The visits of volunteers to the classroom are important events in the lives of many of the boys at the school. Reporter Rene Sanchez described the scene when a volunteer, twenty-nine-year-old architect Ron Casey, arrived at the second-grade classroom of teacher Tenin Sutherland:

One recent afternoon, Sutherland's second-graders were in a class matching numbers with letters to spell words such as "flower," "cake," and "apple." Sutherland patrolled the room. . . . But some students were still goofing off. Then Ron Casey, the architect, arrived. The boys erupted in a chorus of cheers. They left their desks and tugged at his arms and waist to show good grades on homework or ask for help with the word and number work.[21]

Sutherland sees a real need for the volunteers in her class. "Many of these boys lack family support and aren't being taught to respect each other. Their needs are tremendous." The school's sole counselor, Yolanda Coleman, is equally convinced of the importance of the project. "This is like manna from heaven," she says. "You can see the effect the men have. The students' faces light up. And when the men leave, you hear the boys ask the same question, 'Will you be back? Will you be back?' "

The volunteers themselves can feel the impact of their work. Architect Casey says, "These kids are so intense, they want every last thought you have. But that's great. They really need this kind of help. It's crucial that I keep coming back." Volunteer Albert Pearsall, who works with the U.S. Justice Department, agrees. "We can't save everyone, but we can have an impact. It's so important that these boys be around intellectual black men."

Washington, D.C.'s, Project 2000 has been influential. It has served as the model for programs in several other major cities, including Miami, Baltimore, and Newark.[22] With the majority of black male children being raised by single mothers, Project 2000 has shown that the elementary school can become a key intervention point where men can mentor young minority male children. Moreover, with around 85 percent of all elementary teachers being women, and less than 2 percent of male elementary school teachers being African American, there is a good chance that an African-American boy can go through his entire elementary school education without being taught by a man, and a near certainty that African-American boys will complete their early grade education having had little interaction with an African-American male teacher, counselor, or volunteer.[23] Mentoring then becomes a key strategy in reaching these millions of boys.

To combat the destruction of young inner-city males, other initiatives are being tried. Some school districts have attempted to institute all-male elementary schools primarily for young African-American boys. The hope was that the male academies, which would feature a predominantly male teaching corps, would help combat the fatherlessness and lack of male role models that disproportionately affect African-American males. This concept had strong support in local communities in Detroit and elsewhere. Unfortunately the opening of these schools was effectively blocked by the ACLU and the NOW Legal Defense Fund, which claimed that the schools would violate state and federal discriminatory laws.[24]

As many programs and activists work with minority boys in the attempt to spare them from compulsive masculinity's destructive lifestyles, others are working with teens and young men. A special task for activists is attempting to foster responsibility and self-respect in minority unwed fathers. The majority of black children are now born to unwed mothers, and too often the father is gone even before the birth.

MENTAL POVERTY

Charles A. Ballard is fond of quoting the line of Scripture "And he shall turn the hearts of fathers to their children, and the hearts of children to their fathers."[25] But Ballard is not waiting for divine intervention; he has initiated one of the nation's most ambitious projects involving working with young minority unwed fathers. According to Ballard, many black fathers, especially the large number of unwed fathers, are afflicted with a problem equal to their economic disenfranchisement—"mental poverty." The destructive compulsive-masculinity syndrome has led many of these young men into a dysfunctional lifestyle where they glorify the sex-and-drug culture and eschew any responsibility for the children they father.

Ballard bases his approach to counseling these young men on an old African proverb: "The ruin of a nation begins in its homes." But he adds a new line: "And the ruin of homes begins in the heart of the father." And that is where Ballard begins his work. Ballard's group, the National Institute for Responsible Fatherhood and Family Development (NIRFFD), situated in Cleveland, Ohio, specializes in a unique "nontraditional" counseling method. The group's outreach specialists, called Sages, provide services in the home of the young man being counseled that often allow them to get to the core of the problem in a way no traditional counseling could. The program also focuses on changing the risk-laden compulsive-masculinity lifestyle into a "no-risk" model. For NIRFFD "no risk" means no alcohol, tobacco, other drugs, abusive behavior, sex outside of marriage, obesity, or other high-risk behaviors. Ballard and all other team members live the no-risk lifestyle that they encourage their protégés to embrace. Ballard often has the young men he is counseling come into his home. He is a firm believer in the role-modeling method of teaching.

Besides one-on-one counseling Ballard's organization provides group and family counseling, family outreach, fathering skills, health and nutrition information, medical and housing referrals, and career guidance. Importantly they assist fathers with paternity establishment, the process by which a child is legally acknowledged by the father in probate court. Through this process the child may take on the father's name and is entitled to his estate.

Ballard's unique counseling approach was born of personal experience. Ballard was himself separated from his father at three years of age. After a stint in the army he began a self-destructive phase that led to a jail term and a health crisis. Ballard remembers a doctor whom he was seeing in those years, an elderly white-haired doctor who kept insisting that he change his lifestyle. Soon after, during a hospital stay, Ballard remembers the doctor coming into his room and saying, "Now I've got you." Over the next weeks Ballard, who was still at the hospital, had no choice but to go on the doctor's regime—no heavily fried foods, alcohol, or unnecessary fats. Soon Ballard saw his health return. He could run, his complexion cleared, and many of his nagging physical problems evaporated. "That's when I understood about personal responsibility," Ballard remembers. "The old doctor taught me that mental poverty could be overcome by each person, no matter how poor or troubled." It was a lesson that changed Ballard's life and ultimately the lives of the hundreds of men, women, and families he counsels.

Independent evaluations have demonstrated that Ballard's nontraditional program works. In a survey of more than 150 former NIRFFD clients, investigators found that the program helped 70 percent of young male parents (aged fifteen to twenty-five, more than 93 percent African American) complete twelve years of education, 12 percent get at least one year of college, 62 percent gain full-time employment, 96 percent experience an improved relationship with the child's mother, and 97 percent spend more time with their children and provide financial support. Before entering the program only 7.8 percent of the young fathers had legitimized their children. By the end of the program 84.4 percent had taken this important step.

As men like Spencer Holland and Charles Ballard fight to save one elementary school class and one unwed father at a time, it is well to remember that the problems with young black men and the black family are quickly becoming problems we see throughout society. One in four white children are now being born out of wedlock. As described in Chapter Ten, the same type of technological unemployment that made the black male irrelevant is now doing the same to millions of white workers in corporations and factories around America. The white unemployed are experiencing much of the despair, family breakup, suicide, disease, and violence that black men have experienced for decades. Rampant fatherlessness is becoming as endemic in white families as it was for blacks at the time of the Moynihan Report. If white men who are becoming increasingly irrelevant to the family and to the high-technology global economy want to know about their future, they need only speak with their African-American brothers, who for so long have been virtually invisible, but waiting to be seen and heard.

15

THE UNTOUCHABLES

*People just don't understand—there are ex-policemen, former
schoolteachers and college students among us.*
> —Ray Ragland, former steel-mill worker, currently
> homeless in Washington, D.C.[1]

*The homeless as a group represent a menace, not only because of the
high crime rate which exists among them, but also because of their
psychological impact on those brought into contact with them.*
> —Dennis Mitchem, chairman of the Phoenix, Arizona,
> Downtown Crime Task Force[2]

It's the evening rush hour during winter. People pour from office
buildings toward the parking lots and commuter train stations.
They are bundled in coats against the cold night air, hurrying to
cars or trains that will take them home. A homeless man stands in
the middle of the sidewalk facing the crowd of passersby. He is
African American, in his mid-thirties, and is dressed in what appears
to be torn, battered fatigues. Under his misfitting Russian-style winter
cap his hair is matted and in disarray. His face is obscured by a
week's beard growth. He mutters constantly under his breath. Occasionally he holds out his hand toward those passing by him. At other

times he stands with his arms folded. This is his temporary home and has been for several days. A few yards from where he is standing are two heavy blankets and a crammed backpack held together with rope. The blankets are laid out near a metal air vent in the sidewalk.

Most of the commuters walk by or around the man, their gait unchanged. For them he is simply part of the urban scenery. Others are visibly apprehensive and displeased by his presence. Their attitude is apparent: The man is either crazy, a failure, or both; he should get a job. Others hesitate, a flash of compassion in their eyes; it is after all a cold night. Yet perhaps they gave that day to the disabled vet that sits in his wheelchair outside the station every morning, or to the homeless woman who always stands singing spirituals beside the automated cash machine during lunch hour. You can't give to everybody. They, too, pass by.

Variations on this scene are commonplace throughout America. The national disgrace of homelessness pervades our urban areas. A 1990 *New York Times* poll revealed that 68 percent of urban Americans come in contact with the homeless on a daily basis. Nationally over 54 percent of people see the homeless as part of their daily routine, a figure up 50 percent in four years.[3] This level of contact is not surprising: Currently close to one million U.S. adults and children are homeless on any given night.

Homelessness does not shock most Americans and seems to leave our policymakers cold. In the United States, shelter has never been one of the rights we hold to be self-evident. (Currently only two states, New York and West Virginia, guarantee all their citizens some form of shelter.) Throughout U.S. history "boom and bust" cycles have always created homelessness. The "Gay" 1890s were followed by a depression and homelessness. Even more devastating was the depression and mass homelessness that followed the "Roaring" 1920s. The current surge of homelessness follows this same pattern as society, and especially the poor, "pay" for the excesses of the 1980s.

The increasing homeless crisis also follows the older pattern of homelessness caused by a transition in society's means of production. In Chapter Three we saw how the transition from an agrarian to an industrial society created millions of economic refugees who became the first urban homeless. We are now in a technological transition as profound as that from agriculture to industry in past centuries. The United States is rapidly changing from an industrial to a postindustrial society. Workers in the traditional manufacturing industries of the past are losing their jobs and are not being trained for the new kinds of jobs available in the new information-age workplace. Unemployment and homelessness result.

The increasing loss of traditional family and community structures in recent years has added to our current homeless woes. In his 1992 work, *The Visible Homeless*, researcher Joel Blau writes,

> Bad times have happened before, and they have made people homeless. But the risk incurred by poor and working people in this economic recovery has been significantly increased by . . . the decline of social networks and the loss of community. In the past when workers lost jobs, there were people to take them in— friends, neighbors and family. Now, however, these networks have shrunk, and people who are at risk of homelessness have much less to fall back on.[4]

Who are the current victims of homelessness? The legal definition of a homeless person is "one who lacks a fixed permanent nighttime residence or whose nighttime residence is a temporary shelter, welfare hotel, or any public or private place not designed as sleeping accommodations for human beings."[5] The exact number and nature of the homeless who fit this definition are not easy to quantify or describe with precision. The homeless population is diverse and of course mobile.

For many of us the most compelling homeless are the women and children in the streets. Those seeking support for the homeless usually focus our attention on the large numbers of homeless families and women. This is a good strategy and is based on solid evidence that families are a fast-growing subset of the homeless. Moreover it is a truism of any fund-raising effort on social issues (from animal protection to world hunger) that Americans respond best when their sympathy for "innocent victims" is tapped.

Yet an examination of research on the homeless reveals that the majority of the homeless are not women or children, or even women and children combined. About 10 percent of our homeless are children, another 10 percent are adults with children (a majority of whom are women). The rest, approximately 80 percent, are single adults. Out of that total about 80 percent are single men. From these statistics a picture of the homeless emerges that is different from that usually portrayed. Of all the homeless adults, single or with families, 70 percent are men. And of all homeless people—adults or children—58 percent are single men.[6]

It in no way diminishes the suffering of homeless women or children to note the importance of understanding that the vast preponderance of the homeless problem involves men, and a majority of the problem involves single men. As stated by noted researcher on the homeless Peter Marin, "The fact remains, despite the claims of advocates, that the problem of chronic homelessness is essentially a problem of *single adult men*. Far more single adults than families, and far more men than women, end up in our streets. Until we understand how and why that happens, nothing we do about the homeless will have much of an impact." (Emphasis in the original.)[7]

Who are these hundreds of thousands of homeless men? The statisticians tell us that their average age is thirty-five, their life expectancy at most fifty-one years. Slightly over 50 percent are African American. Veterans make up about one-third of the male homeless, with Vietnam veterans up to 43 percent of that total.[8] Twenty-four percent are engaged in full- or part-time work. These men are often afflicted with alcohol and drug addiction, as well as serious diseases such as high blood pressure, tuberculosis, and AIDS.[9]

Beyond the statistics are of course the real men so many of us pass on the street each day. Unfortunately, few of us have stopped to hear their stories. To better understand these men, we must begin to listen.

THE WHITE HOUSE HOMELESS

There is no better or more symbolic place to meet the homeless men of the United States than in the nation's capital. At any given time there are several thousand homeless men within an hour's walking distance of the White House. Many travel to D.C. hoping for work. Often they cannot find steady employment and are forced into the streets.

Such was the case with the two homeless men *Washington Post* columnist Courtland Milloy picked up in late December 1990. The two men talked with the reporter as he gave them a ride to a soup kitchen nearby. The men discussed their plans for the imminent New Year. "I'll be sleeping outdoors and using the bathroom in the bushes," said forty-seven-year-old Doc Higgenbottom. For years Higgenbottom had been a supervisor at a warehouse in Landover, Maryland, but he lost his job after suffering a stroke. He had been on the streets for three months. "I'll probably have to fight for a peanut butter sandwich that tastes like dirt," added Doc's friend, Ray Ragland, with a slight laugh. Ragland, thirty-nine, had worked in a steel mill in Pittsburgh. But the mill closed, and Ragland's fruitless search for work brought him to Washington, D.C.[10]

For both men the descent from decent work to despair was rapid. And there was no safety net to catch them. Once the paychecks stopped, it took only a few months before they were in the streets urinating in bushes and fighting for scraps of food.

In a recession unskilled African Americans like Doc and Ray face a grim future in attempting to find new work. "You go for a job and don't have a telephone number because you live in a shelter and that's the end of that," Higgenbottom remarks. "It's Catch 22. Nobody wants to help me because I need help."[11]

Past and future illness is also constantly on the minds of Doc and Ray. "One day I had a home, a car, a job—and then had a stroke, and no medical insurance," Doc recalls. "No damn insurance." Over 85 percent of the homeless in the United States are without any health insurance.[12]

Becoming jobless and homeless in 1990 made both men fear not only for their physical survival but also for their mental stability. "I have seen people go crazy out here," Ragland says. "It doesn't take long. You start talking to yourself, and the next thing you know, you just lose it."[13]

The homeless routine for Ray and Doc involves daily trekking to various food lines, a circuit that can require up to twenty miles a day of walking. "I feel like I'm part of the cattle drive, being herded from one soup line to the next," Higgenbottom continues. "Here I am sick, hard of hearing, and they kick me out of the shelter at 6 A.M.—rain, shine, sleet or snow."[14]

Ragland notes that he used to give quarters to homeless people but did not give much thought to their plight. "The reality is much worse than anything I could have imagined," Ragland says. "If it wasn't for the kindness of shelter and soup kitchen operators, this city would be in total chaos, overrun by starving men and women. Being homeless is the hardest job I ever had."[15]

Meanwhile the men pray for a better future. "We went to Bible study on Sunday and prayed for the weather to hold," Ragland says. "I also asked God to give Doc a hearing aid and both of us a job. But we'd settle for a room and a hot plate."[16]

Those seeking work in Washington, D.C., often come from places far more distant than Maryland or Pennsylvania. Typical are the hundreds of Hispanic construction workers who have only intermittent employment in the District's Virginia suburbs. As construction jobs decline, more and more of these workers are added to the homeless. Pastor Meija, forty, one of the unemployed workers, is ashamed of his homeless status. "I feel humiliated. Every time I see somebody I know, I stop them and ask them for money or food."[17] As the temperatures drop, some resort to criminally breaking into vacant buildings for shelter. "It is wrong, but there is nothing [I] can do," says one of the men "[I] can't die on the street . . . and freeze out."[18] The concern is not hypothetical. Each year many homeless do die in the streets from exposure or disease.

Even the mighty, or semimighty, can fall into the growing ranks of the homeless men in Washington. John F. King had been termed a GOP "wunderkind." King was a Vietnam veteran who had been awarded three Bronze Stars. During the 1970s the clean-cut veteran put himself though college and graduate school and then entered the two-fisted world of West Virginia politics. Within a short time the feisty (some would say mean) King ascended to the top of the Mountain State's Republican party. His tough and often questionable tactics earned him a comparison with then–national GOP strongman Lee Atwater. R. Lane Bailey, chief of staff of Sen. John D. Rockefeller IV, notes, "In that Lee Atwater was sometimes unfair and unrelenting, I would agree with the comparison."[19]

King more than lived up to his unsavory reputation. As part of one campaign fight King collected over nineteen thousand copies of an opponent's direct-mail solicitation and mailed back the enclosed envelopes with blank pieces of paper because the rival had to pay thirty-nine cents in postage for every one returned. During another campaign he started rumors that an opponent was gay—rumors that caused the candidate's children to get involved in playground brawls to defend their father. King was delighted with the "success" of his whispering campaign.[20]

In 1988 King decided to abandon political life in West Virginia and make it big in Washington. King, then thirty-nine, set up a one-man firm called Palladin Consulting. He used post office boxes, fancy letterheads, and "smoke and mirrors" to create the impression that his company was a large and growing concern. Unfortunately for King his overly intense personality and blunt, semiabusive style alienated him from the Republican clients he needed to woo if his business was to succeed.

Over several months King's business and life unraveled. Unpaid bills began mounting up, and King simply could not keep up. Checks started to bounce. King sent out his resume but had no serious takers. Finally in October 1989 he was evicted from his $725-a-month apartment in a posh apartment complex called the Boulevard in Alexandria, Virginia. King recalls that on the night following his eviction he "ended up standing at the Boulevard and remembering I couldn't go in. So I walked down [the street], went to the park, sat down and I was exhausted. So I just lay down and went to sleep."[21]

The next day King went to a shelter in Alexandria. In his gray three-piece suit he made an incongruous appearance amid the other homeless men in their ragtag clothing. Soon, however, he was following the regular schedule of the homeless, rooming with three men (all with criminal records) at the shelter, being kicked out in the morning and returning at night, told when to eat, when to sleep, and when to wake. He earned the nickname "The Professor" because he often read Faulkner and other American classics to the men.

Unlike many other homeless men King did have others to turn to—his ex-wife, parents, brothers, friends. But for the former political prodigy the shame of returning to his relatives or friends as a failure was even worse than withstanding the shelter ordeal. "I couldn't face it," he remembers. "I had become everything I had loathed all my life. I just wanted to become anonymous and withdraw."[22]

As do many homeless men, King actively looked for work. However, despite his former employment status, King faced the same problem getting a job as the less illustrious homeless. While he was able to get occasional menial jobs, no one seemed interested in giving a "failure" a real chance. In a society where men are judged by their success in the job market, being down and out is thought of as a fatal disease, one that just might be catching. No one wants to hire, or even come near, someone living in a shelter. "You try and explain it," King said. "But people treat you like you're unclean, like you're contagious. 'God, keep away, I don't want to get that.' That's the exact feeling you get from people."[23]

After three months of life in shelters and on the street, King swallowed his pride and began hopping from one friend's house to another. "Cleaned up," he continued looking for jobs. His experience on the street caused King to reevaluate his past road to success as a GOP hatchet man. "I wanted to be Henry Thoreau as a kid," he remembered. "I ended up being George Patton with a little Marquis de Sade thrown in for character." Though still a conservative on some issues, King's view of economic impoverishment, the homeless, and racism had changed. However briefly, he had been there. With a grim laugh he remembers the old saying, "We have met the enemy and he is us."[24]

THE POETRY OF THE STREETS

Kevin Rasberry was another homeless man in Washington, D.C. Commuters driving to the suburbs from the city might have seen him walking the streets in Washington's Georgetown section or huddled in his cardboard-box shelter near the Key Bridge, which spans the Potomac River and connects many of Washington's top officials' workplaces with their homes in northern Virginia's numerous bedroom communities. Rasberry, thirty years old, was a former Marine and corrections guard. He had been on the streets since a painful separation from his wife. Rasberry often acted as a leader to the small cadre of men who made their homes under the freeway ramps leading to the bridge and who often begged from passing motorists stopped at the lights during rush-hour traffic. Rasberry had an additional avocation: He was a poet.[25]

One day in early 1991 Rasberry was confronted with an odd sight. A well-dressed teenage boy was making his way to Rasberry's homemade shelter. Even stranger, the boy spoke with a distinct German accent. "What can I do for you? Do you need clothes, some shoes?"[26]

The young man was Christoph Leonhard, age eighteen, the son of the naval attaché at the German embassy in D.C. Leonhard's life was a stark contrast to Rasberry's. The young German attended an exclusive private school run for children of German parentage in the Washington, D.C., area. He spent his nights in a spacious house in McClean, Virginia.

For several weeks Leonhard had been attempting to help the homeless. He had initiated a volunteer program in his school. As part of the program, students acting on their own and spending their own money provided food and clothing to the homeless. "I wanted to do something," said Leonhard in his German dialect. "I'm here. I live well. We have no problems to get things to eat, to drink. Those people are unfortunate . . . to be homeless. It is just fate that this happened." However, Leonhard was not satisfied just to feed the homeless; he wanted to know them. "I wanted to do something directly for the homeless, not just standing in a kitchen peeling potatoes, but to go to the homeless and talk to them."[27]

Rasberry's answer to Leonhard's query as to what he needed must have been a surprise to the student. More than clothes or shoes, Rasberry said, he wanted help publishing his poetry. He showed the young German a tattered collection of twenty-six poems, written during the years he spent on the streets. Rasberry wanted them published so that he could sell them to customers on the sidewalks he lived on. Soon Leonhard and Rasberry were meeting regularly to discuss plans for issuing the poetry collection. After several weeks the poetry was published in a small, professionally prepared booklet entitled *The Way to Utopia*. The proceeds from a reading of the book by Rasberry at Leonhard's school helped defray the publishing costs. Meanwhile Leonhard helped collect enough money for Kevin to afford him a bus trip to his family in Houston, where he found work and "a second chance at life." On the dedication page of his poetry booklet Rasberry left an enduring thank-you to his young friend. "True love is giving, seeking nothing in return. To you may I express my utmost gratitude."[28]

BORN TO LOSE?

A glimpse into the lives of some of the "White House homeless" helps answer the perplexing question of why so many more men than women are on the street. Before becoming homeless men like

Ray, Doc, and Kevin found work as steel-mill workers, warehouse operators, security guards, and pickup construction workers. Throughout our history, jobs such as these and others allowed men to survive at the edges of the economy. Whether dispossessed by family, kicked out of school, fleeing failed marriages or failed jobs, men could still survive. Now, however, as we complete the transition into a postindustrial economy, most of these jobs have disappeared and been replaced by low-paying service-sector jobs. Women and young people are considered far more attractive candidates for these new jobs than are the unskilled male workers who traditionally did the nation's roughest and most dangerous work. As described in Chapter Ten, over just the last five years more than 1.1 million prime-age male workers have become permanently unemployed, most from blue-collar industries.[29] While the old jobs have vanished, the men remain visible as the homeless so many of us see every day.

The bureaucratic and arcane workings of the federal welfare system are also in part responsible for sending men into the streets. The system literally creates homelessness for many men as a by-product of its aiding, albeit minimally, women and children. Witness the Aid to Families with Dependent Children (AFDC) program. It is what we commonly call welfare and covers over 11.4 million people. The program was initiated as part of Franklin Roosevelt's response to the Depression, and was refined during Lyndon Johnson's Great Society push in the 1960s. The AFDC is essentially a program for women, children, and households headed by women (the racial breakdown is 38 percent white, 40 percent African-American, and 16 percent Latino).[30]

Under the program if an adult male remains in a household as a father, mate, or even companion, the program usually does not provide aid to the woman or family. Women are consistently faced with the bizarre choice of receiving aid for themselves and their children, or living with men. Men are in an even more macabre position. The AFDC regulations as currently written force men into a competition with the state for the women they love. One woman involved in the

AFDC program commented, "Welfare changes even love. If a man can't make more at a job than I get from welfare, I ain't even gonna look at him. I can't afford it."[31] Author Peter Marin chronicles the result of this misguided welfare approach:

> Everywhere in America poor men have been forced to become ghost-lovers and ghost-fathers, one step ahead of welfare workers ready to disqualify families for having a man around. In many ghettos throughout the country you find women and children in their deteriorating welfare apartments and husbands, fathers and male companions, in even worse conditions: homeless in gutted apartments and abandoned cars, denied even the minimal help granted the opposite sex.[32]

Recently some alterations in AFDC requirements have allowed men to remain in the household if their work history satisfies certain federal guidelines. However, in many poor areas typical levels of unemployment result in few men being able to satisfy the new requirements, and men remain outside the welfare system. Some recent changes in the AFDC have further hurt men. These changes mandate automatic child-support deductions from paychecks of absent fathers. No one would quarrel with the moral imperative of fathers supporting their children. However this provision simply renders many fathers of AFDC children even more emotionally and financially impoverished. First the law has turned them into "ghost fathers," next it further reduces the money they have to live on. As noted by researcher Joel Blau, "The problem is that many fathers of children receiving AFDC are poor, and their failure to contribute to their child's support stems at least as much from their own meager paycheck as it does from a faulty sense of moral responsibility."[33]

It is interesting to note that when welfare was first made federal policy during the Depression, it was accompanied by work programs for men such as the Civilian Conservation Corps and the Works Progress Administration. Welfare for women is still with us, but the work programs for men have disappeared. No group currently lobbies or requests the reinstatement of these programs, though they would do much to alleviate the living nightmare of men like Ray, Doc, Pastor, and Kevin.

A variety of other factors also contribute to the high rate of male homelessness. For one, women's public and private shelters as well as services are superior to those of men. Additionally the streets are a dangerous place; some men can survive the violence and abuse of street living, but women, understandably, will do almost anything to avoid it. Moreover researchers have found that women more easily ask for help from relatives or friends when faced with the prospect of homelessness.

Ultimately much of the reason for male homelessness comes down to our attitudes about men. It is no accident that we have no job programs for men, that welfare programs effectively exclude men, that shelters and services for men are inferior, and that men do not feel able to become financially dependent on women, friends, or relatives as a last resort. As we have seen time and again in describing the hidden crisis, the masculine mystique defines men to a great extent by their financial success and ability to provide for themselves and others. Even political "star" John King found that after the failure of his consulting firm and a personal breakdown he was treated as a social leper. As noted before, we react to the breakdown of men with the same abhorrence with which we react to that of machines.

Underlying our view of homeless men is the implicit competition-man, Social Darwinist view that the best men survive and flourish in the competitive market system, while the "unfit" fail. Failure means that you are less of a man. And for men there is no greater indicator of failure than dependency. Men are simply not allowed to be dependent. Worse, they are by definition expected to take care of others as well as themselves.

As one observer has noted: "Simply by being in need of help, men forfeit the right to it."[34] Veterans, many African-American men, fathers dispossessed of their children, disabled workers, the homeless, and many other men are caught in a social underworld created by this irony.

The societal view of men as "success objects" not only controls government and social policy on the homeless, it also affects the perceptions of most men and women. Of course, homeless men create more fear in most of us than homeless women, though attacks on people by the homeless are very rare. But the real difference in our treatment of homeless men, as opposed to women, has to do with our view that the masculine gender bears the burden of success, and is defined by its ability to come out on top in the battle of life, and avoid dependency. In this regard homeless advocate Peter Marin invites us to go through a consciousness-raising exercise:

> Try something here. Imagine walking down a street and passing a group of homeless women. Do we not spontaneously see them as victims and wonder what has befallen them, how destiny has injured them? Do we not see them as unfortunate and deserving of help and *want* to help them?
>
> Now imagine a group of homeless men. Is our reaction the same? Is it as sympathetic? Or is it subtly different? Do we have the same impulse to help and protect? Or do we not wonder, instead of what befell them, how they have got themselves where they are?[35] (Emphasis in original.)

PART V

A NEW
MASCULINITY

16

REDEFINING MASCULINITY

If technology is not to play a wholly destructive part in the future of Western Civilization we must now ask ourselves, for the first time, what kind of society and what kind of man are we seeking to produce?
—Lewis Mumford[1]

Unless we change direction, we are likely to end up where we are headed.
—Chinese Proverb[2]

Men are now at a critical crossroad in understanding and dealing with their gender. As has been described over the last several chapters, many men are courageously struggling to lessen the suffering and heal the wounds that society and its masculine mystique have inflicted on so many boys and men. Their important work constitutes a new manifesto for the men's movement and masculinism. However, it is not only men who need healing and rehabilitating but also masculinity itself. As men are being buffeted by a whirlwind of painful new employment realities, gender-role reversals, family breakdowns, and demeaning public and media perceptions about maleness, they remain confused about the very nature of masculinity itself. The result is mass male vertigo—no one, it seems, knows what it means to be a "man" today.

In the midst of this confusion several divergent paths are being suggested to men as a solution to the crisis in the definition of masculinity. Many commentators are suggesting that one way for men to reclaim masculine identity is a staunch resistance to change. Men are urged to stay in the harness and continue to follow, by intent or inertia, the dictates of the masculine mystique. This means the continued glorification of productivity, competition, the profit motive, and technological power. It will mean the embracing of the hidden crisis as an inevitable cost of being a modern man, accepting the destruction of boys and men as the necessary transaction costs of doing business in our society. It will mean that men will continue to project their "masculinity" into machines, leaving precious little for themselves. It means that they will likely live lives of servility, in constant fear of losing employment and thereby being stripped of the only remaining badge of masculinity in our culture. It will mean that they will experience daring, adventure, power, sexuality, and the wilderness primarily as voyeurs sitting before flickering screens in the hours not consumed by work in the industrial and postindustrial workplace.

Those advocating the reaffirmation of the masculine mystique see men working to change society's concept of the masculine as a collection of "crybabies" and "wussies," reminiscent of the same type of ridicule tendered to the early environmentalists (tree-huggers) and feminists (bra-burners). Even veterans and noncustodial fathers who fight for their rights or complain of their treatment are viewed, in the best tradition of Social Darwinism, as a bunch of "losers," men who should stop "whining" and "suck it up" or "move on."

Some men argue for a very different way of dealing with the current crisis. They reject the masculine mystique by joining the rising chorus of those who view masculinity as essentially dysfunctional. These men advocate an implicit or explicit "misandry." They share the sexist assumption that male genes, hormones, physiology, and psychology are responsible for war, environmental devastation, rape, physical abuse, and on and on. They advocate the mistaken notion that the masculine mystique is how men have always been and will always be. They view the oppressive and destructive elements of our current social system not as antithetical to real masculinity but rather as the final collective expression of maleness and "patriarchy." The destruction of fatherhood and the oppression of the vast majority of men under this system are generally ignored. Even the societal abuses that women take part in, whether in the realms of politics, business, spousal or child abuse, consumerism, or destruction of nature, are laid at the feet of masculinity. In fact for many misandrists maleness itself is viewed as an "ontological evil."[3]

Since the 1970s many men especially in academia have purveyed misandry. Men who follow the misandrist path are caught in a debilitating bind: They view themselves as oppressors, yet like most men experience victimization on the personal and social level. Moreover to the men who live under this ideological regime, their very masculinity is seen as an intrinsic negative, a physical and spiritual "minus sign" that must be expiated and purged. Paradoxically for them, being a man requires the destruction of masculinity. As was described in Chapter Two, the chilling extreme conclusion of this approach is that men need to be subjected to mass behavior or genetic modification for the good of society.

Some men reject both the masculine mystique and the misandrist paths by taking up the cudgels for what can be termed equal-opportunity masculinism. This wing of masculinism is founded on the idea that "traditional" male-female roles have become dysfunctional in the last few decades due to modern economics and technology. The more enlightened thinkers in this camp see both men and women involved in a "gender transition" away from their biological mandates and into a new gender reality free of sexism, one that provides equal opportunity for all regardless of gender. These men generally applaud the feminist movement for freeing women to become effective participants in the economic system. However, they now claim that the pendulum has swung too far in the feminist direction. They see men still stuck in their traditional "chivalric" roles in regards to women. This results in equal opportunity for women but also in a continuation of the reality that men still do the dangerous jobs, bear the primary burden in breadwinning, die earlier of stress diseases, commit more suicide, and are killed in battle. These activists look for equal participation by men and women in the armed forces, in the workplace, in the home, and in the marketplace. They urge men to eschew outmoded "chivalry" and to change laws and practices so that the genders are on a truly equal playing field.

While often eloquent in their attack on inequality in awarding custody to fathers, and in their defense of men's health, these masculinists have few structural criticisms of our current economic system and offer men no real vision of what it means to be a man. Rather they seem to be advocating that both genders become a new breed of androgynous competitors in the technological state. Further, while these equal-opportunity masculinists often fight valiantly against injustice to men, their view can quickly degrade into a simple sibling rivalry between equal-opportunity masculinists and equal-opportunity feminists over who is getting the worse deal from the system.

As men search for direction, it is increasingly apparent that none of the paths outlined above offer a sustainable future for masculinity. Neither surrendering to the masculine mystique nor obeying the siren call of misandry will suffice to quell the current crisis in defining masculinity. Nor will calls for equal-opportunity masculinism.

There is, however, yet another path, one that might be termed deep (or transformative) masculinism. Transformative masculinism calls for a gender revolution based on the rediscovery of masculinity as a primal generative and creative force. It involves an historic analysis of the masculine mystique and its decimation of older traditions of masculinity. It does not romanticize past cultures but does attempt to preserve from them traditions that might contribute to a sustainable masculinity in the twenty-first century. It seeks to provide a variety of masculine ethics that both protect the masculine and enable men and society to find real-life solutions to the profound structural problems that have created the hidden crisis for men.

The significant contribution of the mythopoetic wing of the

men's movement to this deep masculine perspective is its understanding that every revolution has to be in part a revival, that the
men's movement must face the current crisis of their gender with a
call to reawaken lost images and ethics of masculinity. A men's
movement cannot by definition be involved in the annihilation of the
essence of masculinity that has been distilled over countless generations of men. It cannot fall into the view that all past cultural traditions of masculinity have been made obsolete by modernity, and
ignore the hunger among men for a recovery of masculine meaning
in their lives and work.

A rediscovery of traditional concepts of masculinity, and the
discovery of a new, relevant masculinity for our times, must begin
by rejecting the machine-, competition-, profit-, and power-men
myths of the masculine mystique. Transformative masculinity advocates empathy over the masculine mystique's idolization of efficiency; cooperation, and community over the competition obsession;
generativity and generosity over the profit motive; stewardship of
life over technological exploitation; and replacing destructive power
with "nutrient" power.

As part of the recovery of masculinity, Robert Bly and others
have also called for a recognition and reaffirmation of the "Wild
Man"—a call for modern men to come to terms with their sexuality
and power and reject the cerebral, desiccated world of the efficient
managers of modernity. Sam Keen has expounded the virtues of
wonder, moral outrage, a "heartful mind," and communion. Yet
there is one ethic that stands out above all others as the key to the
transformation of masculinity. It goes farther than other masculine
traditions in repairing the Procrustean amputation of the masculine
that took place during the industrial age. It is also an antidote to the
infantilism and sibling bickering that have become more frequent in
current gender confrontations. Moreover it also retains the best of
the hard-won masculinity of prior ages and yet creates the basis for
a masculinist political platform for the next century. It stands as a
central concept leading to the reconnection of men to each other, to
family, community, and the earth. It is the ethic of husbandry.

HUSBANDRY

The word *husbandry* is derived from a combination of the Old English *husbonda* ("bonded to home"), and the Old Norse word *bua* ("to dwell"). The "husband" was a term originally used to distinguish the household dweller from the nomad. Husbandry later came to be synonymous with the craft of farming. For the husbandman the masculine was seen in terms of a deep relationship to wife, children, community, and soil. Jungian psychologist and author Robert Mannis has been among the most eloquent proponents of a reawakening of husbandry:

> The essence of husbandry is a sense of masculine obligation— generating and maintaining stable relationships to one's immediate family and to the earth itself. At its heart, husbandry reflects a bonding to both family and nature through a clear appreciation of the responsibility inherent in the role of provider, caretaker and steward. As men have increasingly been wrenched from their families and the earth upon which they worked, they have lost their appreciation for what it meant to live the role of the steward of the land and caretaker of our resources. Over the generations there has been a considerable erosion in the sustaining identity of the role of husband.[4]

The gross reduction in the meaning of the word *husband* over the last several centuries—from a term signifying a rich group of masculine relationships to family, community, earth, and animals to a pale term for one part of the diminished nuclear family—parallels the pauperization of the meaning of masculinity in the lives of modern men. Of course it would be impracticable, if not impossible, for most of us to return literally to the role of husbandmen to animals and the soil. However, the spirit of this relationship can be applied to men in contemporary life. In its renewed sense, drawn from its historical ancestry, husbandry implies the caring for others, one's family and community as well as the larger biotic community with whom we share the natural world. Moreover husbandry also suggests a sense of pride for men, a pride gained in the purposeful care of their own health and that of their families and friends, and in the stewardship of the earth's land and its limited resources. Husbandry reflects the ultimate expression of masculine generativity and power and thus is an ethic around which a community of men can grow. It brings a renewed sense of purpose, relationship, and meaning that is lost to many men of today. As Sam Keen writes,

> I know of no single honorific that defines a man so much as the verb "to husband." . . . A husbandman may or may not plow and sow crops, but he certainly must take care of the place with which he has been entrusted. To husband is to practice the art of stewardship, to oversee, to make judicious use of things, and to conserve for the future. The image is as central to gay men, bachelors, and widowers living in high rise apartments as it is to married or landed householders. Psychologically, the husbandman is a man who has made a decision to be in place, to make commitments, to forge bonds, to put down roots, to translate the feeling of empathy and compassion into an action of caring.[5]

To actively husband, without domination or exploitation, can reawaken the male spirit from defeat and isolation. A renaissance and revolution of husbandry will help heal the woundedness of body and spirit men now suffer. A masculinist revolution, one based in husbandry, will need to be in part a quiet one as men listen to one another and to their bodies, and study the meaning of masculinity in other cultures and times. But it must also be a noisy one. For such a social movement will require a near-constant confrontation with current economic and social structures. It will oppose the defective view of masculinity espoused by the masculine mystique and will fight the growing trend toward misandry. It will struggle to recover fatherhood, real work, male community, and stewardship.

This "deep" masculinist revolution has already begun. In the last sections we witnessed its vanguard in action: men who are risking their success in the workplace to become teaching and nurturing fathers; men who are struggling to mentor young men in inner-city schools; men who gather in the wilderness to recapture a deeper understanding of themselves and of the wilderness itself; men who struggle, often for years, against a court system to retain a relationship with their children; men who fight for veterans and for the homeless; men who struggle against the powerful forces destroying the natural environment; men working to reduce the number of hours in the workplace; men providing holistic health for men.

However, for the work of deep or transformative masculinism to succeed, it will have to be supported by many more communities of men. A beginning has been made but far more remains to be done. The task of community building therefore is the most important, and in many ways the most difficult, hurdle men face in addressing the masculine mystique.

17

BUILDING A
COMMUNITY OF MEN

*With the breakdown of the community of men, we no longer have
access to relationships that restore a feeling of connectedness and
belonging. We are left with the perception that it is up to us to endure
alone, without the solace of male friendship.* —Francis Weller[1]

One of the most tragic casualties of the masculine mystique is
the male community. In virtually every premodern culture,
men lived as part of male groups. Much of men's lives were
spent in mutuality and communion with other men in a group
setting. As enclosure destroyed traditional communities, these male
communities were also lost. As men became the primary actors in
the market system, the relationship of the employment and sales
contract replaced the traditional bonds between men. As men sold
their labor to avoid destitution, each man became isolated from the
other in a fierce competition for livelihood. The new "community"
for men was the factory or corporation.

To be sure, traces of traditional or tribal male bonding survived
into the industrial age. Freemasons, Elks, and similar societies were
common until they were undermined by the Great Depression of
1929. These men's societies often engaged in elaborate ritualized
initiation ceremonies. The use of various masks and animal cos-

tumes—reminders of the premodern ancestry of the groups—was routine. Even today certain forms of male community are still promoted, especially for young men prior to their being absorbed into the labor market. School sports, college fraternities, and even the military offer some sense of male bonding. It is ironic that despite the destruction of boys and men that is endemic to many sports and the military, numerous men still remember these experiences, no matter how abusive or traumatic, as "the best days" of their lives.

Their time in the military holds a special significance for many men. Stephen Crane described an army as "[A] mysterious fraternity born out of smoke and danger of death."[2] Even in the mechanized wars of our century, combat offered one of the few opportunities in which men could hold each other and weep and mourn openly for one another without shame. No matter how brutal and impersonal, battle offers a forum in which men can fight together and die for one another. Many veterans belong to societies that commemorate their former military units and meet yearly to reestablish the sense of community lost when war is ended.

A central task of the men's movement and transformative masculinism is to attempt in a variety of ways to reestablish male community, albeit in the face of an economic and social system structurally antithetical to the attempt. Over the last decade various wings of the men's movement have nurtured forms of masculine community that act as pockets of resistance to the masculine mystique. Some of these attempts are meeting with unexpected success even among those in our society who are the most oppressed and enclosed.

THE SHAWANGUNK REDEMPTION

"This is the only time that I'm holding hands with men and don't feel corny," says Louis Velez, an inmate at Shawangunk Maximum Security Prison serving twenty-five years to life.[3] Velez is speaking about what is believed to be the first chapter of the men's movement established inside a penitentiary. In 1991 a dozen prisoners started regular meetings in this Wallkill, New York, facility. At the gatherings they discuss their daily needs and fears, reflect on the role models that were forced on them before and after their incarceration, and explore how the timeless myths about men from a variety of cultures can inform their current lives.

The meetings take place every two weeks. After several minutes of silence and meditation, a participant begins the session by inviting all present to come together with a sense of brotherhood and solidarity. This is often followed by a prayer ("Let us empty our minds of that whirlwind of chaos out there. Feel a place inside where each of us is always free, never imprisoned"). The men sit in a circle to symbolize equality of power and the desire to experience true community.

One man then calls the others to speak. Each person is recognized and given an opportunity to share experiences and feelings uninterrupted.

The men speak without braggadocio or the required "cool pose" of the streets. "This here is an oasis," says Jalil Bottom, who is serving thirty-five years to life for the killing of a police officer. "We're battling the psychology of criminality and trying to become new human beings."[4] Bottom finds the meetings a place where he can shed the masks required to survive in prison and reveal his "true self." Randy Hinds, who is partway through a ten-to-twenty-year prison sentence, also feels the redemptive potential of the meetings. "Being a human being is a process. . . . I may have murdered somebody, sold drugs—that was me then. But I'm a human being and I'm not static."[5] The two-hour sessions end in a circle of fraternity, each man standing and holding the hand of the man on his right and on his left. One convict states simply, "It's an honor to be part of the circle and to be among men." Another convict says, "This is a blessing."[6]

This unique chapter of the North American Federation of Men's Councils was initiated by Robert Vosper. Vosper, a longtime employee of the prison, supervises the facility's grievance program. Brought up in a tough blue-collar neighborhood in Queens, New York, Vosper has empathy and understanding for many of the inmates with whom he works on a daily basis. On occasion he even sees prisoners he knew growing up. Vosper joined a men's group in Woodstock, New York, in order to deal with many of his own concerns, and through his work in the group began to feel that a men's group in the prison might be helpful to many of the men he was seeing. Vosper was able to recruit several prisoners whose trust he'd gained over time to give the idea a try.[7] Harris Breiman, a professional therapist and holistic-health advocate who ran the men's council in Woodstock, New York, generously offered to take the nearly hour-long trip every two weeks to the prison and facilitate the meetings without charge. He now cofacilitates the sessions with author-activist Onaje Benjamin. Breiman, like Vosper, was convinced that the men's movement, with its ability to get men to mentor each other and crack the masculine mystique's insistence that each male fight the other for economic and personal survival, was particularly relevant to the often-grim reality of prison life. He feels strongly that men's work needs to grow "to become inclusive, multi-racial and reach the men in the trenches." His work in the prison combines his two major passions: "soul-making and social justice-making."[8]

Because he is an employee of the prison, it is not appropriate for Robert Vosper to attend the meetings he helped initiate. Yet he is buoyed by their success. The growing success of the group is also an affirmation for Vosper, who went out on a limb with his superiors to create the group. "The best part of it is there's no carrot involved— no required credits for a parole hearing or anything else at stake. This is totally their own volition, something personally gainful." Vosper also feels that the Shawangunk prison group demonstrates the appeal of the men's movement beyond its usual white middle-class constituency. He notes the strong positive force of male bonding even in the prison environment. "This group shows that even in jail there can be a sense of community. Men can feel a oneness and sameness."[9]

The meetings are also a measure of the tolerance and flexibility of the New York prison system. The New York system, at least in comparison with the correctional bureaucracies of other states, is willing to try a variety of approaches to attempt "rehabilitation" and to achieve a more positive atmosphere inside prisons. Now, however, as the Shawangunk men's group is publicized, prisons both in New York State and around the country are interested in using it as a model for their own programs.[10]

As the prisoners involved in the group grapple with their personal psychic journey and the extraordinary difficulties of prison life, they also feel that they are learning valuable lessons that need to be shared with others, especially young men in the streets. "Today's youth does not respond to their elders," says Philip White, thirty-seven, who is doing thirty years to life. "It would be useful to have a group like us make contact with these kids. We have to return something back to them."[11] Robert L. Jones, fifty-two, a lifer, also finds the current initiation of boys in the streets deeply disturbing. "There's a different type of kid now whose rite of passage is a 9-millimeter pistol and a vial of crack."[12] Many in the group feel that their meetings could be a model for those attempting to resist the pressure to commit violence and take drugs. As pointed out by one of the group, "It takes a certain type of man not to respond to peer pressure." Robert E. Sawyer, with seventeen years in prison toward a twenty-five-to-life term, remembers with pride the process of initially getting the gathering together. "It has taken a long time to really create itself and get the feeling we're generating now." He also looks forward to a time when the newly gained understandings of the men can reach past prison walls. "We have to put in a lot more energy and share our feelings with the larger population."[13]

The Shawangunk group now calls itself the Fellowship of the King of Hearts. The name symbolizes the men's commitment to act as role models in service and positive leadership for other men. They are living up to their name. Members of the council have committed themselves to mentoring younger inmates, taught African and Latino studies classes, facilitated in Alternatives to Violence workshops, helped other inmates in the law library, promoted early release legislation, mediated prison disputes, and been active in the Christian and Muslim communities. Harris Breiman summarizes the accomplishment of the men. "These men have survived the madness in the belly of the beast. They are using prison as a positive rite of passage by aspiring to the noble side of human nature and by bringing gold out of the ashes of incarceration."[14]

THE FIRST STEP

For many men male community can be established through joining, and perhaps helping to transform, church or community men's groups or by becoming part of men's activist and rights groups. Additionally the North American Federation of Men's Councils has a directory of all the established councils across the country. However, often initiating a men's community will be up to individuals. Breaking the masculine mystique and starting a men's group is not easily done. As we have seen, through its very structures our society breeds competition and mistrust, as opposed to fraternity, among men. Robert Vosper was successful at starting a group at Shawangunk because for many years he had earned the trust of the long-term inmates at the maximum-security prison. Starting a group without a prior relation of trust to men in a community can be harrowing. In 1984 Doug Hufnagel did just that in Camden, Maine. Hufnagel, full of "frustration and discontent" about his lack of male comradeship, after weeks of hesitation put a classified ad in the *Camden Herald*. The ad read, "Changing with times? The New Man, relationships, children, Vietnam, the 60s, sex, power, work, divorce, anger, sports. If you are interested in forming an ongoing men's group to discuss, study and explore these or any of our issues in 1984, please respond to Box H, c/o the Camden Herald."[15]

Hufnagel remembers his feeling waiting for responses to arrive:

> At the time I didn't have the slightest idea of what a men's group was or even if anyone might be interested in such a thing. I was pretty nervous about the ad and could only wait for the response. The first week I got no letters. How depressing, I thought; maybe this is just too strange for men. The second week I got two letters,

both nasty. As I recall now one went something like, "Are you crazy? . . ." Very depressed I thought about canceling the ad, but since I had run it for a month I decided to let it ride. Week three—a breakthrough. Two short notes, both cautious and hesitant. One had a number, the second only an address. I called up one and wrote the other. Both men were as excited and apprehensive as I was, but we agreed to meet.[16]

Hufnagel's group grew slowly, with several men joining and others leaving. After three years the group decided it was time to do outreach again into the community. After weeks of talk they decided to hold a men's potluck supper. Once again there was anxiety over whether men would come forward:

No one knew what to expect when that cold Friday evening in February rolled around. Would anyone show? We all got there early and waited. It was Box H angst revisited. Slowly men began to wander in, carrying their hot dishes under aluminum foil. Within an hour 35 men were sitting around eating and laughing. Across the table I caught the eye of the original member of the Box H group from four years before. He was shaking his head in disbelief at the responses. That night three new men's groups were formed.[17]

Each men's group or community is a potential political and social force. As each is organized from the larger community, it must eventually return to share what has been learned. For centuries men have entered the political arena blind to the extent to which they have been indoctrinated by the masculine mystique and unaware of the defective mythologies of masculinity and power under which they act. Men's groups are in the process of freeing themselves from these pathologies and grounding themselves in a healthier, more sustainable masculinity. Men's groups can therefore provide a new kind of male activist, one who has obeyed the axiom "Healer, heal thyself." With its new paradigms of masculinity, the men's movement could act as a unique support base to affiliate with local men's groups organized around various gender issues and with other groups on more general social and community concerns.

Clearly if men's groups follow this political and activist path, new skills will have to be learned. Along with the many experiences and techniques that men have learned in the new communities must come the skills required for effective political action. Learning these political skills will allow communities of men to become politically active without losing their "heart." It will permit men to be honest to the social implications of their passions while remaining honest to themselves and to one another.

18

A MANIFESTO FOR MEN

In every man's heart there is a revolution. —G. K. Chesterton[1]

The current generation of men face a unique moment in history. While most men are still trapped by economic coercion, and the psychological co-option of the masculine mystique, many men are beginning to see that they can no longer submit to the dictates of a social system steeped in the masculine mystique. They have found that the destruction it exacts on their bodies and psyches is no longer bearable, that its undermining of fatherhood and family is too painful, that the pressures it puts on boys is too cruel, that its using and discarding of men's lives and work is too inhumane, that its sacrificing of millions of young men in wars is genocidal, that its rejecting men because they are vulnerable or ill is unacceptable, that its destroying male friendship is emotionally impoverishing, that its exploiting the natural world is far too dangerous.

Perhaps the most dominant and immediate factor in the consciousness raising among men is their current economic plight. As has been noted, since 1989 the rate of labor force participation—those working or looking for work—has dropped sharply for men. Conservative estimates indicate that some 1.1 million more prime-age male workers are out of the labor force as compared with five years ago. Additionally, over the last two decades, while the earnings of college-age women have increased dramatically, the earnings of college-educated men have remained stagnant and the earnings of men who have a high school degree have declined precipitously (13 percent). The result is a substantial increase in the number of men living in or near poverty.

The situation for male workers is likely to worsen as the United States experiences a continuing decline in manufacturing jobs. Virtually all economists agree that the majority of new workers entering the job force in the next decade will be women. As this occurs, more and more men will begin to question the bargain that the masculine mystique offers. They will question whether their diminishing economic role is really worth the costs in degradation of health, of emotional isolation, divorce, demeaning work, separation from their children, and destruction of the earth. They will increasingly question the gods of profit, technology, competition, productivity, and consumption.

Men's new gender consciousness is also a product of the emphasis by so many men on being better and more generative fathers. Though the average male works many more hours than his father, he is also attempting to be a far better and more involved parent than his father. Yet in the divorce and custody setting men see a court system that still clings to both the masculine mystique and the motherhood mystique and continues to discriminate against fathers.

The movement among men is also being generated by the millions of men who, having devoted their lives to work and family, have grown weary of the continuing assault on their gender identity. They no longer find our society's misandry and constant scapegoating of men acceptable. For many years they have endured male bashing in relative silence. However, many are now proclaiming, "We're not going to take it anymore!"

Men's growing anger at the system was graphically displayed in the 1994 election results. The vast majority of men, fed up with current economic and social realities, joined those far to their right, with whom they have little in common, in order to protest their condition.

This protest vote is both significant and potentially liberating. It undoubtedly portends the new age of the politics of masculinity. However, as discussed in Chapter Sixteen, the anger among men has the potential to become reactionary. Instead of focusing on the real needs of men, addressing the hidden crisis and the masculine mystique, the movement could be led astray into tangential and misguided campaigns against purported enemies. Many reactionaries have already called for warfare against feminists and encouraged xenophobic campaigns against immigrants.

The real politics of masculinity must avoid the path of reaction and instead be a vehicle through which men can find a sustainable masculinity that can transform men and create a more humane and just society. What follows is a review of some of the basic goals and strategies of such a masculinist movement. This summary is intended as an outline of a personal and political platform for men, a brief manifesto with which men can begin the process of organizing themselves as a positive political force for the coming century.

A FATHER POLICY

The greatest irony of our industrial and postindustrial system is that it has been universally referred to as "patriarchal." Yet, from the start it accomplished the ruthless and efficient destruction of real fatherhood, both personal and social. Earlier in this work we recounted the history of the enclosure of common lands that forced men away from lives lived in constant contact with their children and spouses and resulted in the enclosure of men into the industrial workplace. We saw how violence and coercion are used to continue the worldwide enclosure of men today. Alexander Mitscherlich's "invisible father" is rapidly becoming a global phenomenon.

The recovery of fatherhood is an individual effort, and it must also be a collective one. Erasing the structural fatherlessness that besets our nation will require a viable men's movement that can act as a powerful constituency to pass laws and change current legal trends.

Restoring fatherhood will require nothing less than a concerted social and legal program, one designed to transform the way we work, to promote family policies, and to revise divorce and custody law.

■ *Men must fight for reduced work hours.* The most important single step that men can take as part of the masculinist revolution—and the restoration of fatherhood—is to fight alongside labor leaders, feminists, parents' organizations, and others in the struggle for reduced work hours. Real liberation for men is only possible if they begin to reverse the enclosure into the workplace which occurred so many generations ago and has had such profound consequences. Only by having more time away from work, but still sufficient income, can men truly recover fatherhood and return as real presences in their families and communities.

■ *Men must struggle inside the business world to develop profather policies.* Men must work together to initiate family-leave policies which actually work for male employees, to create available flextime arrangements, to encourage job sharing, and to make home-based employment possible for those employees whose jobs lend themselves to such arrangements. Men must also stand up for those who are being fired or discriminated against because they insist on balancing work and home.

■ *Men need to fight the discrimination they face in family courts around the country.* Even if men achieve a shorter workweek and other workplace "father policy" reforms, they will still be separated from their children and remain on the family's periphery unless they win equal treatment in custody cases. Courts and judges (and lawyers) still discriminate against men in custody decisions. Divorcing fathers face a court system whose custody philosophy is "Daddy pay and go away." Grassroots organizations, lobbys, and pro bono legal networks will all be necessary if men are to erase the discrimination they currently face in custody decisions.

■ *Men need to fight for custody legislation that "demilitarizes" divorce and allows both parents maximum contact with children after divorce.* The current competition system of divorce and custody has been a disaster for men, families, and children. Important battles to initiate a new demilitarized regime of divorce include requiring alternate dispute resolution (ADR) for any divorcing couple, the submission of a "parenting plan" prior to the granting of a divorce decree, minimum-access guidelines (as an insurance policy against the continuing judicial policy of granting virtually automatic custody to mothers), and civil and criminal penalties for false allegations of child and spousal abuse. Moreover, federal and state governments as well as private charities should be lobbied to contribute heavily to access counseling programs for divorced parents, such as the pioneering program of the Fathers for Equal Rights (see Chapter Nine). In the custody, child support, and visitation environment nonlitigation solutions will almost always be preferable to court solutions.

■ *Laws must also be enacted that encourage unwed fathers to play a central role in their children's lives.* The plight of unwed fathers also needs to be addressed. The current laws which discriminate against unwed fathers should be rescinded and replaced by legislation that will give unwed fathers presumed rights as fathers.

■ *Federal, state, and local governments and the private sector should be encouraged to support expanded counseling and job-training programs for unwed fathers.* Counseling programs for unwed fathers, like that of the National Institute for Responsible Fatherhood (see Chapter Fourteen), need to be supported and expanded. Men should volunteer to help in these programs if possible and should lobby government and the private sector to give counseling and job training programs additional financial support.

■ *Welfare reform must include changes that eliminate the current antifather bias.* Under current Aid to Families with Dependent Children (AFDC) rules, the low-income father who wishes to be a physical and emotional asset to his children also becomes a financial liability by disqualifying them from most government assistance. The welfare system needs to be fundamentally altered to decrease the number of "driven-away" dads, forced out of their homes so that their female companions can receive AFDC payments. New Jersey has proposed a plan to encourage marriage by continuing AFDC benefits to children if their natural parents marry and live together in the home, as long as their income does not exceed state eligibility standards. Another concept as yet untried is to provide a large, one-time bonus to any woman who marries, leaves the AFDC rolls, and stays off for an extended period of time.

■ *Federal programs should encourage establishment of paternity.* Federal programs—beginning with the Women, Infants, and Children (WIC) program—should make reasonable attempts to establish paternity. In-hospital paternity forms should encourage parties to voluntarily establish custody and visitation as well as financial support. Increasing the fathers' involvement and encouraging maintenance of two-parent families will decrease poverty and welfare dependence.

■ *The men's movement must be at the forefront in educating parents on the potential risks posed to children in single-parent families.* Many adults continue to subscribe to the myth that children do as well with one parent as two, more specifically, that fathers are unnecessary. The public must be made aware that children who grow up with only one parent are at an increased risk for emotional problems, of becoming high school dropouts or teen mothers, and having difficulty in finding a steady job as compared with children raised with both parents. Men need to educate society that the growing number of single-parent households (usually an absent father) puts children at risk, and that those risks are present regardless of socioeconomic status. Further, men must be in the forefront of those challenging the current "culture of divorce."

■ *Federal tax policies should be changed to encourage the mainte-nance of two-parent families.* Tax laws must be changed to be more profamilies and profathers. For example, the United States is the only Western industrialized country that does not have a child al-lowance. Instead, there is an income tax child deduction that helps middle-income families but is often no help to poor, two-parent fam-ilies. Medium- and low-income families should be given a child al-lowance worth $500 per child.

■ *Each father and son can take action within their own family.* Each father who struggles to defeat the demands of the workday— and the separation often caused by divorce—to become a better fa-ther is a key part of restoring fatherhood. When a father teaches his children in whatever area he can—music, sports, poetry, science, crafts—he defeats the masculine mystique's view of fatherhood. Every instance in which the "teacher" father is substituted for the "temperament" father begins the personal and social recovery of fatherhood.

The restoration of fatherhood in the family sometimes has to be initiated by sons and daughters. Many older men still trapped in the masculine mystique cannot express their feelings to their children and especially to their sons. They often feel guilty for having spent so little time with their children, for not being as affectionate as they wanted to be, for not being the teachers they could have been, or for divorces they might have caused or prevented. But they also feel an-gry and alienated by the perceived lack of gratitude and under-standing they receive from their children despite decades of labor dedicated to supporting their families. These conflicting emotions of shame and anger make a move toward intimacy with their grown children difficult for many aging fathers. When this happens it is up to the son to make the first move.[2]

Creating a father policy for the United States will not be easy. As is clear when reviewing the ambitious agenda of such an attempt, it will meet stiff opposition, and will require significant mobilization of men. Moreover, making the personal choices necessary to become a more involved and generative father, or to reconcile with an estranged father, are also not easy. Yet there is no more important goal for a deep masculinist movement than the recovery of fatherhood for this and succeeding generations.

MENTORING

Men are not only absent from America's homes but also from its schools and virtually all other child care. The restoration of the teaching man is not solely a task for fathers. All men, whether fathers or not, must break the masculine mystique to become teachers, mentors, and initiators to young men. A vital task for the masculinist movement is that each man should take on the duty and privilege of guiding young men through the stages of manhood. Amid the current confusion about the masculine, most young men yearn for a final affirming experience of manhood. As Aaron Kipnis writes, "Our young men need to know that there are men in the community other than their fathers, to whom they can relate, from whom they can learn, and by whom they can be accepted and admired."[3]

■ *Men must launch a national effort to recruit men as teachers, especially for the elementary school grades, and halt the practice of not hiring men for these jobs.* Along with the invisible father, the near-invisible male elementary school teacher is among the most shocking testaments to the reduction of the masculine role in our society. The masculine mystique leaves some men and women in our society with the bizarre view that teaching our children is "unmanly." A 1992 survey by the National Education Survey showed that the percentage of men teaching at all grade levels (K–12) has decreased to 28 percent, the lowest of any year since the association began such surveys in 1961.[4] However, each year over half (54 percent) of individuals seeking teaching positions are male, yet only 23 percent of those hired each year are men.[5] These disturbing statistics have been consistent for several years. This discrimination against hiring men as public school teachers must stop.

- *Men should devote as much time as possible to volunteering as teachers in their local schools.* Most schools welcome participation of men volunteers and will encourage them to act as teaching assistants. Moreover, programs like Project 2000 (see Chapter Fourteen)—in which professionals are volunteering to help adolescents finish school; identify career goals; and avoid trouble with crime, drugs, or unwanted parenting—have proven to be enormously helpful to boys.

- *Men should lobby states and localities to institute apprentice programs in schools.* Unemployment and low pay have reached epidemic proportions among high school–educated men. Apprenticeship programs could help young men and provide them with more employment opportunities. One program initiated in a few states and worthy of men's movement support has students learning about various apprenticeship possibilities in the ninth and tenth grades and entering workplace apprenticeships in the eleventh grade.

- *Each man can become a mentor.* Men can volunteer for community-based mentoring programs. Boys clubs, scout troops, sports leagues, and big brother programs have achieved significant success in helping to impart various skills and self-esteem to male children. Additionally, many men have "adopted" young men in their own communities and taught them jobs, skills, or crafts.

Volunteer mentoring may not be easy for many men. It often will require time and energies working men cannot easily spare. It may also require that men learn to drop their competitive feelings toward younger men. For the apprentice, the struggle may involve getting over innate hostility to an older man in authority. Whatever the difficulties, a mentor can play a unique role not only in helping boys with school or work but also in helping them come to understand the deeper mysteries of manhood. Unmentored boys are more prone to suicide, steroid and other drug abuse, and mental illness.

WORKING AND NOT WORKING

Issues of employment and unemployment remain the central concerns for most men. Their lives, far more than women's, are defined and limited by their identification with work and the requirement that they be successful breadwinners. Though economic trends no longer favor the male worker, the masculine mystique still has society judging men by their financial success. As long as men remain "success objects," a masculinist work policy is a central component of male liberation.

■ *Men should lobby for legislation to shorten the workweek.* A shorter workweek is not only a central goal for a father policy in the United States but also a key component in helping men break the masculine mystique's view of men as disposable working machines. In the past legislation has been introduced to amend the Fair Labor Standards Act, reducing the number of hours worked weekly from forty to thirty over an eight-year period. Such bills also increase overtime pay from time and a half to double time to deter employers from using overtime as an alternative to hiring additional workers. Such legislation should become a centerpiece of a working policy for the men's movement. Reducing working hours for the overworked employed male will allow more time for family, recreation, and education. Additionally, reducing the workweek will spread employment over a greater number of employees and reduce joblessness for the rapidly increasing number of men who are currently unemployed.

■ *Men need to initiate and support small businesses and lobby for proentrepreneurial legislation.* Small businesses—including manufacturing, crafts, and small farms—allow greater independence and dignity for men. Unfortunately, the economic trend is toward ever-larger businesses and less control for workers. Men must work to re-verse this trend. One key goal is to support legislation that provides significant tax incentives for self-employment.

■ *Men need to lobby for employment and training targeted to low-income men, especially fathers.* Skyrocketing unemployment for blue-collar workers and for low-income groups, including African Americans, must be reversed. Increasing numbers of these men are becoming homeless. Additionally, this massive new unemployment forces many men to abandon their roles as fathers, leading to in-creases in fatherless children, families headed by single women, welfare payments, and less payment of child support. Throughout the recent discussion of welfare reform, child support, and out-of-wedlock births, the plight of these unemployed men has been ig-nored. Initiation of national employment and training programs for these men is long overdue.

■ *Men must oppose international trade agreements that cost jobs, undermine worker's wages and safety, compromise the environment, and lead to the exploitation of foreign workers.* The competition man ethic has brought us misguided international trade agreements such as the North American Free Trade Agreement (NAFTA) and the General Agreement on Tariffs and Trade (GATT) (see Chapter Five). In the name of global competition these agreements cost thou-sands of American jobs, lead to the undermining of workers' eco-nomic and physical well-being, and result in diminishment of environmental protection as they force the United States to compete with countries that have lower wages and fewer safety and environ-mental regulations. The agreements additionally usurp the power of national governments by setting up international trade bureaucra-cies that can impose sanctions on national legislation which is viewed as anti–free trade. They also undermine local crafts, busi-nesses, and agriculture that simply cannot compete with the mass production capability of global corporations. Of equal importance, these agreements encourage "developing" countries to accelerate the process of enclosure of agricultural lands (described in Chapter Three), which leads to the impoverishment and exploitation of peasants and workers throughout the world. A men's worker policy should seek the rescission of NAFTA and GATT and oppose other similar international agreements in the future.

■ *Men must work to increase job safety.* Workplace accidents kill and injure tens of thousands of people each year, the large majority of whom are men. Over 90 percent of those working in our country's most dangerous professions are men. Unfortunately, the priority given to workplace-accident prevention by government and many businesses is low. The Occupational Safety and Health Administration (OSHA) must be urged to increase the number of monitors of workplace safety and to work cooperatively with the businesses which employ men in dangerous jobs so that preventive measures can be taken to increase job safety. Additionally, appropriations cuts to the agency must be reversed.

■ *Men must lobby for local, state, and federal programs that provide counseling for unemployed men.* Unemployment is traumatic for any worker. Over the last few years a disproportionate number of laid-off workers have been men. Additionally (as has been described in Chapter Ten), men suffer uniquely when unemployed, in large part because of the masculine mystique's equation of masculinity with employment. Statistics demonstrate that unemployment among men causes a reciprocal rise in suicide, family violence, family breakup, and emotional and physical disease. Yet we have virtually no programs to help counsel men through this difficult experience.

TAKING CARE OF OURSELVES

Encouraging men to take care of their bodies must become a major objective of the masculinist movement. Changes in lifestyle, eating habits, workplace environment, and strategies to promote early disease detection are critical if men are to defeat the "machine man" archetype and recover their health.

■ *The government must be encouraged to play a more aggressive role in protecting men's health.* Currently, the National Institutes of Health (NIH) spends twice as much money on women's health issues as it does on men's. The agency has just initiated a new "Office of Research on Women's Health"; a similar office for men's health is urgently required. Such an office could begin research on crucial men's health issues that no health agency has adequately studied, such as suicide, male-specific cancers (prostate, testicular), Ritalin use on boys, steroid use, male depression, and male-specific genetic disorders. (These and other male health issues are described in Chapter Eleven.)

■ *Men need to encourage health professionals to become more involved in the male health crisis.* Health professionals need to be encouraged to emulate men like Dr. Kenneth A. Goldberg and a few other pioneers who have designed clinics and health centers for men (see Chapter Eleven). Over 2,000 such clinics are operating for women, yet less than a handful exist for men. Men desperately need medical care tailored to the denial and fear of illness that the masculine mystique has inculcated.

■ *Corporations should be encouraged to initiate workplace screening for their workforce.* Due to the masculine mystique, many men will not see doctors; however, they will take a few minutes at work to get screened for serious diseases. Workplace screening could save the lives of tens of thousands of men each year. For men, workplace screening should at a minimum include tests for prostate cancer, high blood pressure, and heart disease.

■ *Companies need to be encouraged to initiate aggressive health promotion/disease prevention programs in the workplace.* As has been described, men lag behind women in most health promotion and disease prevention categories. Several companies have pioneered employee health promotion/disease prevention programs that involve daily exercise, dissemination of nutrition information, and medical advice and assistance. Once again, given time constraints and their masculine mystique–fostered reluctance to care for themselves, men are more likely to participate in health promotion if it is initiated in the workplace.

■ *A national study of the growing crisis in male education needs to be initiated, and public and private schools need to be encouraged to set up young men's health programs.* Despite myths to the contrary, our nation's educational systems have taken a significant and disproportionate toll on young men (see Chapter Eleven). The Department of Education needs to launch a national study of the growing crisis for boys in our schools. Additionally, schools need to become far more active in helping promote male physical and mental health at all grade levels. The programs should also actively instruct young men on a variety of important subjects often ignored in today's education. These include diet, violence, physical and mental health maintenance, risks of sports injuries, the threat of substance abuse (including steroids and hormones), and suicide.

■ *Men need to support and become involved with local and national groups that provide information on men's health issues.* Currently, there is a tragic lack of health-care information for men. Numerous programs alert women to the dangers of breast cancer, cervical cancer, etc. These groups actively encourage women to examine themselves for female-specific diseases and to have regular checkups. No effective campaign exists that is devoted to awareness and prevention of many of the leading killers of men. However, several groups, including the Men's Health Network (see Chapter Eleven), have begun to initiate national awareness campaigns on men's health.

■ *Men must work for adequate health care for veterans.* The government support for veterans' physical and mental health borders on the negligent. The Government Accounting Office and others have published reports noting that federal programs, including hospitalization and psychological care for veterans, have been grossly inadequate. Additionally, the Veterans' Administration (VA) often takes several years to adjudicate veterans' health claims. Vets often have to sue the VA for negligence in health care delivery. Men need to support veterans and their advocacy groups (see Chapter Fourteen) to change policy on veterans. It is clear that we have failed these men, to whom our society owes so much. The physical and mental health of our veterans must become a national priority.

ECOLOGY AS MASCULINE POLITICS

Among the masculine mystique's most damaging effects is its alienation of men from nature. This alienation has been further intensified by the continuing identification of masculinity with technology and femininity with the organic (see Chapter Four). Restoring the traditional male ethic of husbandry is a central task of the masculinist movement.

■ *Men should be at the forefront of struggles to protect the natural world.* The environmental movement of our time offers men a unique forum in which to express their traditional roles as careful stewards and husbands of the earth. Men's groups around the country need to organize to support environmental legislation on the local and national level. The gender gap in environmental issues is a constant reminder of the continuing power of the masculine mystique.

■ *Men should involve themselves in lobbying and grassroots organizing to protect wilderness areas and the species that inhabit them from further destruction.* The masculine mystique's alienation of men from their primal roots has deprived men of the "heart of wilderness." As part of the reexperience of the wild in themselves, men should actively become involved in experiencing the wilderness. By hiking, camping, and fishing many men recapture a relationship with the mountains, streams, and wilderness. These experiences should be shared with their sons and daughters. Of equal importance, men need to organize support for wilderness- and species-protection legislation.

■ *Men need to be adamant in their call for appropriate limitations on use of pesticides and herbicides.* An important aspect of the masculine ethic is the defense of earth and family. Pesticides and other toxic pollutants—which poison our food, water, and air—can represent a real danger, especially to children.

■ *To the extent possible, men should become involved in farming and gardening and initiate and support legislation that sustains our farming communities.* If men are to recapture a true sense of stewardship and husbandry and affirm the "seed-bearing" creativity of the primal male, they must reacquaint themselves with the soil and farming and gardening.

■ *Men should promote appropriate, human-scale technologies, including renewable energy sources.* Devolving technology is a key element of the men's manifesto. It reflects the recognition by men that industrial and other inappropriate technologies led to men's dispossession, degradation—and increasingly their unemployment.

HELPING MEN WITHOUT HOPE

All men need to come to the aid of those who have lost the most in the competition for profit and power that has marked the reign of the masculine mystique. We have seen men like Harris Breiman working in the prisons, Charles A. Ballard bringing young minority unwed fathers into his home, and young Christoph Leonhard devoting himself to a homeless man. Each of us individually and as part of a male community must help these men. If they cannot get help from their brothers, who will provide it?

- *Whether it is the unemployed, minority men, disabled veterans, men in prison, or the homeless, a central focus of the men's movement must be to include and help serve these men.* By serving men who are suffering or who are victims of discrimination men roll back the Social Darwinist "competition man" dogma of winners and losers, successes and failures and assure men that they can ask for help and find it.

Moreover, no group of men is more economically dispossessed than African-American men. All men should support and network with African-American and Hispanic men's groups around the country who are seeking answers to the unique and terrible problems that face minority men in this country. Nor can we continue to abandon our homeless who also suffer physical and mental disorders at many times the rate of the rest of the population, and who are predominantly men. In 1992, less than $1.5 billion was allocated to the federal government's HOME program to provide assistance to state, county, and local governments to rehabilitate substandard housing, revitalize inner-city neighborhoods, and provide financial help for low-income families to purchase homes. This is less money than the cost of a single high-tech fighter plane. Clearly these efforts need to be greatly expanded if we are to reverse the process of social disintegration in our inner cities and address homelessness. We need to view shelter as fundamental right, and men's activists need to recall that the large majority of those being deprived of homes are men.

Ultimately, those men who share the deep masculine vision have a difficult responsibility. For they, along with feminists who seek a new vision of society, have the task of transforming the productive paradigm, which has dominated men for so long, into a generative one. They must balance the efficiency ethic with one of empathy, the market ideology with one of cooperation, the exploitation of nature with one of husbandry, the rigors of the workplace with the freedom of the wild. These men must follow the adage of men's activist Harris Breiman and become driven "not by the profit motive but rather by the motive of prophecy."[6]

As we have seen in the courageous actions described in this book, individual and social change is possible, and there is a world to gain. Acting individually and in groups, men can begin the long process of the recovery of a true masculinity.

Shortly after World War I, author Ford Maddox Ford depicted twentieth-century men as continually pinned down in the trenches, unable to stand for fear of annihilation. As the century closes men remain pinned down by an economic and political system that daily forces millions into meaningless work, powerless lives, and self-destruction. Worse, men have through generations of indoctrination in the masculine mystique become accomplices in their own oppression.

The time has come to recapture and resurrect the generative concept for masculinity lost in the trauma of enclosure. Men must begin now to help fashion a world without the daily frustration and sorrow of having to view each other as a collection of competitors instead of a community of friends. As we face a new century, the time has come to aid our sons, brothers, fathers, and friends in the political struggles necessary to address the crisis we face together. We can no longer passively submit to the destruction of the household and the father; the demise of self-employment and good work; the disintegration of fatherhood, the family, and the community; and the desecration of the earth. The time has come for men to stand up.

NOTES

INTRODUCTION

1. Elaine Partnow, ed., *The Quotable Woman*, 2 vols. (Los Angeles: Pinnacle Books, 1977), vol. 2, p. 252.
2. Myron Benton, *The American Male* (New York: Coward-McCann, 1966), p. 13.
3. This phrase is taken from the title of the first chapter of Betty Friedan's *The Feminine Mystique*, 20th anniversary ed. (New York: Dell, 1983), p. 15.

CHAPTER 1

1. As of 1920 the life expectancy for men was 53.6 years; for women 54.6 years. National Center for Health Statistics, U.S. Department of Health and Human Services, *Life Tables: Vital Statistics of the United States* (Washington, D.C.: U.S. Government Printing Office), 1990, vol. 2, section 6.
2. Life-expectancy statistics are as of 1991 (Source: National Center for Health Statistics).
3. *Vital Statistics*, 1991, p. 44.
4. *Cancer Facts and Figures* (Atlanta, GA: American Cancer Society, 1994), pp. 5, 6, 13.
5. "NCI Seeks Answers on Prostate Cancer," fact sheet issue by National Cancer Institute, National Institutes of Health (Bethesda, MD, 1995), p. 1.
6. *Criminal Victimization in the United States, 1992*, A National Crime Victimization Survey Report, March 1994 NCJ-145125, U.S. Department of Justice, Washington, DC, p. 22, table 3; p. 25, table 7. The rates of all personal crimes per 1,000 persons aged twelve and over are white males—97.5, black males—134.8, white females—80.4, black fe-

males—91.0. *Criminal Victimization in the United States, 1992*, U.S. Department of Justice, Washington, DC, p. 22, table 3; p. 25, table 7.

7. "Two Thirds of Women Violence Victims Are Attacked by Relatives or Acquaintances," U.S. Department of Justice press release, Jan. 30, 1994, p. 2.

8. *Bureau of Justice Statistics Sourcebook of Criminal Justice Statistics—1993*, U.S. Department of Justice, Washington, DC, p. 385.

9. U.S. Department of Labor, 1992; *Washington Post*, "Health," Nov. 23, 1993, p. 5.

10. "Work Injuries and Illnesses by Selected Characteristics, 1992," U.S. Department of Labor press release, April 26, 1994, p. 2.

11. See Warren Farrell, *The Myth of Male Power* (New York: Simon & Schuster, 1993), pp. 105, 106.

12. *Bureau of Justice Statistics Sourcebook of Criminal Justice Statistics—1993*, p. 430, table 4.9; see also Farrell, *The Myth of Male Power*, p. 396, footnote 26.

13. Don Colburn, "Doctors Detect Depression More in Women Than in Men," *Washington Post*, "Health," Dec. 10, 1991, pp. 5, 6.

14. Source: National Center for Health Statistics, U.S. Department of Health and Human Services, 1993.

15. *Cancer Facts and Figures—1994*, American Cancer Society, p. 18.

16. Richard Majors and Janet Mancini Billson, *Cool Pose* (New York: Lexington Books, 1992), pp. 12, 13.

17. *Criminal Victimization in the United States, 1992*, U.S. Department of Justice, p. 18; see also *Bureau of Justice Statistics, Crime Data Brief, Young Black Male Victims*, Dec. 1994, pp. 1, 2.

18. See Aaron Kipnis, *Knights Without Armor* (Los Angeles: Tarcher, 1992), pp. 23, 24; Diane Divoky, "Ritalin: Education's Fix-It Drug?" *Phi Delta Kappan*, April 1989, p. 603.

19. *The World Almanac and Book of Facts, 1995* (Mahwah, N.J.: Funk & Wagnalls, 1994), p. 960; U.S. Department of Health and Human Services, *Annual Summary of Births, Marriages, and Deaths: 1990*, p. 13, table 4.

20. U.S. General Accounting Office, "Drug Misuse: Anabolic Steroids and Human Growth Hormone" (GAO/HRD—89–109), Aug. 1989, p. 4.

21. See *Men's Health Advisor*, ed. Michael Lafavore (Emmaus, PA: Rodale Press, 1993), pp. 129–134; see also "Facts on Male Health" (Dallas, TX: The Male Health Center, 1991).

22. Cited by Diane Ravitch, former Secretary of Education, in "Blackboard Bungle," *Men's Health*, Oct. 1994, p. 110.

23. National Center for Education Statistics, U.S. Department of Education, *Digest of Education Statistics, 1991*, p. 167.

24. See Ravitch, "Blackboard Bungle."
25. Frank Swoboda, "Workers Generally Worse Off Than a Decade Ago, Study Finds," *Washington Post*, Sept. 7, 1992, p. A25.
26. Ibid.
27. "Worker Displacement Increased Sharply in Recent Recession," Bureau of Labor Statistics, U.S. Department of Labor press release, Aug. 19, 1992; Sylvia Nasar, "More Men in Prime of Life Spend Less Time Working," *The New York Times*, Dec. 1, 1994, p. A1.
28. *Household Wealth and Asset Ownership, 1991*, "1991 Survey of Income and Program Participation," U.S. Bureau of Census.
29. See Majors and Billson, *Cool Pose*, pp. 14, 15; Marc Mauer, *Young Black Men in the Criminal Justice System* (Washington, DC: The Sentencing Project, 1990), p. 4; Sam Roberts, "Black Women Graduates Outpace Male Counterparts," *The New York Times*, Oct. 31, 1994, p. A12.
30. Joel Osler Brende and Erwin Randolph Parson, *Vietnam Veterans: The Road to Recovery*, (New York: Plenum Press, 1985), p. 75.
31. Arthur Egendor et al., *Legacies of Vietnam: Comparative Readjustment of Veterans and Their Peers* (Washington, DC: U.S. Government Printing Office, 1981). Also David Gelman, "Treating War's Psychic Wounds," *Newsweek*, Aug. 29, 1988.
32. Peter Marin, "Born to Lose: The Prejudice Against Men," *The Nation*, July 8, 1991, p. 46.
33. See Elizabeth Harvey Stephen, Vicki A. Freedman, and Jennifer Hess, "Near and Far: Contact of Children with Their Non-Residential Fathers" (unpublished thesis Feb. 1992), p. 1. Also Lee Bombria, et al., "New Hampshire, Men and Divorce," June 1988, Coalition Organized for Parental Equality (COPE), p. 2.; Wendy Rieboldt and Sharon Seiling, "Factors Related to Men's Award of Custody," *Family Advocate*, Winter 1993, p. 42. Texas Divorce Statistics (75 percent of mothers make the decision to divorce) provided by Texas Children's Rights Coalition, Austin, TX.
34. See Report of the New York Task Force on Women in the Courts, 15, *Fordham Urban Law Journal* pp. 11, 15, 16, 23–25 (footnote 21), 49, 102 (1986–87); also R.L. Associates, "Attorneys' Perceptions of Gender Bias Within the New York State's Judicial System", (unpublished study, Dec. 1985), p. 48; New York Office of Court Administration, 1992 Report of the Chief Administrator of the Courts Pursuant to Judiciary Law Section 216(4), table 4.
35. Stephen, Freedman, Hess, "Near and Far, p. 25, table 1. Also David Blankenhorn, *Fatherless America* (New York: Basic Books, 1995), p. 149.
36. Jack C. Smith, James A. Mercy, and Judith M. Conn, "Marital Status and the Risk of Suicide," *American Journal of Public Health* 78, no. 1 (Jan.

1988), p. 79, fig. 3; Jennifer Steinhauer, "Big Benefits in Marriage, Studies Say," *The New York Times*, April 10, 1995, p. A10.

37. "Survey, How Fathers Feel . . . ," *Parents Magazine*, Dec. 1993, p. 234.

38. Blankenhorn, *Fatherless America*, p. 113.

39. "State and Federal Prison Population Tops One Million," U.S. Department of Justice press release, Oct. 27, 1994, pp. 2, 3.; *Bureau of Justice Statistics Sourcebook of Criminal Justice Statistics—1993*, U.S. Department of Justice, p. 430, table 4.5; Farrell, *The Myth of Male Power*, pp. 240–244; "Capital Punishment 1993," U.S. Department of Justice, Bureau of Justice Statistics Bulletin, p. 1 (thirty-eight prisoners were executed in 1993; none were women).

40. Barbara Vobjeda, ". . . As Single Fathers Head More Families," *Washington Post*, May 13, 1992, p. A21.

41. "Alcohol Problems Prevalent Among Elderly," *Washington Post*, Sept. 8, 1993, p. A5; *Suicides by Age, Race, and Sex*, National Center for Health Statistics, 1993.

CHAPTER 2

1. Anne Moir and David Jessel, *Brain Sex: The Real Difference Between Men and Women* (New York: Lyle Stuart, 1991), p. 166.

2. Jerry Mander, *Four Arguments for the Elimination of Television* (New York: Quill, 1978), p. 239.

3. See, for example, Inge Braverman et al., "Sex Role Stereoptypes: A Current Appraisal," *Journal of Social Issues* 28, no. 2 (1972): p. 59; Cris Evatt, *He & She: 60 Significant Differences Between Men and Women* (Berkeley: Conari Press, 1992), pp. 150–51; Sam Keen, *Fire in the Belly* (New York: Bantam Books, 1992), p. 199.

4. Andrea Dworkin, quoted in Sarah Crichton, "Sexual Correctness: Has It Gone Too Far?" *Newsweek*, Oct. 25, 1993, p. 54.

5. Marilyn French, cited in Gail Jennes, "Out of the Pages," *People*, Feb. 20, 1983.

6. Daphne Patai and Noretta Koertge, *Professing Feminism* (New York: Basic Books, 1994), p. 105.

7. Ibid., p. 83.

8. Sally Miller Gearhart, "The Future—If There Is One—Is Female," in *Reweaving the Web of Life*, ed. Pam McAllister (Philadelphia: New Society Publishers, 1982), p. 271.

9. Quoted in *Wingspan: Inside the Men's Movement*, ed. Christopher Harding (New York: St. Martin's Press, 1992), p. xi.

10. Quoted from *Morning Edition*, National Public Radio, Aug. 28, 1992.

11. George Gilder, *Naked Nomads* (New York: Quadrangle/The New York Times Book Co., 1974), p. 91.

12. Ibid., pp. 77–78.
13. R. G. Ratcliffe, "Not a Tender Gender? Jordon Says Men Lack CARE Package," *Houston Chronicle*, Sept. 28, 1991.
14. Jack Kammer, "Jordon Should Help Bridge Gender Gap for Dems," *New York Daily News*, "Opinions," July 12, 1992.
15. Moir and Jessel, *Brain Sex*, p. 6.
16. Ibid., p. 166.
17. Ibid., p. 202.
18. See, i.e., Karl Polanyi, *The Great Transformation* (Boston: Beacon Press, 1944), pp. 269–279; Bronislaw Malinowski, *Argonauts of the Western Pacific* (New York: Dutton, 1922); David D. Gilmore, *Manhood in the Making, Cultural Concepts of Masculinity* (New Haven: Yale University Press, 1990); see also Ivan Illich, *Gender* (New York: Pantheon, 1982), pp. 70–80.
19. Gilmore, *Manhood in the Making*, pp. 229–230.

CHAPTER 3

1. Ivan Illich, *Gender* (New York: Pantheon, 1982), p. 175.
2. Robert L. Heilbroner, *The Worldly Philosophers* (New York: Simon & Schuster, 1972), p. 30.
3. Alex Shoumatoff, *The World Is Burning* (Boston: Little, Brown, 1990), p. 5.
4. Heilbroner, *The Worldly Philosophers*, p. 29.
5. Illich, *Gender*, pp. 106–110.
6. J. L. Hammond and Barbara Hammond, *The Village Laborer, 1760–1832* (London: Longmans Green, 1912), p. 10.
7. Gilbert Slater, *The English Peasantry and the Enclosure of the Common Fields* (New York: Augustus M. Kelley, 1968), p. 1.
8. Hammond and Hammond, *The Village Laborer*, pp. 82, 218.
9. Heilbroner, *The Worldly Philosophers*, p. 31.
10. Bruce Rich, *Mortgaging the Earth: The World Bank, Environmental Impoverishment and the Crisis of Development* (Boston: Beacon Press, 1994), p. 155.
11. See Clarence Maloney, "Environmental and Project Displacement of Population in India, Part I: Development and Deracination," University International Field Staff Report, 1990–1991, no. 14, p. 1.
12. See Allan C. Carlson, *From Cottage to Work Station* (San Francisco: Ignatius Press, 1993), pp. 25–64.
13. Gary Cross, *Time and Money: The Making of Consumer Culture* (London: Routledge, 1993), p. 167.
14. D. B. Lynn, quoted in Nancy Chodorow, *The Reproduction of Mothering* (Berkeley: University of California Press, 1978), p. 176.

15. Quoted in Juliet B. Schor, *The Overworked American* (New York: Basic Books, 1992), p. 53.

CHAPTER 4

1. Carlyle, Thomas, "Signs of the Times," *Edinburgh Review*, 49 (June 1829) p. 439.
2. Herb Goldberg, *The Hazards of Being Male: Surviving the Myth of Masculine Privilege* (New York: NAL, 1987), pp. 43–44.
3. Patrick M. McGrady, Jr., *The Love Doctors* (New York: Macmillan, 1972), p. 281.
4. Judith Rodin, "Body Mania," *Psychology Today*, Jan.–Feb. 1992, pp. 55, 56.
5. Robert T. Grieves, "Muscle Madness," *Forbes*, May 30, 1988, p. 216.
6. Robert Ho, "Men Try to Put a New Face on Careers," *Wall Street Journal*, Aug. 28, 1991, p. B1.
7. Goldberg, *The Hazards of Being Male*, pp. 43–44.
8. Quoted in Ashley Montagu and Floyd Matson, *The Dehumanization of Man* (New York: McGraw-Hill Book Company, 1983), p. 10.
9. Ibid., p. 10.
10. Juliet B. Schor, *The Overworked American* (New York: HarperCollins, 1992), p. 44.
11. Ibid., p. 45.
12. Sidney Pollard, *The Genesis of Modern Management* (Middlesex, England; Baltimore, MD: Penguin Books, 1968), p. 190.
13. Ibid., p. 162.
14. Ibid., p. 161.
15. Ibid.
16. Ibid., p. 196.
17. Michael Adas, *Machines as the Measure of Men* (Ithaca: Cornell University Press, 1989), p. 209.
18. Quoted in Anson Rabinbach, *The Human Motor* (Berkeley: University of California Press, 1992), p. 74.
19. Pollard, *The Genesis of Modern Management*, pp. 229, 230.
20. Ibid., p. 243.
21. Quoted in E. F. Schumacher, *Good Work* (New York: Harper & Row, 1979), p. 119.
22. Quoted in Montagu and Matson, *The Dehumanization of Man*, p. 15.
23. Jeremy Rifkin, *Biosphere Politics* (New York: Crown Publishers, 1991), p. 106.
24. David J. Rogers, *Waging Business Warfare: Lessons from the Military Masters in Achieving Corporate Superiority* (New York: Charles Scribner's Sons, 1987).
25. Floyd Matson, *The Broken Image* (Garden City, NY: Anchor Books, Doubleday, 1966), p. 6.

26. Ibid.
27. Quoted in Rabinbach, *The Human Motor*, p. 64.
28. Quoted in David F. Channel, *The Vital Machine* (New York: Oxford University Press, 1991), p. 40.
29. Quoted in Aram Vartanian, *Diderot and Descartes* (Westport, CT: Greenwood Press, 1953), pp. 205, 206.
30. See Channel, *The Vital Machine*, p. 44.
31. Ibid., p. 67.
32. Rabinbach, *The Human Motor*, p. 2.
33. Ibid., p. 68.
34. C. George Benello, Clifford G. Christians, and Jay M. Van Hook, eds., "Technology and Power: Technique as a Mode of Understanding Modernity," Chapter 5 in *Jacques Ellul: Interpretive Essays* (Urbana, IL: University of Illinois Press, 1981).
35. Jeremy Rifkin, *Time Wars* (New York: Simon & Schuster, 1987), pp. 106, 107.
36. Warren Farrell, *The Myth of Male Power* (New York: Simon & Schuster, 1993), pp. 52, 53.
37. For example, in 1991, among married couples with preschool children, 28 percent of mothers were employed full-time, year-round as contrasted with 77 percent of all fathers who were employed full-time, year-round. Source: U.S. Department of Labor Statistics, "Current Population Survey," March 1992.
38. Far more men than women work full-time. Even for men and women working full-time, men work over 440 hours more per year. However, women's work hours are increasing. See Schor, *The Overworked American*, pp. 29–32 (tables 2.1, 2.2).
39. Jeremy Rifkin, *The End of Work* (New York: Tarcher-Putnam, 1995), p. 5.
40. Schor, *The Overworked American*, p. 22.
41. Erich Fromm, *The Anatomy of Human Destructiveness* (New York: Holt, Rinehart and Winston, 1973), p. 350.
42. Wayne Hearn, "Real Men Don't Get Sick," *American Medical News*, Dec. 28, 1992, p. 1.
43. Quoted in Alan Riding, "Sartre Soldier: Musing, Writing," *The New York Times*, Feb. 13, 1995, p. C20.
44. Both quotes from Farrell, *The Myth of Male Power*, p. 126.
45. Quoted in John Tierney, "Porn, the Low Slung Engine of Progress," *The New York Times*, "Arts and Leisure," Jan. 9, 1994, p. 18.
46. George Basalla, quoted in Tierney, "Porn."
47. For example, *People* magazine entitled one article on the case, "Severence Pay," *People*, Dec. 13, 1993, Vol. 40, Issue 24, p. 92.
48. Quoted in Tierney, "Porn."

CHAPTER 5

1. Quoted in D. Stanley Eitzen, "The Dark Side of Competition in American Society," in *Vital Speeches of the Day*, Jan. 1, 1990, p. 184.
2. Cris Evatt, *He & She* (Berkeley: Conari Press, 1992), p. 38.
3. "Remarks of the President after the House NAFTA Vote," White House press release, Nov. 17, 1993.
4. Quoted in Evatt, *He & She*, p. 38.
5. Alfie Kohn, *No Contest: The Case Against Competition* (Boston: Houghton Mifflin, 1986, 1992), p. 1.
6. Quoted in ibid, pp. 142–43.
7. Quoted in ibid, p. 143.
8. Quoted in ibid, p. 123.
9. Marshall D. Sahlins, "The Origins of Society," *Scientific American*, Sept. 1960, pp. 80, 82.
10. See Kohn, *No Contest*, pp. 34–39.
11. Robert Harry Lowie, quoted in Karl Polanyi, *The Great Transformation* (Boston: Beacon Press, 1944), pp. 269, 270.
12. Ibid.
13. Richard Hofstadter, *Social Darwinism in American Thought* (Boston: Beacon Press, 1955), p. 6.
14. Ibid., p. 66.
15. William G. Sumner, *The Challenge of Facts and Other Essays* (New Haven: Yale University Press, 1914), p. 68.
16. Quoted in Hofstadter, *Social Darwinism*, p. 63.
17. Ibid., p. 54.
18. Ibid., p. 58.
19. William G. Sumner, *What Social Classes Owe Each Other* (New York: Harper Bro., 1883), pp. 22–24.
20. Quoted in Hofstadter, *Social Darwinism*, p. 120.
21. Quoted in Kohn, *No Contest*, p. 21.
22. Goldberg, *The Hazards of Being Male*, p. 77.
23. Quoted in Kohn, *No Contest*, p. 81.
24. Jacques Ellul, *The Technological Society* (New York: Knopf, 1964), p. 383.
25. Source: National Athletic Trainers Association, from records kept 1986–89; see also "Sidelined: How Injuries Take Student Athletes Out of the Game," *Washington Post*, "Health," Sept. 12, 1989, p. 5.
26. See *Drug Misuse: Anabolic Steroids and Human Growth Hormone*, U.S. General Accounting Office, 1989, p. 4.
27. See "Unsafe at Work," *Washington Post*, "Health," Nov. 23, 1993, p. 5.

CHAPTER 6

1. Quoted in Mark Gerzon, *A Choice of Heroes* (New York: Houghton Mifflin, 1992), p. 129.
2. The New Scofield Reference Bible, Authorized King James Version (New York: Oxford University Press, 1967).
3. Quoted in Laurence Shames, *The Hunger for More* (New York: Times Books, 1989), pp. 100–101.
4. Earl Shorris, *A Nation of Salesmen* (New York: W. W. Norton & Company, 1994), p. 25.
5. Ibid., p. 270.
6. Quoted in Suzanne Gordon, *Prisoners of Men's Dreams* (Boston: Little, Brown, 1991), p. 25.
7. Ibid., p. 20.
8. Quoted in Cris Evatt, *He & She* (Berkeley: Conari Press, 1992), p. 14.
9. Ibid.
10. Andrea Dworkin, *Pornography*, quoted in *Time*, Feb. 14, 1994, p. 58.
11. Quoted in George Dalton, ed., *Primitive, Archaic and Modern Economies, Essays of Karl Polanyi* (Boston: Beacon Press, 1968), p. ix.
12. Quoted in Karl Polanyi, *The Great Transformation* (Boston: Beacon Press, 1957), p. 269.
13. Ibid., pp. 269–70.
14. Ibid., p. 270.
15. Ibid., p. 43.
16. Robert L. Heilbroner, *The Worldly Philosophers* (New York: Simon & Schuster, 1972), p. 22.
17. Both quotes from Shorris, *A Nation of Salesmen*, p. 61.
18. Thomas Chobham, *Summa Confessorum*, ed. F. Broomfield (Paris: Louvain, 1968), p. 505.
19. Raymond Williams, *Keywords* (New York: Oxford University Press, 1983), p. 331.
20. Quoted in Robert Nelson, *Reaching for Heaven on Earth* (Savage, MD: Rowman & Littlefield, 1991), p. 97.
21. Heilbroner, *The Worldly Philosophers*, p. 35.
22. Ibid.
23. Adam Smith, *The Wealth of Nations* (Chicago: University of Chicago Press, 1976), p. 18.
24. Polanyi, *The Great Transformation*, p. 135.
25. Jeremy Rifkin, *Biosphere Politics* (San Francisco: HarperSanFrancisco, 1991), p. 173.
26. Ibid., p. 96.
27. Max Weber, *Economy and Society*, vol. 2, ed. Guenther Roth and Claus Witich (New York: Bedminster Press, 1968), p. 636.

28. Quoted in Juliet B. Schor, *The Overworked American* (New York: Basic Books, 1992), pp. 120–121.
29. Harvey Wasserman, *American Born and Reborn* (New York: Collier Books, 1983), p. 110.
30. Benjamin Hunnicut, *Work Without End: Abandoning Shorter Hours for the Right to Work* (Philadelphia: Temple University Press, 1988), p. 76.
31. William Green, "Editorial," *American Federationist* 34 (Nov. 1927), p. 1,300.
32. A. Link, *American Epoch* (New York, 1955), p. 238.
33. Elbert H. Gary, *Monthly Labor Review*, Dec. 1926, p. 1,168.
34. Quoted in Jeremy Rifkin, *The End of Work* (New York: Tarcher/Putnam, 1995), p. 20.
35. Hunnicut, *Work Without End*, pp. 47, 48.
36. Ibid., p. 42.
37. John Kenneth Galbraith, *The Affluent Society*, 4th ed. (Boston: Houghton Mifflin, 1984), p. 127.
38. Schor, *The Overworked American*, p. 119.
39. Jackson Lears, *Fables of Abundance: A Cultural History of Advertising in America* (New York: Basic Books, 1994), p. 227.
40. Ibid., p. 228, fig. 7.4.
41. Schor, *The Overworked American*, p. 119.
42. Hunnicut, *Work Without End*, p. 44.
43. Ibid., p. 121.
44. John A. Ryan, "High Wages and Unemployment," *Commonweal* 13, (Jan. 3, 1931): p. 261.
45. Alan Durning, *How Much Is Enough?* (New York: W. W. Norton & Company, 1992), pp. 21, 22.
46. John Judis, "The Jobless Recovery," *The New Republic*, March 16, 1993, p. 22.
47. Schor, *The Overworked American*, pp. 108, 109; Judis, "The Jobless Recovery," p. 22; "Consumer Credit Up Again but the Monthly Pace Eases," *The New York Times*, March 8, 1994, p. D16.
48. Schor, *The Overworked American*, pp. 28–31.
49. Stuart Ewen, *Captains of Consciousness* (New York: McGraw-Hill, 1976), p. 133.
50. Shorris, A Nation of Salesmen, pp. 331–332.
51. See Diane Crispell, "The Brave New World," *American Demographic*, Jan. 1992, p. 38.
52. The study is cited in Warren Farrell, *The Myth of Male Power* (New York: Simon & Schuster, 1993), p. 33.
53. Keith Bradsher, "Gap in Wealth in U.S. Called Widest in West," *The New York Times*, April 17, 1995, p. A1.

54. Lawrence Mishel and Jared Bernstein, *The State of Working America 1992–93* (Washington, D.C.: M. E. Sharpe, 1993), pp. 131–134.
55. Jason De Parle, "Sharp Increase Along the Borders of Poverty," *The New York Times*, March 31, 1994.
56. "U.S., Others Struggle with the Choice of Creating More or Good Jobs," *Washington Post*, July 11, 1993.

CHAPTER 7

1. Rollo May, *Power and Innocence* (New York: W. W. Norton & Company, 1972), p. 105.
2. "A Master Class in Radical Change," *Fortune*, Dec. 13, 1993, p. 82.
3. Ibid.
4. Ibid.
5. Richard Barnet and Robert Muller, *Global Reach: The Power of the Multinational Corporations*, (New York: Simon & Schuster, 1974), pp. 72–73.
6. Ibid., p. 15.
7. "Executive Pay: The Party Ain't Over Yet," *Business Week*, April 26, 1993, pp. 56–62; see also, "That Eye-Popping Executive Pay: Is Anybody Worth This Much?," *Business Week*, April 25, 1994, pp. 52–58.
8. Barnet and Muller, *Global Reach*, pp. 13–14.
9. Suzanne Gordon, *Prisoners of Men's Dreams* (Boston: Little, Brown, 1991), p. 21.
10. Cris Evatt, *He & She* (Berkeley: Conari Press, 1992), p. 40.
11. Ibid.
12. May, *Power and Innocence*, p. 109.
13. James Burnham, *The Machiavellians* (Washington, DC: Regnery Gateway, 1987), p. 300.
14. Ibid., p. 106.
15. Ibid., p. 69.
16. Ibid., p. 59.
17. Ibid., p. 49.
18. Ibid., p. 278.
19. Francis Bacon, *Novum Organum*, vol. 2 of *The Works of Francis Bacon*, ed. byJames Spedding, Robert Leslie Ellis, Douglas Devon Heath, 14 vols. (London: Longmans Green, 1870), p. 246.
20. Ibid., pp. 320, 325.
21. Ibid., p. 296; see also Carolyn Merchant, *The Death of Nature* (San Francisco: Harper & Row, 1980) pp. 164–190.
22. C. George Benello, ed. "Technology and Power: Technique as a Mode of Understanding Modernity," in *Jacques Ellul: Interpretive Essays* (Urbana, IL: University of Illinois Press, 1981), p. 98.

23. Carroll Pursell, "The Rise and Fall of the Appropriate Technology Movement in the United States, 1965–1985," *Technology and Culture*, July 1993, pp. 635–37.
24. Michael L. Smith, "Selling the Moon," in Richard Wightman Fox and T. J. Jackson Lears, eds., *The Culture of Consumption* (New York: Pantheon Books, 1983), pp. 184–85.
25. Quoted in Smith, "Selling the Moon," p. 209.
26. Scott Russell Sanders, *The Paradise of Bombs*, (Athens: University of Georgia Press, 1987), p. 113.
27. Joseph Heller, *Something Happened* (New York: Ballantine, 1975), p. 76.
28. S. Kelly, "Some Social and Psychological Aspects of Organic Sexual Dysfunction in Men," *Sexuality and Disability* 4 (1981): p. 126.
29. Ibid.
30. Barbara Ehrenreich, "Angry Young Men," *Utne Reader*, May–June 1991, p. 80.

CHAPTER 8

1. Robert Bly, *Iron John, A Book About Men* (Reading, MA: Addison-Wesley, 1990), p. x.
2. Quoted in Dan Oldenburg, "Getting a Life: The Movement Takes a Pragmatic Turn," *The Washington Post*, October 12, 1993, p. C5.
3. Andrew Ferguson, "America's New Man," *The American Spectator*, Jan. 1992, p. 27.
4. Ferguson, "America's New Man, p. 27."
5. Laura S. Brown, "Essential Lies: A Dystopian Vision of the Mythopoetic Men's Movement," in *Women Respond to the Men's Movement*, ed. Kay Leigh Hagan (San Francisco: Pandora, HarperSanFrancisco, 1992), p. 94.
6. Ibid., p. 96.
7. Trip Gabriel, "Call of the Wildmen," *The New York Times Magazine*, Oct. 14, 1990, p. 47.
8. Gerzon, *A Choice of Heroes* (Boston: Houghton Mifflin, 1992), pp. 273, 274.
9. Mitscherlich, *Society Without the Father* (New York: HarperCollins, 1993), p. 147.
10. Ibid. p. 155, 156.
11. Ibid. p. 156, 157.
12. Herb Goldberg, *The Hazards of Being Male: Surviving the Myth of Masculine Privilege* (New York: Penguin Books/NAL, 1976, 1987), p. 90.
13. Significant works include Warren Farrell's *The Myth of Male Power* (New York: Simon & Schuster, 1993); Mark Gerzon's pioneering 1982 work *A Choice of Heroes* (Boston: Houghton Mifflin, 1982, 1992); Sam Keen's *Fire in the Belly* (New York: Bantam Books, 1991); and Aaron Kipnis's

Knights Without Armor (New York: Tarcher, 1991). An important part of the growing literature on men is that of African-American men, including Elijah Anderson's study *Streetwise* (Chicago: University of Chicago Press, 1990) and Richard Major and Janet Mancini Billson's *Cool Pose* (New York: Lexington Books, 1992).

14. Bly, *Iron John*, p. 19.
15. Ibid., p. 97.
16. Sharon Doubiago, "Enemy of the Mother: A Feminist Response to the Men's Movement," *Ms.*, March/April 1992, p. 82.
17. Diane Johnson, "Something for the Boys," *The New York Review of Books*, Jan. 16, 1992, p. 17.
18. Quoted in Oldenburg, "Getting a Life."

CHAPTER 9

1. David Blankenhorn, "The Good Family Man: Fatherhood and the Pursuit of Happiness in America," Institute for American Values, Publication No. W.P. 12, Nov. 1991, p. 8.
2. Rich Blake, "Father Says System Is Unfair to Men in Custody Battles," *Alexandria Port Gazette Packet*, Oct. 22, 1992, p. 5.
3. Ibid.
4. Personal interview with Russell Peverell by author, March 6, 1993.
5. Ibid.
6. Ibid.
7. Blake, "Father Says System Is Unfair," p. 5.
8. Ibid.
9. Jan Hoffman, "Divorced Fathers Make Gains in Battles to Increase Rights," *The New York Times*, April 26, 1995, pp. A1, B5.
10. "Putting Working Moms in Custody," *Newsweek*, March 13, 1995, p. 55.
11. Blankenhorn, "The Good Family Man," p. 6.
12. Quoted in Richard A. Warshak, *The Custody Revolution* (New York: Poseidon Press, 1992), p. 31.
13. Ibid.
14. Ibid.
15. In *J.B. v A.B.*, 242 S.E.2d 248 (W.VA., 1978).
16. For a recent discussion of this issue see Ronald K. Henry, " 'Primary Caretaker': Is It a Ruse?" *Family Advocate*, Summer 1994, pp. 53–56.
17. Ibid., p. 33.
18. Joseph H. Pleck, "Family Supportive Employer Policies: Are They Relevant to Men?" unpublished, August 12, 1991, pp. 1–2.
19. Robinson, "Caring for Kids," *Demographics*, July 1989, p. 52.
20. Quoted in Blankenhorn, "The Good Family Man," p. 19.
21. Warshak, *The Custody Revolution*, p. 50.

22. David Blankenhorn, *Fatherless America* (New York: Basic Books, 1995), p. 149.

23. Julie Bonnin, "Shadows of a Dad," *Austin American Statesman*, March 8, 1992, p. G1.

24. Joyce A. Arditti, "An Overview of Policy and Resources," *Family Relations*, Oct. 1990, p. 460.

25. Quoted in Bonnin, "Shadows of a Dad," p. G13.

26. Arditti, p. 461.

27. Ibid.

28. Quoted in Bonnin, "Shadows of a Dad," p. G13.

29. Author interview with Mike K., December 13, 1992.

30. Quoted in Warshak, *The Custody Revolution*, p. 79.

31. Blankenhorn, *Fatherless America*, pp. 18, 19., tables 1.2 and 1.3.

32. Urie Bronfenbrenner, "Discovering What Families Do," in David Blankenhorn, Steve Bayme, and Jean Bethke Elshtain, eds., *Rebuilding the Nest: A New Commitment to the American Family* (Milwaukee: Family Service America, 1990), p. 34.

33. Irwin Garfinkel and Sara S. McLanahan, *Single Mothers and Their Children: A New American Dilemma* (Washington, D.C.: Urban Institute Press, 1986), pp. 30–31.

34. *Interstate Child Support: Mothers Report Receiving Less Support from Out-of-State Fathers*, Jan. 1992, General Accounting Office, GAO/HRD/92-39FS, p. 19.

35. Steven A. Holmes., "Low-wage Fathers and the Welfare Debate," *The New York Times*, April 25, 1995, p. A12.

36. Elaine Sorensen, "Noncustodial Fathers: Can They Afford to Pay Child Support?," *The Urban Institute*, Feb. 1995, pp. 3–4.

37. Rick Bragg, "Georgia, Pursuing Child Support, Discovers Its Potential and Limits," *The New York Times*, April 14, 1995, p. A1.

38. Quoted in Bonnin, "Shadows of a Dad," p. G13.

39. *Interstate Child Support: Mothers Receiving Less Support.*

40. Ellen Hopkins, "Trumped-up Charges of Child Abuse Are Divorce's Ugly New Weapon; Father on Trial," *New York*, Jan. 11, 1988, p. 45.

41. Ibid.

42. Ibid.

43. Ibid., p. 42.

44. Ibid.

45. Quoted in Grace Wong, "A Bitter New Issue," *Maclean's*, Oct. 3, 1988 p. 52.

46. Ibid.

47. Hopkins, "Trumped-up Charges," p. 44.

48. Ibid.

49. Ibid.

50. Ibid., p. 49.
51. Ibid.
52. Texas Department of Protective and Regulatory Services, "Protective Services for Families and Children," 1991 Status Report, fig. 15. See also statistics provided by Oregon Children Services Division, New Jersey Division of Youth and Family Services, Virginia Child Protective Services, Michigan Department of Health and Human Services, and Alaska Division of Family and Youth Services.
53. Cited in Katherine Dunn, "Just as Fierce," *Mother Jones*, Nov./Dec. 1994, p. 38.
54. Murray A. Strauss, "Assaults By Wives on Husbands: Implications for Primary Prevention of Marital Violence," paper presented at the American Society of Criminology, 1989, p. 9.
55. Gloria Robinson-Simpson and R. L. McNeely, "The Truth About Domestic Violence: A Falsely Framed Issue," *Social Work*, Nov.–Dec., 1987, p. 486; Murray A. Strauss and Richard J. Gelles, "Societal Change and Change in Family Violence from 1975 to 1985 as Revealed by Two National Surveys," *Journal of Marriage and the Family*, vol. 48, Aug. 1986, pp. 465–79.
56. Strauss and Gelles, "Societal Change."
57. Ibid. See also Armin A. Brott, "When Women Abuse Men," *Washington Post*, Dec. 28, 1993, p. C5.
58. Ibid.
59. Robinson-Simpson and McNeely, "The Truth About Domestic Violence: A Falsely Framed Issue," p. 485.
60. Dunn, "Just as Fierce," p. 39.
61. Quoted in Bonnin, "Shadows of a Dad," p. G13.
62. Blankenhorn, *Fatherless America*, pp. 19–20, 129–130.
63. Adoption of Baby Doe, 492 So. 2d 508, 511 (1986).
64. Rickie M.'s last name has been withheld to protect him and his child.
65. Declaration of Rickie M., Case Nos. A9982 & A9993, Superior Court State of California, July 3, 1992, p. 2.
66. Ibid.
67. Ibid., p. 6.
68. Ibid., pp. 7–8.
69. See Statement of Decision and Order, *Rickie M. v. Cirri S.*, Aug. 26, 1988.
70. Adoption of Kelsey S., California Supreme Court, 92 Daily Journal D.A.R. 2629, 2640.
71. Declaration of Rickie M., p. 8.
72. Personal interview with Sharon Huddle by author, Dec. 3, 1992.
73. Quoted in Bonnin, "Shadows of a Dad," p. G13.
74. Interview with author, March 8, 1994.
75. Ibid.

CHAPTER 10

1. Herb Goldberg, *The Hazards of Being Male*, p. 1.
2. Sam Keen, *Fire in the Belly*, p. 66.
3. Donald P. Baker, "Roughest Seas for Navy Man Are on Shore," *Washington Post*, Sept. 29, 1992, p. C1.
4. Ibid.
5. Ibid.
6. Ibid.
7. William R. Mattox, "The Parent Trap," *Policy Review*, Winter 1991, p. 9.
8. Quoted in "The Joys and Risks of the 'Daddy Track,'" ABC News *Nightline* transcript, #2668, Aug. 14, 1991, p. 4.
9. Ibid., p. 3.
10. Ibid.
11. Ibid., p. 6.
12. Ibid., p. 1.
13. Earl Harrel, "Together Again," *Men's Health*, April 1991, pp. 65–66.
14. See Guy Toscana and Janice Windau, "The Changing Character of Fatal Work Injuries," *Monthly Labor Review*, Oct. 1994, p. 17; see also "First National Census of Fatal Occupational Injuries Reported by BLS News," U.S. Department of Labor press release, Oct. 1, 1993; see also "Unsafe at Work," *Washington Post*, "Health," Nov. 23, 1993, p. 5; see also "Work Injuries and Illnesses by Selected Characteristics, 1992," News, U.S. Department of Labor press release, April 26, 1994, pp. 1, 2.
15. Ibid.
16. *Handbook of Labor Statistics*, Bureau of Labor Statistics, U.S. Department of Labor, Washington, DC, 1992.
17. Gordon Williams, "Flaming Out on the Job," *Modern Maturity*, Oct.–Nov. 1991, pp. 26–27.
18. Katherine Griffen, "Karoshi in America?" *Health*, May/June, 1993, p. 43.
19. "Multiple Jobholding Unchanged in May 1991," Bureau of Labor Statistics, U.S. Department of Labor, Oct. 28, 1991.
20. Juliet B. Schor, *The Overworked American*, p. 22.
21. Williams, "Flaming Out on the Job," p. 28.
22. Ibid.
23. Robin Herman, "Tougher Jobs Threaten Blood Pressure, Heart," *Washington Post*, "Health," May 19, 1992, p. 5.
24. Aaron R. Kipnis, *Knights Without Armor* (Los Angeles: Tarcher, 1991), p. 33.
25. Charles N. Weaver and Michael D. Mathews, "What White Males Want from Their Jobs: Ten Years Later," *Personnel*, Sept., 1987, p. 62.
26. Goldberg, *The Hazards of Being Male*, p. 96.
27. Kipnis, *Knights Without Armor*, p. 194.

28. Goldberg, *The Hazards of Being Male*, pp. 3–4.
29. "Worker Displacement Increased Sharply in Recent Recession," Bureau of Labor Statistics press release, U.S. Department of Labor, Aug. 19, 1992.
30. Christopher Farrell and Michael Mandel, "The Real Truth About the Economy," *Business Week*, Nov. 7, 1994, p. 110.
31. Sylvia Nasar, "More Men in Prime of Life Spend Less Time Working," *The New York Times*, Dec. 1, 1994, pp. A1, D15.
32. "Worker Displacement Increased Sharply in Recent Recession," Bureau of Labor Statistics, U.S. Department of Labor, Aug. 19, 1992.
33. Ibid.
34. Dale Russakoff, "Lives Once Solid as Steel Shatter in Changed World," *Washington Post*, April 13, 1992, p. A1.
35. Ibid.
36. Dale Russakoff, "The American Dream: Fired Up and Melted Down," *Washington Post*, April 12, 1992.
37. Ibid.
38. Ibid.
39. "Not Home Alone, Jobless Male Managers Proliferate in Suburbs," *Wall Street Journal*, Sept. 20, 1993, p. A1.
40. Ibid.
41. Ibid.
42. Ibid.
43. Quoted in Thomas J. Cottle, "When You Stop, You Die: The Human Toll of Male Unemployment," *Commonweal*, June 19, 1992, pp. 16–17.
44. Ibid.
45. Ibid.
46. Sara S. McLanahan and Jennifer L. Glass, "A Note on the Trend in Sex Differences in Psychological Stress," *Journal of Health and Social Behavior*, vol. 26, Dec. 1985, p. 329.
47. See Ivo L. Abraham and Heide von Koss Krowchuk, "Unemployment and Health," in *The Nursing Clinics of North America*, March 1986, pp. 37–40.
48. Mary Merva and Richard Fowles, "Effects of Diminished Economic Opportunities on Social Stress: Heart Attacks, Strokes, and Crime," Washington D.C., Economic Policy Institute, Oct. 1992.
49. Robert B. Reich, *The Work of Nations* (New York: Vintage Books, 1991), p. 95.
50. Ibid.
51. Jeremy Rifkin, "Watch Out for Trickle Down Technology," *The New York Times*, Op-Ed, Feb. 24, 1993.
52. Quoted in ibid.
53. Quoted in ibid.

54. *Employment and Earnings*, vol. 42, #1, U.S. Department of Labor, Bureau of Labor Statistics, Jan. 1995.
55. "Literacy of 90 Million Is Deficient," *Washington Post*, Sept. 9, 1993, p. A1; also Jonathan Kozol, *Illiterate America* (New York: Anchor Press/Doubleday, 1985), pp. 4, 10.
56. Schor, *The Overworked American*, pp. 12, 13.
57. "Labor Wants Shorter Hours to Make Up for Job Losses," *The New York Times*, Oct. 11, 1993, p. A10.
58. "Let's Fight Together for Shorter Work Time," *Labor Notes*, Oct. 1993, p. 6.
59. Thomas L. Friedman, "World's Big Economies Turn to the Jobs Issue," *The New York Times*, March 14, 1994, p. D1.
60. Elizabeth Mehren, "Who'll Benefit from the Act and When?," *Washington Post*, March 9, 1993, p. C5.
61. Ibid.
62. Ibid.
63. Congressman Lucien Blackwell, U.S. Congress, House of Representatives, *H.R. 3267, The Full Employment Act of 1994*, March 23, 1994.
64. Cited in William McGaughey, "The International Dimensions of Reduced Hours," Society for the Reduction of Human Labor, Newsletter, vol. 1, no.1, p. 6.
65. "VW Plans 4-Day Week in Germany as Sales Stagnate," *Financial Times*, Oct. 25, 1993, p. 1.
66. Letter to President Clinton from Betty Friedan, Dec. 8, 1994.
67. Personal interview with author, Jan. 7, 1994.
68. McLanahan and Glass, "A Note on the Trend in Sex Differences in Psychological Distress," p. 329.

CHAPTER 11

1. Warren Farrell, *The Myth of Male Power* (New York: Simon & Schuster, 1993), p. 183.
2. Quoted in Wayne Hearn, "Real Men Don't Get Sick," *American Medical News*, American Medical Association, Dec. 28, 1992, p. 1.
3. Cited in Farrell, *The Myth of Male Power*, pp. 180–181.
4. U.S. Department of Health and Human Services, National Center for Health Statistics, Division of Vital Statistics, 1988 (unpublished).
5. From "Facts on Male Health"; see also Farrell, *The Myth of Male Power*, p. 396, note 26.
6. Hearn, "Real Men Don't Get Sick."
7. Kim Painter, "Men Less Likely to Notice Their Melanomas," *USA Today*, June 11, 1992, p. D1.

8. Hearn, "Real Men Don't Get Sick."

9. Patricia Anstett, "Real Men Don't Get Sick," *Detroit Free Press*, Feb. 2, 1993, p. 21B.

10. See "NCI Seeks Answers on Prostate Cancer: Causes, Detection, Prevention, and Treatment," *Cancer Facts*, National Cancer Institute, National Institutes of Health, July 26, 1994, p. 1.; see also Robin Herman, "Prostate Cancer Prevention Study Launched," *Washington Post*, "Health," Oct. 19, 1993, p. 9.

11. See Leonore Tiefer, "In Pursuit of the Perfect Penis," *American Behavioral Scientist*, vol. 29, no. 5, May/June 1986, p. 580.

12. Source: "Facts on Male Health."

13. Anstett, "Real Men Don't Get Sick."

14. Reported in Don Colburn, "Doctors Detect Depression More in Women Than in Men," *Washington Post*, "Health," Dec. 10, 1991, pp. 5–6. The study revealed that mental health practitioners underdetected depression in men by 65 percent and overdetected depression in women by 19 percent.

15. Jane E. Brody, "Recognizing Demons of Depression in Either Sex," *The New York Times*, "Health," Dec. 18, 1991, p. C21.

16. "How You Can Tell," *Ladies' Home Journal*, April 1992, p. 104.

17 Quoted in Natalie Angier, "New Malady Found: Is There a Cure for Boyhood?" *Toronto Globe and Mail*, July 26, 1994, A17.

18. Alfie Kohn, "Suffer the Restless Children," *Atlantic Monthly*, Nov. 1989, p. 90.

19. Diane Divoky, "Ritalin: Education's Fix-It Drug?" *Phi Delta Kappan*, April 1989, p. 603.

20. Kohn, "Suffer the Restless Children," p. 90.

21. "Do Doctors Too Often Medicate 'Hyper' Children?" *Washington Post*, "Health," Jan. 12, 1993, p. 10.

22. Author interview with Richard Woods, March 9, 1994.

23. Kohn, "Suffer the Restless Children," p. 92.

24. Ibid., p. 98.

25. Ibid.

26. Ibid.

27. Divoky, "Ritalin: Education's Fix-It Drug?" p. 602.

28. Kohn, "Suffer the Restless Children," p. 602.

29. Daniel J. Safer, M.D., John M. Krager, M.D., M.P.H., "A Survey of Medication Treatment for Hyperactive/Inattentive Students," *JAMA*, vol. 260, no. 15, Oct. 21, 1988, p. 2,256.

30. Natalie Angier, "New Malady Found: Is There a Cure for Boyhood?" *Toronto Globe and Mail*, July 26, 1994, p. A17.

31. "Drug Misuse: Anabolic Steroids and Human Growth Hormone," General Accounting Office (GAO/HRD-89-109), Aug. 1989, p. 14.

32. Ibid., pp. 14–16, 21, 41.
33. Committee on the Judiciary, United States Senate: "Steroids in Amateur and Professional Sports—The Medical and Social Costs of Steroid Abuse." One Hundred First Congress, First Session, April 3, 1989, May 9, 1989, pp. 1–4.
34. Ibid., p. 4.
35. GAO Report, "Drug Misuse," p. 4.
36. Steve Coursen and Lee R. Schreiber, *Steelers and Steroids, False Glory* (Stamford, CT: Longmeadow Press, 1991), p. 55.
37. GAO Report, "Drug Misuse," p. 4.
38. Committee on the Judiciary, "Steroids in Amateur and Professional Sports," pp. 12, 13.
39. Joanne M. Schrof, "Pumped Up," *U.S. News & World Report,* June 1, 1992, p. 55.
40. "Facts on the Male Health Center" (Dallas, TX: The Male Health Center, 1992).
41. Hearn, "Real Men Don't Get Sick," p. 1.
42. Ibid.
43. "Facts on the Male Health Center," p. 3.
44. Hearn, "Real Men Don't Get Sick," p. 1.
45. Ibid.
46. Personal interview with Ron Henry, Feb. 2, 1993. The author is a co-founder of the network.
47. Interview with James Sniechowski by author Feb. 10, 1993.
48. See James F. Fries, C. Everett Koop, et al., "Reducing Health Care Costs by Reducing the Need and Demand for Medical Services," *The New England Journal of Medicine,* July 29, 1993, p. 322.
49. Michael Specter, "Male Smokers Seen Losing 18 Years," *Washington Post,* May 13, 1990, p. A4.
50. See Mary Harvey, R. William Whitmer, James C. Hilyer, Kathleen C. Brown, "The Impact of a Comprehensive Medical Benefit Cost Management Program for the City of Birmingham: Result at Five Years," *American Journal of Health Promotion,* March/April 1993, pp. 296–303.
51. Ibid., p. 299.
52. Ibid., pp. 300–303.
53. Cited in "Employers Recognizing What Stress Costs Them, UN Report Suggests," *Washington Post,* March 28, 1993, p. H2.

CHAPTER 12

1. Quoted in "Spiritual Warrior," an interview with Joseph Jastrab, in *Wingspan: Inside the Men's Movement* (New York: St. Martin's Press, 1992), p. 177.

2. Aaron R. Kipnis, "The Blessings of the Green Man," in *Wingspan: Inside the Men's Movement* (New York: St. Martin's Press, 1992), p. 161.
3. See Wendell Berry, "A Rescued Farm," in *To Be a Man*, ed. Keith Thompson (Los Angeles: Tarcher, 1991), p. 219.
4. Ibid., p. 221.
5. Ibid.
6. Ibid., p. 222.
7. Ibid.
8. "The Estrogen Complex," *Newsweek*, March 21, 1994, p. 76.
9. Ibid.
10. Sam Keen, *Fire in the Belly* (New York: Bantam Books, 1992), p. 183.
11. Quoted in Tom Melham, *John Muir's America* (Washington, DC: National Geographic Society, 1976), p. 194.
12. Ibid., p. 186.

CHAPTER 13

1. Richard Holmes, *Acts of War: The Behavior of Men in Battle* (New York: Free Press, 1985), p. 393.
2. Ray Raphael, *The Men from the Boys: Rites of Passage in Male America* (Lincoln: University of Nebraska Press, 1988), pp. 118, 121.
3. Martin Van Creveld, *Technology and War* (New York: The Free Press, 1989), p. 171.
4. Richard Rubenstein, *The Cunning of History* (New York: Harper & Row, 1978), p. 9.
5. Holmes, *Acts of War*, p. 178.
6. Ibid., p. 99.
7. Ibid., p. 392.
8. Ibid., p. 372.
9. Ibid., p. 402.
10. Michael Uhl and Tod Ensign, *GI Guinea Pigs* (New York: Playboy Press, 1980), pp. 176–177.
11. Quoted in David Gelman, "Treating War's Psychic Wounds," *Newsweek*, Aug. 29, 1988, pp. 62–64.
12. Ibid.
13. Ibid.
14. Ibid.
15. Lucinda Franks, "Soldiers Pay," *The Nation*, Oct. 25, 1990, p. 397.
16. Doug Magee, "The Long War of Wayne Felde," *The Nation*, Jan. 2–9, 1982, p. 11.
17. Ibid.
18. Ibid.

19. Uhl and Ensign, *GI Guinea Pigs*, p. 128.
20. "Citizen Soldier Sues to Stop Agent Orange Settlement," *Citizen Soldier*, no. 8, April 1985, pp. 1, 6.
21. Quoted in statement of Senator Thomas Daschle, Congressional Record, Nov. 21, 1989.
22. A new suit against Agent Orange makers was filed by veterans whose diseases occurred subsequent to the 1984 settlement. In February 1994, the case was dismissed by the Supreme Court. This means that thousands of veterans who were victims of Agent Orange will now receive no compensation as the money settled on in 1984 has been exhausted.
23. Personal interview with author, August 12, 1993.

CHAPTER 14

1. Richard Majors, Janet Mancini, Billson, *Cool Pose* (New York: Lexington Books, 1992), p. 55.
2. Brent Staples, "Just Walk on By," excerpted in *Harpers* Magazine, Dec. 1991, p. 19.
3. *Criminal Victimization in the United States, 1991*, U.S. Department of Justice, table 19, p. 40.
4. Eloise Salholz and Gregory Cerio, "Short Lives, Bloody Deaths," *Newsweek*, Dec. 17, 1990, p. 33.
5. Majors and Billson, *Cool Pose*, p. 21.
6. Ibid., p. 14. Milwaukee study cited in Michelle Collison, "Black Male Schools: Yes," *Black Enterprise*, Feb. 1991, p. 18.
7. Rochelle Sharpe, "Unequal Opportunity," *Wall Street Journal*, Sept. 14, 1993, p. A1. Salim Muwakkil, "Are Black Males an Endangered Species?" *Utne Reader*, Nov./Dec. 1988, p. 46.
8. Quotes in Muwakkil, "Are Black Males an Endangered Species?" p. 46.
9. Quoted in Sidney M. Willhelm, *Who Needs the Negro?* (Cambridge, MA: Schenkman Publishing Company, 1970), p. 2.
10. Ray Stannard Baker quoted in Willhelm, *Who Needs the Negro?*, p. 2.
11. Willhelm, *Who Needs the Negro?* p. 141; see also Willis Peterson, Yoav Kislev, *The Cotton Harvester in Retrospect: Labor Displacement or Replacement* (St. Paul, MN: University of Minnesota, Sept. 1991).
12. David Cohn quoted in Nicholas Lemann, *The Promised Land: The Great Black Migration and How It Changed America* (New York: Vintage Books, 1992), p. 51.
13. UAW testimony, "Hearings before the United States Commission on Civil Rights," Dec. 1960 (Washington DC: U.S. Government Printing Office, 1961), pp. 63–65.
14. Julius William Wilson, *The Truly Disadvantaged* (Chicago: University of Chicago Press, 1987), p. 30.

15. Willhelm, *Who Needs the Negro?* p. 162.
16. Personal interview with Richard Majors, December 12, 1992; see also Majors and Billson, *Cool Pose*, pp. 34–35.
17. Rene Sanchez, "Adding Gentle but Firm Persuasion," *Washington Post,* Feb. 8, 1990, p. A1.
18. See Concerned Black Men, Inc., Washington, DC, Chapter, "Adopt-A-School Committee, Project 2000, 1992–1993 School Year Plan," Stanton Elementary School, Naylor Road and Alabama Avenue, S.E., Washington, DC 20020, p. 4.
19. Sanchez, "Adding Gentle but Firm Persuasion."
20. See Project 2000, p. 5.
21. Ibid.
22. For more information about Project 2000 contact Concerned Black Men, Inc., 655 15th Street, N.W., Suite 300, Washington, DC 20005.
23. A 1992 survey by the National Education Association showed that the number of men teaching at all grade levels (K–12) has decreased to 28 percent, the lowest of any year since the Association began such surveys in 1961. However, each year over half (54 percent) of individuals seeking to teach are male, yet only 23 percent of those newly hired each year are men.
24. Alan L. Adler, "Detroit Told to Admit Girls to Male Academies," *Washington Post,* Aug. 16, 1991, p. A3.
25. Personal interview with Charles A. Ballard, February 21, 1994. Scripture cited is Malachi 4:6.

CHAPTER 15

1. Courtland Milloy, "Homeless Pair Rings in a New Year on the Same Old Streets," *Washington Post,* Jan. 1, 1991, p. B3.
2. Joel Blau, *The Visible Poor: Homelessness in the United States* (New York: Oxford University Press, 1992), p. 3.
3. Ibid., p. 3.
4. Ibid., p. 10.
5. Ibid., p. 8.
6. Peter Marin, "Born to Lose, The Prejudice Against Men," *The Nation,* July 8, 1991, p. 46.
7. Ibid.
8. Blau, *The Visible Poor*, pp. 26–30.
9. Amy Goldstein, "Lower Life Expectancy Found Among the Homeless," *Washington Post,* Dec. 22, 1990, p. A24.
10. Courtland Milloy, "Homeless Pair Rings in a New Year on the Same Old Streets," p. B3.
11. Ibid.

12. Ibid.
13. Ibid.
14. Ibid.
15. Ibid.
16. Ibid.
17. Pierre Thomas, "Scores of Alexandria Hispanics, Far from Home, Now Homeless," *Washington Post*, March 16, 1991, p. B1.
18. Ibid.
19. Peter Baker, "A GOP Wunderkind's Free Fall to Poverty," *Washington Post*, April 19, 1991, p. A1.
20. Ibid.
21. Ibid.
22. Ibid.
23. Ibid.
24. Ibid.
25. Retha Hill, "Street Poet, Diplomat's Son Forge Alliance of Hope," *Washington Post*, June 3, 1991, pp. D1, D6.
26. Ibid.
27. Ibid.
28. Hill, "Street Poet, Diplomat's Son Forge Alliance of Hope," also telephone conversation between author and Anja Schulmann, Nov. 9, 1992.
29. "The Real Truth About the Economy," *Business Week*, Nov. 7, 1994, pp. 110–111.
30. Blau, *The Visible Poor*, p. 52.
31. Marin, "Born to Lose, The Prejudice Against Men," p. 47.
32. Ibid.
33. Blau, *The Visible Poor*, p. 53.
34. Marin, "Born to Lose, The Prejudice Against Men," p. 48.
35. Ibid.

CHAPTER 16

1. Lewis Mumford, "Technics and the Future," *Interpretations and Forecast: 1922–1972* (New York: Harcourt Brace Jovanovich, 1973), p. 290.
2. Quoted in Kirk B. Smith, "Home Economics," in *The Green Lifestyle Handbook* (New York: Henry Holt & Co., 1990), p. 1.
3. See, for example, Germaine Greer, "The Backlash Myth," *The New Republic*, Oct. 5, 1922, pp. 20–22.
4. Robert Frank Mannis, "Husbandry, Reawakening a Lost Masculine Ethic," *Utne Reader*, May/June 1991, pp. 70–71. Also personal conversation, September 4, 1993.
5. Sam Keen, *Fire in the Belly* (New York: Bantam Books, 1991), p. 180.

CHAPTER 17

1. Francis Weller, "Ashamed to Be Male," in *To Be a Man*, ed. Keith Thompson (Los Angeles: Tarcher, 1991), p. 72.
2. Francis X. Clines, "Men's Movement Challenges Prison Machismo," *The New York Times*, Feb. 23, 1993, p. B1.
3. Ibid., p. B6.
4. Ibid.
5. Ibid.
6. Interview with Robert Vosper by author, March 25, 1993.
7. Interview with Harris Breiman by author, March 26, 1993.
8. Interview with Robert Vosper by author, March 25, 1993.
9. Ibid. Harris Breiman has now initiated OASIS, The National Prison Council Project (P.O. Box 31, Woodstock, NY 12498).
10. Clines, "Men's Movement Challenges Prison Machismo," p. B6.
11. Ibid.
12. Ibid.
13. Doug Hufnagel, "Box H," in *Wingspan: Inside the Men's Movement*, ed. Christopher Harding (New York: St. Martin's Press, 1992), p. 84.
14. Harris Breiman, "Creating a Men's Council Behind Bars, The Fellowship of the King of Hearts," *Wingspan*, Dec. 1994–March 1995, pp. 1, 6. Also personal interview with the author, February 16, 1995.
15. Hufnagel, "Box H," p. 84.
16. Ibid.
17. Ibid., p. 86

CHAPTER 18

1. G. K. Chesterton, *Varied Types* (New York: Dodd, Mead and Company, 1908), p. 251.
2. Psychologist and author Ken Druck fought through resistance and reconciled himself with a distant father. From his experience he created a "credo" for sons reaching out to the father. See Ken Druck, *The Secrets Men Keep* (Garden City, NY: Doubleday, 1985), pp. 92–93.
3. Kipnis, *Knights Without Armor* (Los Angeles: Tarcher, 1992) p. 175.
4. Mary Jordan, "Shortage of Minority, Male Teachers Reported," *Washington Post*, July 7, 1992, p. A4.
5. C. Emily Feistritzer, *Who Wants to Teach* (Washington, DC: National Center for Education Information, 1992), p. 17.
6. Interview with author, March 26, 1993.

INDEX

Peverell, Rusty, 145–47, 151–52, 154
play, 84, 219–20
  see also sports
Pleck, Joseph, 150–51
politics:
  and building community of men,
    309–10
  custody cases and, 156, 171
  employment and, 204–6
  homelessness and, 279, 284–86,
    290–91
  and manifesto for men, 312–13,
    320–22, 325–26, 328
  and man's relationship with nature,
    239–42
  men's movement and, 134, 139, 142
  power man archetype in, 117–24,
    126–27, 139
  and redefining masculinity, 297,
    299
  veterans and, 254, 261
Pollard, Sidney, 52, 55
pornography, 69, 128
post-traumatic stress disorder (PTSD),
    228, 254–57, 262
poverty, xii
  competition man archetype and, 72,
    80, 86
  employment and, 185, 199
  enclosure and, 31, 33, 35, 37
  gender identity and, 19, 26
  homelessness and, 279–80, 286,
    289
  and manifesto for men, 312, 316–17
  men's movement and, 142
  profit man archetype and, 110
power and power man archetype,
    111–30
  and appropriate-technology
    movement, 123–24
  and building community of men,
    308–9
  and custody cases, 153
  definitions of, 116, 118
  and employment, 111–16, 126–28,
    130, 186–87, 199–200
  and health care, 213, 231
  and impotence, 128–29
  and industry, 111–16, 122, 124–26
  knowledge as, 121–22
  and men's movement, 137, 139
  and nature, 120–26, 128, 236–37
  objectivity and neutrality in, 122

paradox of, 124–30
  in politics, 117–24, 126–27, 139
  and redefining masculinity, 296,
    299, 301
  Prince, The (Machiavelli), 118–19
prisons, *see* imprisonment
profit man archetype, 87–110
  advertising and, 102–4, 107–8
  consumerism and, 101–10
  demeaning impact of, 107–10
  and doctrine of self-interest, 95–98
  dominance of, 97–98
  employment and, 87, 89–90,
    98–110, 199–200
  and gap between haves and have-
    nots, 109
  and manifesto for men, 312
  and meaning of success, 90
  objections to, 98–102
  origins of, 92–96
  power man archetype and, 112–15,
    125–26
  and redefining masculinity, 296,
    299
  and treadmill of work and spend,
    102–3, 105–10
Project 2000, 272–74, 319
prostate disease, 212–13, 225,
    227–28, 322
Protestantism:
  employment and, 192
  machine man archetype and, 54–55,
    58
  profit man archetype and, 103

Ragland, Ray, 278, 282–83, 288, 290
Ranch Hand, Operation, 258–59
Rasberry, Kevin, 286–88, 290
Reagan, Martin W., 177–78
Reich, Robert, 110, 199, 202
religion:
  and building community of men,
    307–8
  competition man archetype and, 79
  custody cases and, 149, 153
  employment and, 187, 192
  enclosure and, 36, 39
  gender identity and, 15, 18
  homelessness and, 283
  machine man archetype and, 54–55,
    58–59
  and man's relationship with nature,
    237, 239, 241–42